Debacle

Debacle

*Obama's War on Jobs
and Growth and
What We Can Do Now
to Regain Our Future*

Grover G. Norquist
John R. Lott Jr.

WILEY

John Wiley & Sons, Inc.

Published by John Wiley & Sons, Inc., Hoboken, New Jersey.
Published simultaneously in Canada.

For general information on our other products and services or for technical support, please
contact our Customer Care Department within the United States at (800) 762-2974,
outside the United States at (317) 572-3993 or fax (317) 572-4002.

Wiley also publishes its books in a variety of electronic formats. Some content that appears
in print may not be available in electronic books. For more information about Wiley
products, visit our website at www.wiley.com.

Library of Congress Cataloging-in-Publication Data:

Norquist, Grover Glenn.
    Debacle : Obama's war on jobs and growth and what we can do now to regain our
future / Grover G. Norquist and John R. Lott, Jr.
        p. cm.
    Includes index.
    ISBN 978-1-118-18617-6 (cloth); 978-1-118-24047-2 (ebk);
    978-1-118-22753-4 (ebk); 978-1-118-26520-8 (ebk)
        1. United States—Economic policy—2009-   2. United States—Economic
conditions—2009-   3. United States—Politics and government—2009-
4. Global Financial Crisis, 2008–2009. I. Lott, John R. II. Title.
HC106.84.N675 2012
330.973—dc23
                                                                    2011053434

Printed in the United States of America
10 9 8 7 6 5 4 3 2 1

To Harold Demsetz and Ben Klein, who helped teach me how to apply economics to everyday life.

—John Lott

Contents

Acknowledgments

Many individuals provided helpful comments and assistance in putting this book together. Among them are Gertrud Fremling, Robert Hansen, Anna Henderson, Maxim Lott, Sherwin Lott, Ryan Ellis, Mattie Duppler, Adam Radman, Christopher Prandoni, Kelly William Cobb, Patrick Gleason, Joshua Culling, and William Upton. Alexander Hoyt, our agent, as well as Debra Englander and her colleagues at John Wiley & Sons, have also been very helpful.

Introduction

The Players

P resident Obama campaigned in 2008 on bringing the country together, promising to "turn the page on the ugly partisanship in Washington."[1] On many issues, he campaigned as a sensible moderate and even repeatedly advocated conservative positions such as cutting the size of government spending and deficits.

But once in office, he took a hard left turn: overseeing a massive 21 percent increase in federal government spending from 2008 to 2011. Creating the largest deficits that the United States had ever seen, with virtually every possible project on Democratic wish lists getting funding. Generating multibillion dollar wealth transfers to unions. Unleashing a flood of new regulations—a 40 percent increase over George Bush's last term in so-called major regulations costing $100 million or more.

But these actions by Obama were no surprise to those who knew him. One of the authors of this book, John Lott, had the dubious distinction of getting to know Barack Obama while they both worked at the University of Chicago Law School.

At Chicago, Obama was neither the type who wanted to bring people together, nor was he moderate. As Lott tells of a meeting in 1996:

> When I was first introduced to Obama, he said: "Oh, you're the gun guy."

1

I responded: "Yes, I guess so."

"I don't believe that people should be able to own guns," Obama replied.

I then suggested that it might be fun to have lunch and talk about that statement sometime.

He simply grimaced and turned away, ending the conversation. That was the way numerous interactions with Obama went.

At the one faculty seminar that I saw Obama attend, he asked a question, but it didn't appear that the speaker understood the point. After the seminar, I went up to him telling him that I thought that he had an interesting point but that it might have been clearer if he phrased it differently. Obama's response was simply to turn his back.

It was very clear that Obama disagreed on the gun issue and acted as if he believed that people who he disagreed with were not just wrong, but evil. Unlike other liberal academics who usually enjoyed discussing opposing ideas, Obama simply showed disdain.

With that background, it's not too surprising that Obama was caught during what he thought was an off-the-record conversation in April 2008 with supporters in San Francisco about how Americans in "small towns . . . cling to guns or religion."[2] Or that he was later caught privately telling Sarah Brady, with a group that supported gun bans in Washington, DC, and Chicago, about his under-the-radar efforts at gun control.[3]

But Obama can be good at the political game. He has taken various antigun positions: bans on importing semiautomatic rifles, support for the UN Arms Trade Treaty, putting more regulations on the sale of rifles and defining any rifle more than a .22 as "high-powered," and the appointment of judges to the Supreme Court and lower courts who do not believe that there is an individual right to self-defense. Nevertheless, he has convinced the media of his moderate views on the issue. An Associated Press article in November 2011 supportively quotes the Obama administration as saying their goal is to "protect the

Second Amendment rights of law-abiding citizens" and claims that the administration has done nothing to push more controls.[4]

He assembled a group of very bright academics with no experience outside of academia or government, elitists who think they know what is best for others, that from their ivory towers they think that they can micromanage people's lives. It isn't just a question over whether people can be trusted to own guns, but it goes to issues such as health care and how people spend their own money.

Take Larry Summers, a very bright Harvard professor, a former president of Harvard, and a former Clinton administration official. Summers became Obama's chief economic adviser during the beginning of his administration. Explaining why universal health care wasn't going to increase the deficit, Summers told NBC's *Meet the Press* in April 2009 that the government needed to step in and reduce the number of surgeries people are getting. Summers claimed: "Whether it's tonsillectomies or hysterectomies . . . procedures are done three times as frequently [in some parts of the country than others] and there's no benefit in terms of the health of the population. And by doing the right kind of cost-effectiveness, by making the right kinds of investments and protection, some experts that we—estimate that we could take as much as $700 billion a year out of our health care system."[5]

But surgeries aren't just done to increase life expectancy. Tonsillectomies have primarily been done because of acute or chronic throat pain.[6] Where different people are willing to draw the line between pain and surgery is a choice that we have traditionally left up to patients, but unless you know something about the patient's preferences, it is hard to claim that a surgery was a "mistake."

This sure seems like rationing. Total health care expenditures in the United States in 2008 came to $2.4 trillion, implying that Summers believes that the proper government regulations can cut health care expenditures by almost 30 percent. That would cut back health care a lot. Summers softened the blow by saying that right now the government wouldn't have to cut expenditures by more than a third of that $700 billion.

Obama and his advisers have consistently demonstrated an extreme willingness to shade the truth when it helps the cause. Take one particularly bright individual, Austan Goolsbee. In college, he had excelled as one of the nation's top debaters, ranking third at the 1991 World Championships.[7] Goolsbee was also a professor at the University of Chicago during the time that Obama was there, and he served as an economics adviser ever since Obama ran for the U.S. Senate in 2004. Goolsbee later ran Obama's Council of Economic Advisers.

In one instance, during the 2008 presidential campaign, Obama adviser Austan Goolsbee caught the national spotlight when he reportedly told Canadian diplomats in private that they could ignore Obama's anti-NAFTA rhetoric, saying that it was just blather told to win the support of Democratic primary voters. But he explicitly denied this when confronted, telling the *New York Observer:* "It is a totally inaccurate story."[8]

Yet, after Goolsbee had sworn multiple times that the incident never happened, the Associated Press discovered a memo proving that the meeting had taken place.[9] The memo was written by Joseph DeMora, a Canadian consulate staffer, as a record of Goolsbee's February 8 meeting with a man named Georges Rioux, the Canadian Consul General in Chicago.

Additionally, confirming what Goolsbee had told the Canadians, Obama later disowned the promises he had made the voters regarding NAFTA. Obama explained away the change by telling CNN: "Sometimes during campaigns the rhetoric gets overheated and amplified."[10]

It is also hard to forget Goolsbee's weird definition of taxes during the health care debate.[11] During the 2008 campaign, Obama had promised: "I can make a firm pledge. Under my plan, no family making less than $250,000 a year will see any form of tax increase. Not your income tax, not your payroll tax, not your capital gains taxes, not any of your taxes."[12] So how do you raise money to pay for the very expensive health care bill? Goolsbee solved the problem by claiming that penalties that the administration planned to impose on those refusing to buy health insurance didn't really constitute a tax. According to Goolsbee's logic, defending the administration, the penalty wasn't really a tax because if those without health insurance get hurt and require health care, costs are imposed on everyone else.

Of course, by Goolsbee's logic, gasoline taxes wouldn't really be taxes because people are using the roads. And our income taxes wouldn't really be taxes because we all are getting benefits from national defense or other government spending.

But the administration disowned Goolsbee's argument when a new political problem arose: States were challenging the health insurance mandate as unconstitutional. The solution seemed simple. Declare that the health insurance mandate isn't a mandate, but a tax. The government may not have the authority simply to penalize people who don't buy health insurance, but the government has broad authority to levy taxes. Even the administration has conceded that mandates are constitutionally questionable. The Supreme Court is expected to decide in its 2011–2012 term whether Obama can relabel the penalties as taxes whenever it is politically convenient.

These bright guys often seem to act as if the normal rules don't apply to themselves and that they can slyly obscure issues. Misleading Americans is viewed as all right as long as it is for a good cause.

But so how have Obama's policies of these best and brightest worked out?

Why was unemployment still at least 9 percent 30 months into Obama's economic recovery? Why has median household income fallen and poverty risen by record amounts despite a recovery? Why has our economy gotten so much worse than others, such as Canada's, right after Obama passed the Stimulus?

Obama may have a lot of bright academics advising him, but they, and he, have little real-world experience and are willing to go to any extreme to accomplish what they deem to be the morally right policies. As we shall see in this book, the result has been disastrous.

Notes

1. Congressional Quarterly Transcripts, "Sens. Obama and Biden Deliver Remarks in Springfield, Ill.," *Washington Post,* August 23, 2008, www.washingtonpost.com/wp-dyn/content/article/2008/08/28/AR2008082803216.html.

2. Saira Anees, "Obama Explains Why Some Small Town Pennsylvanians Are 'Bitter,'" ABC News, April 11, 2008, http://abcnews.go.com/blogs/politics/2008/04/obama-explains-2/.

3. Jason Horowitz, "Over a Barrel? Meet White House Gun Policy Adviser Steve Croley," *Washington Post,* April 4, 2011, www.washingtonpost.com/lifestyle/style/over-a-barrel-meet-white-house-gun-policy-adviser-steve-croley/2011/04/04/AFt9EKND_story.html.

4. Associated Press, "Gun Issue Represents Tough Politics for Obama," Fox News, November 24, 2011, www.foxnews.com/politics/2011/11/24/gun-issue-represents-tough-politics-for-obama/.

5. David Gregory, *Meet the Press* transcript for April 19, 2009, NBC News, www.msnbc.msn.com/id/30291720/page/2/.

6. Reasons for tonsillectomy, www.scribd.com/doc/4705075/Reasons-for-Tonsillectomy.

7. Alec Brandon, "Austan Goolsbee: The College Years," *Chicago Maroon,* October 11, 2007, http://chicagomaroon.com/2007/10/11/austan-goolsbee-the-college-years/.

8. Byron York, "Is Obama Lying about NAFTAGate?" *National Review Online,* March 4, 2008, www.nationalreview.com/articles/223826/obama-lying-about-naftagate/byron-york.

9. Jennifer Parker, Teddy Davis, and Kate Snow, "Obama Campaign Denies Duplicity on Trade," ABC News, March 3, 2008, http://abcnews.go.com/Politics/DemocraticDebate/story?id=4380122&page=1#.TtWZS2AeI0M. "Subject: Report on U.S. Elections—CHCGO Meeting with Obama Advisor Austan Goolsbee," ABC News, http://abcnews.go.com/images/Politics/Canwest%20News_1.pdf.

10. Nina Easton, "Obama: NAFTA Not So Bad after All," CNN Money, June 18, 2008, http://money.cnn.com/2008/06/18/magazines/fortune/easton_obama.fortune/index.htm?postversion=2008061810.

11. Editorial, "Obama's Taxing Logic," *Washington Times,* September 27, 2009.

12. PolitiFact.com, "No Family Making Less than $250,000 Will See 'Any Form of Tax Increase,'" *St. Petersburg Times,* updated April 8, 2010, www.politifact.com/truth-o-meter/promises/obameter/promise/515/no-family-making-less-250000-will-see-any-form-tax/.

Chapter 1

The Financial Crisis

"You've picked the wrong people. I don't understand how you could do this. You've picked the wrong people!"[1] Senator Byron Dorgan (D–North Dakota) shouted at President-elect Obama in a private meeting shortly after Obama announced his economic team back in December 2008.

Dorgan—along with many other Democrats—was upset about Obama's choice of Larry Summers as director of the National Economic Council, and Tim Geithner as Treasury Secretary.[2] Dorgan blamed these two men for having helped cause the crisis by persuading President Clinton to deregulate banks.

Summers and Geithner did play a big role in creating the crisis, but not because they once supported deregulation.[3]

Summers and Geithner bore responsibility for the crisis in another, much more direct and obvious way. They had a hand in encouraging risky home-mortgage lending and ensuring that the federal government would cover any losses Fannie Mae and Freddie Mac would bear. And with a loss of $141 billion as of October 2011, these two organizations were at the center of the mortgage collapse.[4]

Fannie and Freddie are government-sponsored enterprises—corporations created by the government but run, for profit, as private enterprises. They provide extreme examples of what happens when private companies are allowed to gamble with taxpayer money. If Fannie and Freddie won, they got to keep the money. If they lost, taxpayers picked up the bill.

As Alan Greenspan, the former Federal Reserve chairman, testified before the Financial Crisis Inquiry Commission on April 8, 2010, about the events back in 2008: "While the roots of the crisis were global, it was securitized U.S. subprime mortgages that served as the crisis's immediate trigger. The surge in demand for mortgage-backed securities was heavily driven by Fannie Mae and Freddie Mac, which were pressed by the Department of Housing and Urban Development and the Congress to expand affordable housing commitments."[5]

Greenspan also witnessed, firsthand, this pressure on banks during the 1990s and 2000s to issue mortgages to people they thought were too risky to lend to: "I sat through meeting after meeting in which the pressures on the Federal Reserve—and on, I might add, all of the other regulatory agencies—to enhance lending were remarkable."

Unfortunately, Fannie and Freddie's problems didn't just end with them pressuring banks to make risky loans. They also committed fraud. As one academic journal, the *Journal of Business & Economics Research,* put it: "In 2003, the Office of Federal Housing Enterprises Oversight (OFHEO) investigated Fannie Mae and found a culture of corruption, arrogance, and pervasive accounting violations in the company. Executives at Fannie Mae cooked books to pocket an extra twenty-seven million dollars in bonuses."[6]

Fannie and Freddie's job has been to purchase and repackage a large share of all private mortgages in the country into mortgage-backed securities—they put lots of mortgages together into bundles that are then resold. Why bundle the mortgages? It is too risky to hold mortgages from just one community. For example, if a major employer goes out of business, all home mortgages in the area could be adversely affected. It is much safer to hold a diversified bundle of mortgages from many different places together.

But it was not done right. To help sell high-risk home mortgages, Fannie and Freddie mislabeled a large number of risky mortgages as safe ones, and got them rated them as AAA. Even when the fraud began to be clear, investors still purchased these mortgages because they thought that Fannie Mae and Freddie Mac, with the financial support of the federal government, stood behind the mortgage-backed securities they issued.

Fannie and Freddie worked alongside the Federal Reserve to gut mortgage-lending standards. The goal was deemed by both Republican and Democratic administrations as a noble goal—making homeownership something everyone could afford. But they did this by gutting mortgage-underwriting standards.

"When we boost the number of homeowners in our country, we strengthen our economy, create jobs, build up the middle class, and build better citizens," President Clinton said in a speech at the White House in June 1995, advocating an increase in homeownership.[7] In virtually identical remarks eight years later, President Bush announced: "This administration will constantly strive to promote an ownership society in America. We want more people owning their own home. It is in our national interest that more people own their own home. After all, if you own your own home, you have a vital stake in the future of our country."[8] Bush was particularly proud of the increase in homeownership by minority and poor individuals and committed his administration early onto this path.[9]

Fannie and Freddie accomplished this by financially rewarding mortgage lenders who provided loans to borrowers who traditionally would have been rejected, such as welfare recipients, the unemployed, and those lacking a credit history.[10] Lenders in urban areas were pushed to use inflated appraisal standards to inflate the perceived value of the home relative to the amount being borrowed.[11] Other special programs were also offered to encourage homebuying by lower-income individuals.[12] This was a politically winning solution for Fannie and Freddie since it gave politicians something they could boast about—expanded homeownership.

It was a give-and-take relationship. In return for Fannie and Freddie giving politicians what they wanted, Fannie and Freddie got to keep their special status with the Federal government. Backed by the full faith and credit of the United States, Fannie and Freddie were able to borrow money at about half a percentage point lower than that paid by private companies.[13] Fannie and Freddie also enjoyed many other privileges compared to normal banks: a low interest rate on a line of credit directly from the U.S. Treasury, exemption from state and local taxes, and exemption from many government regulations imposed on private banks. These subsidies have made it very difficult for private companies to compete against them and gave Fannie and Freddie— as well as Ginnie Mae, another wholly owned government-sponsored enterprise—over 95 percent of the U.S. market for mortgage-backed securities.[14]

Lacking these subsidies, private mortgage bundlers in a competitive market could never have spent money on subsidizing politically desirable loans for risky homebuyers. Those companies would have quickly gone out of business.

These changes in lending standards started back in 1992, when a Boston Federal Reserve study *claimed* to find evidence of racial discrimination.[15] People were outraged. The finding was significant: Out of every 100 blacks and Hispanics applying for mortgages, 17 were rejected but only 11 of these could be explained by conventional underwriting data; the other 6 could not. The lead author, Alicia Munnell, claimed: "The study eliminates all the other possible factors that could be influencing [mortgage] decisions."[16] At a quickly called Senate hearing, Maryland Democrat senator Paul Sarbanes asked representatives of the Federal Reserve: "Gentlemen, the first question I want to put to you is that, clearly, these practices are taking place. Does anyone contest that statement? Well, why aren't we doing more to try to get at them? What's the problem?"[17]

By April 1993, just months later, the Federal Reserve had issued *a manual* for mortgage lenders warning: "Discrimination may be observed when a lender's underwriting policies contain arbitrary or outdated criteria that effectively disqualify many urban or lower-income minority applicants."[18]

So what was on the list of the Fed's "outdated criteria"? It included such discriminatory factors as the borrower's credit history, income verification, and the size of the mortgage payment relative to income. Failure to heed these criteria carried significant risk to the lender. The manual warned:

"Failure to comply with the Equal Credit Opportunity Act or Regulation B can subject a financial institution to civil liability for actual and punitive damages in individual or class actions. Liability for punitive damages can be as much as $10,000 in individual actions and the lesser of $500,000 or 1 percent of the creditor's net worth in class actions."

The penalties were very serious, and would ensure that banks would follow the new rules.

But that was only a small part of the penalties. At the same time that the Federal Reserve was releasing its manual, 10 government agencies under the Clinton administration were responding to the Boston Fed study with their own 20-page "Policy Statement on Discrimination in Lending."[19] The agencies included the Department of Housing and Urban Development, the Department of Justice, the Office of Thrift Supervision, the Federal Trade Commission, and the Federal Housing Finance Board, among others.

The document was quite clear: Applying the same "policy or practice equally to credit applicants" will be defined as having a "disparate impact" if it "has a disproportionate adverse impact on applicants from a group protected against discrimination." Examples included treating income from welfare differently from other income or denying loans based on credit histories or debt ratios.

In case mortgage lenders hadn't picked up the hints from the Federal Reserve manual, the policy statement warned "The Department of Justice is authorized to use the full range of its enforcement authority . . ." and the Department of Housing and Urban development is asked to consider "suspension, probation, reprimand or settlement, against lenders found to have engaged in discriminatory lending practices."

Worse, the study that led politicians to destroy banks' lending standards in the name of ending discrimination turned out to be flawed. Economists discovered that there were *errors in the Boston Fed data* that were used, presumably just due to someone carelessly typing in the data.[20] Some black applicants were listed as having wealth up to hundreds of times greater than they actually had, making it look like wealthy minorities were inexplicably being turned down for loans. Some loans were erroneously listed as having negative interest rates, where the mortgage lenders were supposedly paying the homeowner each month to borrow the money. Some listings showed people receiving mortgages even though they supposedly owed millions of dollars more than they had. Still other loans were shown as being rejected when they were not. The data were a mess.

When the many data errors were corrected, the results reversed: There was no evidence of systematic racial discrimination. Minorities with the same financial background as whites faced slightly lower rejection rates.

But with relaxed lending rules to poorer individuals, there was an expected consequence: Minorities were hit by *higher foreclosure rates*.[21] Ironically, people who point to these higher rates as evidence of discrimination or so-called predatory lending don't understand that the very regulations set up to make it possible to get loans without the qualifications also meant that minorities are more likely to default.

Indeed, the two academics back in 1998, Professors *Ted Day* and *Stan Liebowitz* at the University of Texas at Dallas, found the errors in the Boston Fed study and warned: "After the warm and fuzzy glow of 'flexible underwriting standards' has worn off, we may discover that they are nothing more than standards that lead to bad loans. . . . [T]hese policies will have done a disservice to their putative beneficiaries if . . . they are dispossessed from their homes."[22]

And it wasn't just Democrats who created this problem. One of the prime defenders of the study was Larry Lindsey, a Republican appointed to the Board of Governors of the Federal Reserve by George H.W. Bush and later director of the National Economic Council under George W. Bush. He wanted to make loans based on "fairness" and "not . . . limited to safety and soundness."[23] In an interview, Liebowitz told us that Lindsey "was warned about these errors in this study but the Fed ignored them."[24] Lindsey declined to discuss with us why he didn't follow through on this information.[25]

Unsurprisingly, the lower standards did increase homeownership and inflate prices. As long as housing prices kept rising, the lower standards didn't pose a problem. But with so many people having little or no equity in their houses, as soon as prices started to fall and mortgages were worth more than the value of the house, people would walk away from their homes. Indeed, as more and more people were forced to sell their houses, the effect snowballed and soon enough, prices fell further, causing still more homes to be worth less than their value and forcing even more people to walk away. It is easy to see in the accompanying figure how home prices started falling in the beginning of 2006, well before the recession, and that once they started falling, they really plummeted (see Figure 1.1). With increased foreclosures and declining property values, mortgage specialists, such as Countrywide and IndyMac, as well as major finance and banking firms, such as Citicorp and Merrill Lynch, were financially ruined. Fannie and Freddie became insolvent and were rescued only at a huge cost to taxpayers.

Let us get back to the role of Larry Summers. In 1996, when he was the deputy secretary at Treasury, Fannie Mae and Freddie Mac faced a real threat of losing their perks. At the time, the issue was whether these two organizations should be privatized. The Democratically controlled House and Senate had mandated that a study be done as part of the 1992 Federal Housing Enterprises Financial Safety and Soundness Act's regulations. The report that was scheduled for release was about to show that Fannie and Freddie had a lot of special favors given them

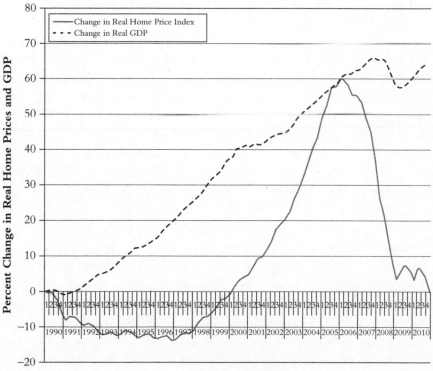

Figure 1.1 How the Drop in Housing Prices Preceded the Recession

by the government. A third of their subsidy was each year disbursed to executives and shareholders, as well as to various friends in Congress.[26] Eliminating these perks would not only dry up this gravy train, it would make it much easier for private companies to compete against Fannie and Freddie.

In their book *Reckless Endangerment, New York Times* reporters Gretchen Morgenson and Joshua Rosner reveal that just a couple of weeks before the Treasury report was scheduled to be released in May, Summers was given oversight of it.[27] Before his takeover, the report was indeed slated to recommend a path toward privatization.

But the fix was in. As one staffer explained: "Nobody has bullied me in my adult life the way that Larry [Summers] did on this one."[28] Summers ordered the staff to rewrite the report. Summers and Robert Zoellick, Fannie's executive vice president, met later privately, and, according to Morgenson and Rosner, Zoellick was seen "floating with euphoria" down the halls of the Treasury department.[29]

Another push to end the government's responsibility for any liabilities that Fannie and Freddie might incur came in 2000. Hearings in the House, headed by Louisiana congressman Richard Baker, tried to push legislation to tighten oversight of the two mortgage giants. Gary Gensler, the undersecretary of the Treasury, unexpectedly gave testimony that shocked everyone. Gensler had been a wonder boy at Goldman Sachs, having become, at the age of 30, one of the youngest partners in the firm's history. Almost immediately after becoming a partner, he left to join the Clinton administration.

While praising Fannie and Freddie for the work they had done, Gensler's testimony noted his concern over the huge $1.4 trillion debts they had already acquired by 2000, and he supported Baker's attempt to revoke their open line of credit from the Treasury.[30] Within 24 hours, with Larry Summers now the secretary of the Treasury Department, the Clinton administration made it clear that they disowned Gensler's remarks. Perhaps it isn't too surprising that former *Wall Street Journal* reporter Ron Suskind wrote that, according to Gensler, Summers and Geithner "often appeared to understand the financial markets better than they actually did."[31]

The Bush administration pushed again to reform Fannie and Freddie. But Timothy Geithner, then president of the New York Federal Reserve, was there to help by providing the right kind of studies to stop reform.

The battle lines were shown in a hearing before the House Financial Services Committee on September 10, 2003. Treasury Secretary John Snow was greatly concerned about the risk that Fannie and Freddie represented, and advocated "a strong world-class regulatory agency to oversee the prudential operations of the [government-sponsored enterprises] and the safety and the soundness of their financial activities."[32] But Democrats on the committee were having none of this. Massachusetts congressman Barney Frank, the top Democrat on the committee, responded:

> Fannie Mae and Freddie Mac are not in crisis. . . . The more people, in my judgment, exaggerate the threat of safety and soundness, the more people conjure up the possibility of serious financial losses to the Treasury, which I do not see. I think that we see entities that are fundamentally sound financially and withstand some of the disastrous scenarios. . . . But the more pressure that there is there, then the less I think that we see in terms of affordable housing.[33]

Soon thereafter, in 2004, Greg Mankiw, chair of the president's Council of Economic Advisers, put the warning about Fannie and Freddie most prophetically: "Because the housing [government-sponsored enterprises (GSEs)] are so large, the risk they face is important for the entire financial system. GSE debt is widely held by other financial institutions. Even a small mistake in GSE risk management could have ripple effects throughout the economy."[34]

Geithner responded with a report that bolstered opponents of reform. At the end of 2004, the New York Federal Reserve published claims that there existed "little evidence to support the existence of a national home price bubble."[35] This assertion received wide coverage in the popular press and helped calm concerns about potential risk in the housing market. It was used as support for those opposed to privatizing Fannie and Freddie.[36]

But Summers obviously had little respect for the likes of Greg Mankiw or others who had served during the Bush administration.

Referring to the transition from Bush to Obama, Summers noted: "We've gone from a moment when we've never had a less social-science–oriented group, to a moment when we've never had a more social-science–oriented group. So . . . we'll see what happens."[37]

Obama's connections with the very people most responsible for the financial crisis extended well beyond Larry Summers and Tim Geithner. Another close adviser during the 2008 presidential campaign was James Johnson, who headed Obama's search for a vice presidential running mate.[38] But in June 2008, documents exposed that Johnson was one of two former Fannie Mae CEOs who had received large below–interest-rate mortgages from Countrywide, with Fannie Mae being the biggest buyer of Countrywide's mortgages. Johnson received one subsidized loan from Countrywide while he was still the CEO of Fannie Mae, and two more loans afterward. All told, they totaled $2.7 million. The apparent conflicts of interest forced Johnson to resign from Obama's campaign.

Johnson ran Fannie Mae from 1991 to 1998, dramatically changing it from a conservatively managed operation to an organization that aggressively pushed homeownership to low-income people, both as a way to grow and as a way to generate political goodwill. Under Johnson, Fannie found an ally in ACORN, the left-wing community-organizing group where Obama obtained success as a community organizer. They joined forces to ease traditional mortgage underwriting standards. The two organizations found success in the 1992 Federal Housing Enterprises Financial Safety and Soundness Act. Instead of the traditional 20 percent down payment that banks had required for houses, the 1992 Act encouraged loans with only 5 percent or less down.

ACORN was also credited with introducing what became known as the "Special Affordable Goal" in the 1992 Act.[39] The provision mandated that a certain percentage of Fannie and Freddie's mortgage purchases in an area had to be done specifically for low-income families. For example, from 2001 to 2003, in most areas, at least 20 percent of the houses financed by Fannie and Freddie's mortgage purchases had to be for those with incomes no greater than 60 percent of an area's median income.[40]

The 1992 Boston Fed study that sparked an effort to end perceived discrimination against minorities and the poor was tailor-made for ACORN. The organization was also deeply involved in generating attention for the results when they came out. ACORN had put out its own study in 1991 claiming that minority applicants were 1.6 to 3.4 times more likely than whites to have their mortgage applications rejected.[41] The organization continued to work closely with Fannie and Freddie for years. Even more than a decade after the 1992 Act, ACORN organizers demonstrated in front of the homes of executives at Household International, a private competitor to Fannie and Freddie.[42] Similar demonstrations were held against many banks across the country.

Of course, Obama's links to ACORN are deep.[43] In 1995, Obama was ACORN's attorney in a case that forced Illinois to implement the federal "motor voter" law. When he ran for the Illinois State Senate in 1996, he filled out a questionnaire listing key supporters by listing ACORN first. During a 2007 speech to ACORN, Obama reminded the group's leaders: "I've been fighting alongside of ACORN on issues you care about my entire career. Even before I was an elected official, when I ran Project Vote in Illinois [1991–1992], ACORN was smack dab in the middle of it, and we appreciate your work."

As mentioned in the beginning of the chapter, Senator Dorgan and many other Democrats might not have liked Summers or Geithner, but with the president's track record, these two individuals were natural choices.

Other Obama economic advisers shared Summers's and Geithner's views. Austan Goolsbee, a long-time Obama friend from the University of Chicago who served as Obama's economic adviser ever since his successful U.S. Senate campaign in 2004, typified these views. When the Democrats moved into regulating financial markets during Obama's first two years in office, Goolsbee dismissed the notion that the legislation should deal with Fannie and Freddie, saying: "I think that's a total red herring to say that [that] ought to be in a bank reform bill."[44] He spoke as if Fannie and Freddie were totally irrelevant to the financial market crisis. Instead, Goolsbee directed his anger more toward U.S. banks. In an edgy comedy routine he gave in late 2009, banks were singled out as the "ungrateful bastards" who "bankrupted your grandma."[45]

Notes

1. Ron Suskind, *Confidence Men: Wall Street, Washington, and the Education of a President* (New York: Harper, 2011).

2. A wide range of Democrat senators from Virginia's moderate Jim Webb to Vermont's socialist Bernie Sanders, along with others such as Iowa's Tom Harkin, Michigan's Carl Levin, and California's Dianne Feinstein, expressed the same concerns about these appointments. Ron Suskind writes: "The reason Dorgan and others in his group wanted to meet directly with the president was precisely because they felt that it was Summers, Geithner, and Gensler who had been instrumental in creating the antecedents of the current financial crisis." See Suskind, *Confidence Men*.

3. The senators faulted them for persuading President Clinton to reduce regulation on banks in 1999 by repealing the Depression-era Glass-Steagall Act. Repealing the act allowed any one bank to offer multiple services. Now, one bank could operate retail banks, sell insurance, and provide investment services. It also allowed them to invest in other types of investments—previously they had been limited primarily to mortgages. The repeal of the Glass-Steagall Act was thus a good move, a deregulation that not only increased competition for customers but also served to make banks' portfolios more diverse and hence less risky. Diversification was a no-brainer for Summers. If banks had kept most of their assets in mortgages, the collapse of the mortgage market would have swept away much more of our banking system.

4. Nick Timiraos, "Fannie, Freddie Bailout Costs Revised Lower," *Wall Street Journal,* October 28, 2011, http://online.wsj.com/article/SB100014240529 702036875045770016534674226674.html.

5. John McKinnon and Randall Smith, "Greenspan Grilled Over Role in Financial Crisis," *Wall Street Journal,* April 8, 2010, http://online.wsj .com/article/SB10001424052702303720604575169650914317956. html?mod=WSJ_hps_LEFTWhatsNews.

6. RamMohan R. Yallapragada, "There Is No Accounting for Fannie Mae," *Journal of Business & Economics Research* 5, no. 7 (2007): 65–69.

7. President William J. Clinton, "Remarks on the National Homeownership Strategy," Speech delivered at the White House on June 5, 1995, www .presidency.ucsb.edu/ws/index.php?pid=51448#axzz1dTH2SDYk.

8. The White House, President George W. Bush, "Expanding Home Ownership," The White House, December 16, 2003, http://georgewbush-whitehouse.archives.gov/infocus/achievement/chap7.html.

9. The White House, Office of the Press Secretary, "President Hosts Conference on Minority Homeownership," October 15, 2002, www.policyalmanac.org/ social_welfare/archive/wh_minority_housing.shtml.

10. Susan E. Rodburg and Richard C. Walker III, "Closing the Gap: A Guide to Equal Opportunity Lending," Federal Reserve Bank of Boston, April 1993, 15, www.bos.frb.org/commdev/closing-the-gap/closingt.pdf.

11. Ibid., 14, 22.

12. Ibid., 17.

13. Gregory Mankiw, "Keeping Fannie and Freddie's Houses in Order," *Financial Times,* February 24, 2004.

14. Deborah Lucas, "Fannie Mae, Freddie Mac, and the Federal Role in the Secondary Mortgage Market," Congressional Budget Office, December 2010.

15. The original Boston Fed study was published as an academic article. Alicia Munnell, G. Tootell, L. Browne, and J. McEneaney, "Mortgage Lending In Boston: Interpreting HMDA Data," *American Economic Review,* March 1996, 25–53.

16. Paulette Thomas, "Boston Fed Finds Racial Discrimination in Mortgage Lending Is Still Widespread," *Wall Street Journal,* October 9, 1992, A3.

17. Robert Stowe England, "Washington's New Numbers Game," *Mortgage Banking,* September 1993, http://findarticles.com/p/articles/mi_hb5246/is_n12_v53/ai_n28630169/pg_6/.

18. Rodburg and Walker, "Closing the Gap," 6.

19. A copy of the "Policy Statement on Discrimination in Lending" is available from the April 15, 1994, Federal Register, www.federalregister.gov/articles/1994/04/15/94-9214/policy-statement-on-discrimination-in-lending-notice-department-of-housing-and-urban-development.

20. Stan J. Liebowitz, "Anatomy of a Train Wreck: Causes of the Mortgage Meltdown," in *Housing America: Building Out of a Crisis,* eds. Benjamin Powell and Randall Holcomb (Transaction Publishers, 2009), http://johnrlott.tripod.com/Liebowitz_Housing.pdf; Theodore E. Day and Stan J. Liebowitz, "Mortgage Lending to Minorities: Where's the Bias?" *Economic Inquiry* 36, no. 1 (1998): 3–28.

21. Juliana Barbassa, "Report: Minorities Hit by Foreclosures," *USA Today,* March 6, 2008, www.usatoday.com/money/economy/housing/2008-03-06-minority-foreclose_N.htm.

22. Day and Liebowitz, 3–28. It should be clear that one of the authors of this book was the editor at *Economic Inquiry* who accepted this paper.

23. Rodburg and Walker, "Closing the Gap," 15.

24. John R. Lott Jr., "Analysis: Reckless Mortgages Brought Financial Market to Its Knees," Fox News, September 18, 2008, www.foxnews.com/story/0,2933,424945,00.html.

25. A call was made to Lawrence Lindsey's office on November 8, 2011.

26. Gretchen Morgenson and Joshua Rosner, *Reckless Endangerment: How Outsized Ambition, Greed, and Corruption Led to Economic Armageddon* (New York: Times Books, 2011), 19.

27. Morgenson and Rosner, *Reckless Endangerment.*

28. Ibid., 80–81.

29. Ibid., 81.

30. Ibid., 164–165.

31. This isn't a direct quote by Gensler, but Suskind's summary of what he said; see Suskind, *Confidence Men.*

32. Treasury Secretary John Snow, "The Treasury Department's Views on the Regulation of Government-Sponsored Enterprises," U.S. House of Representatives, Committee on Financial Services, Washington, DC, Wednesday, September 10, 2003, http://commdocs.house.gov/committees/bank/hba92231.000/hba92231_0f.htm.

33. Fox News Special Report with Brit Hume, September 25, 2008, www.youtube.com/watch?v=LPSDnGMzIdo.

34. Gregory Mankiw, "Keeping Fannie and Freddie's houses in order," *Financial Times,* February 24, 2004.

35. Jonathan McCarthy and Richard W. Peach, "Are Home Prices the Next 'Bubble'?" *FRBNY Economic Policy Review,* December 2004, 12, www.ny.frb.org/research/epr/04v10n3/0412mcca.pdf.

36. According to Morgenson and Rosner, this study had an impact even before its official release in December 2004. They also argue: "The paper also gained traction among mass audiences and was cited in the popular press as evidence that real estate prices were not, in fact, bubblicious." Morgenson and Rosner, *Reckless Endangerment,* 228–229.

37. Suskind, *Confidence Men.*

38. Two CEOs for Fannie Mae, James Johnson and Franklin Raines, received large below–interest-rate mortgages from Countrywide. All four of Raines's loans, totaling almost $4 million, came while he was CEO. See Glenn Simpson and James Hagerty, "Countrywide Friends Got Good Loans," *Wall Street Journal,* June 7, 2008, http://online.wsj.com/article/SB121279970984353933.html?loc=interstitialskip; John Broder and Leslie Wayne, "Obama Aide Quits Under Fire for His Business Ties," *New York Times,* June 12, 2008, www.nytimes.com/2008/06/12/us/politics/12veep.html?pagewanted=all.

39. Robert Stowe England, *Black Box Casino: How Wall Street's Risky Shadow Banking Crashed Global Finance* (Santa Barbara, CA: Praeger, 2011), 42.

40. The rule was actually slightly more complicated than this: "At least 20 percent of the dwelling units financed by each GSE's mortgage purchases should be for very—low-income families (those with incomes no greater than 60 percent of AMI) or for low-income families (those with incomes no greater than 80 percent of AMI) in low-income areas. The corresponding goal was 14 percent for 1997–2000." Issue Brief, "HUD's Affordable Lending Goals for Fannie Mae and Freddie Mac," Office of Policy Development and Research, U.S. Department of Housing and Urban Development, January 2001, www.huduser.org/publications/pdf/gse.pdf.

41. Morgenson and Rosner, *Reckless* Endangerment, 32.

42. Ibid., 241.

43. John Fund, "ACORN Who?" *Wall Street Journal,* September 21, 2009, http://online.wsj.com/article/SB10001424052970204488304574427041636360388.html. See also Stanley Kurtz, "Inside Obama's Acorn," *National Review Online,* May 29, 2008, www.nationalreview.com/articles/224610/inside-obamas-acorn/stanley-kurtz.

44. Kendra Marr, "Goolsbee: 'Total Red Herring,'" *Politico,* April 22, 2010, www.politico.com/politico44/perm/0410/goolsbee_total_red_herring_77fa3584-8e70-4151-9a52-094f28f9ba02.html.

45. Patrick Gavin, "Austan Goolsbee Takes the Prize," *Politico,* October 1, 2009, www.politico.com/click/stories/0910/austan_goolsbee_takes_the_prize.html.

Chapter 2

The Worst Recovery on Record

That is how we will achieve the number one goal of my plan—
which is to create three million new jobs, more than 80 percent of
them in the private sector.[1]

> —*President-elect Obama in his weekly address,*
> *January 3, 2009*

The Obama administration's mantra has been job creation. That
is what they promised with their economic plans. It is the
yardstick they promised to be measured by. This makes it particularly shocking how much worse the job market has gotten during
Obama's recovery plan than it was during the official recession. With
so many people out of work and out of work for so long, it is hardly
surprising that a Rasmussen Reports poll released in late October 2011
found that 70 percent of Americans felt the U.S. economy was still in a
recession. Only 14 percent disagreed and only 18 percent thought the
economy was getting better.[2]

In November 2011, with just a year to go before the 2012 elections,
former Clinton pollster Doug Schoen and former Carter pollster
Patrick Caddell were very succinct: "On the economy, the president
cannot affirmatively make the case that voters are better off now than

they were four years ago. He—like everyone else—knows that they are worse off."[3]

The recession was painful enough. Between when the recession started in December 2007 and ended in June 2009, 6.3 million jobs were lost.[4] After the recession ended and this book was written in October 2011, only 324,000 additional jobs were created—an average of just 11,000 a month over those 29 months.[5] With the working-age population growing by 160,000 a month, this meager job growth failed to make a dent in getting the jobs back, let alone find jobs for the ever-growing population. See Figure 2.1.

It has become common to follow President Obama's lead and call the recent recession the "Great Recession," implying that it has been worse than any other recession since the Great Depression. Obama used this term already back during the 2008 campaign when the unemployment rate was no more than 6.2 percent, and, ironically, he still used it to describe the previous recession in late October 2011, when the unemployment rate was 9.1 percent.[6]

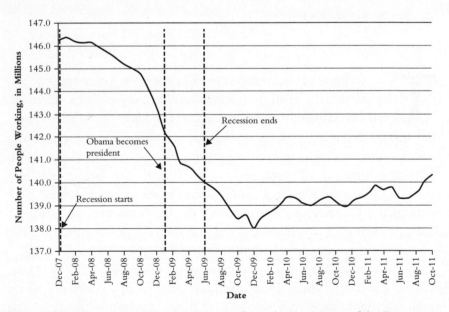

Figure 2.1 Number of People with Jobs from the Beginning of the Recession to October 2011 (Household Survey)
SOURCE: Bureau of Labor Statistics Household Survey.

Despite its widespread acceptance, the term is dubious, as other recessions have been just as bad in many respects. At 18 months, this recent recession is the longest—two months longer than either the 1981–1982 or 1973–1975 recessions. And the drop in GDP was more severe than the drop during the 1981–1982 recession. On the other hand, the 1981–1982 recession was clearly worse in terms of unemployment, which reached 10.8 percent compared to the recent peak of 10.1. We can also measure the state of the economy with the so-called misery index, a frequently referred to measure that adds up the unemployment and inflation rates. That index was almost twice as bad during the 1981–1982 recession.

While this recession no doubt has been one of the worst since the Great Depression, the supposed recovery that followed it has clearly been the worst. Unemployment and job growth have been abysmal. As of October 2011, the unemployment rate was stuck at least at 9.0 percent for 27 out of 29 months. Astoundingly, the unemployment rate during the 29 months of recovery averages three full percentage points higher than the average unemployment rate during the recession. There is no comparable recovery on record since the prolonged period of stagnation during the Great Depression in the 1930s. The Reagan recovery, starting in late 1982, hit a higher unemployment rate, but after the recovery started, it did not take more than nine months for the unemployment rate to dip below 9 percent. Unemployment also fell fairly quickly after the next-worse recession in 1973–1975.

As the Reagan recovery demonstrates, it is very common for any improvement in unemployment to lag a few months after GDP begins to pick up. Since firms delay hiring until they are sure that there is an increase in demand for their products, unemployment often keeps rising at the beginning of a recovery. But that lag is in terms of months, not years. On November 6, 2009, nine months after the Stimulus had passed, President Obama alluded to the traditional lag in reducing unemployment: "history tells us that job growth always lags behind economic growth."[7] But on July 8, 2011, with the release that morning of a new unemployment report showing the unemployment rate still at 9.2 percent, he was still making a similar point: "The economic challenges that we face weren't created overnight, and they're not going to be solved overnight."[8]

Austan Goolsbee, the former head of Obama's Council of Economic Advisers for much of Obama's first term, has been obviously put on the defensive, and he told Sean Hannity in October 2011 that it was "unfair" to evaluate the changes in job creation from the beginning of Obama's administration, that it is only fair to evaluate any changes "since the end of the recession."[9]

But even using his measure, the contrast with the Reagan years is stark. In the first 29 months during the Reagan recovery, the number of jobs grew by 8 percent. In contrast, over the same time, the number of jobs under Obama has grown by just 0.25 percent. See Figure 2.2.

At the end of Reagan's first term in January 1985, there were 6.3 million more jobs than in January 1981. By October 2011, with Obama having been in office for close to three years, there were 1.9 million fewer jobs than when he took office.

But things in America are a lot worse than the simple employment and unemployment numbers indicate because many people have given

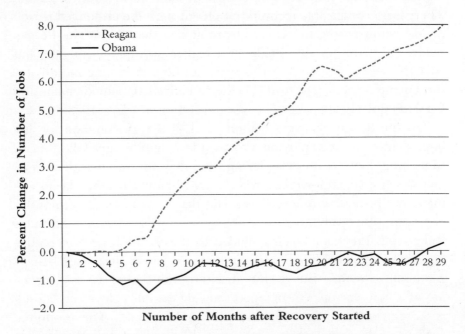

Figure 2.2   Job Creation During the Reagan and Obama Recoveries
SOURCE: Bureau of Labor Statistics Household Survey.

up looking for work and have completely left the labor force, and the government no longer counts people as unemployed after they give up looking for a job. Obviously, lowering the unemployment rate through disillusioned job-seekers giving up looking is not a good thing.

People are supposed to start looking for work during recoveries. It is during recessions that Americans give up looking for work. Unfortunately, under the Obama administration, the reverse has happened (see Figure 2.3a).

There are many good reasons why some adults don't work. Staying home to take care of kids or suffering from an illness are common reasons. But the drop in the rate that people want to work can't be explained by any sudden cultural changes to stay at home with children or of mass illness. Oddly enough, it was only during the Obama recovery that Americans started dropping out of the labor market in droves. In total, 4.7 million people quit looking for work.

There are so-called broader measures of unemployment, measures that include those who have left the labor force because they became discouraged and gave up looking for work or those ending

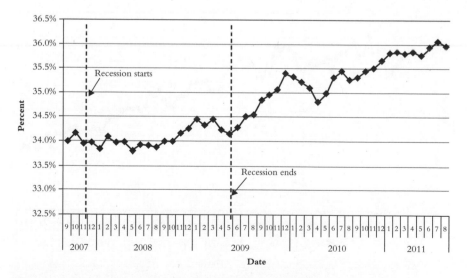

Figure 2.3a   Percentage of Working-Age Population Not in Labor Force during Obama Recovery
SOURCE: Bureau of Labor Statistics Household Survey.

up with only part-time work instead of the full-time work that they wanted. These broader measures of unemployment have averaged a rate of more than 16 percent for the first 10 months of 2011, more than a couple of percentage points higher than at the beginning of the Obama administration.

The contrast with the Reagan recovery is striking (Figure 2.3b). After the Reagan recovery started, millions more people wanted to work than even before the recession started. The sharp drop in the unemployment rate during the Reagan recovery is therefore even more impressive. As more of the unemployed got jobs, more of those who weren't previously working decided to start looking for a job. Yet, despite all those new people looking for work, the unemployment rate fell from 10.8 percent at the end of 1982 to 7.2 percent by the presidential election in 1984. The unemployment rate was lower at the end of Reagan's term than at the beginning. For Obama, even with so many millions of people giving up looking for work, the unemployment rate lingers at more than a percentage point higher than at his inauguration.

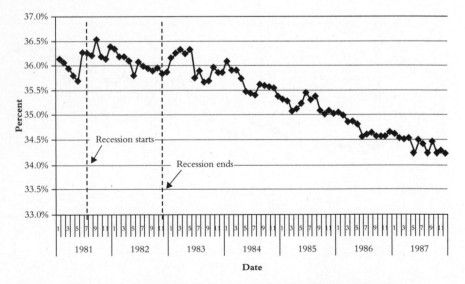

Figure 2.3b   Percentage of Working-Age Population Not in Labor Force during Reagan Recovery
SOURCE: Bureau of Labor Statistics Household Survey.

That so many people have simply given up looking for work under the Obama administration isn't too surprising. They looked for a long time first. The average number of weeks that the unemployed are looking for work has reached record lengths—almost twice the previous record set during the Reagan administration. And things haven't improved on that score: The longest job searches weren't during the recession—the longest searches for jobs were taking place during 2011, two years into the recovery.

By the end of the recession in June 2009, 27 percent of the unemployed searched for work for more than six months (see Figure 2.4). In September 2011, it stood at almost 45 percent.

In general, the more severe the recession, the faster the economic rebound. This argument was used by the Obama administration as a defense of their initial, rosy predictions on how the economy was going to grow after the Stimulus was passed.[10] But since the recovery started in June 2009, annual GDP growth has averaged 2.5 percent, compared to 6 percent over the same length of time under Reagan (see Figure 2.5). During the first three quarters of 2011, the economy had

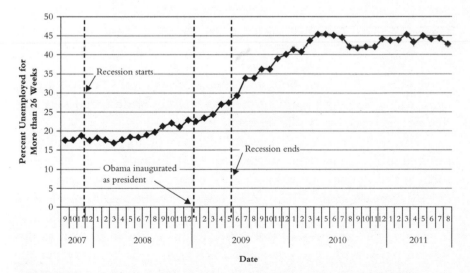

Figure 2.4   Percent of Unemployed Looking for Work for More than 26 Weeks during Obama Recovery
SOURCE: Bureau of Labor Statistics Household Survey.

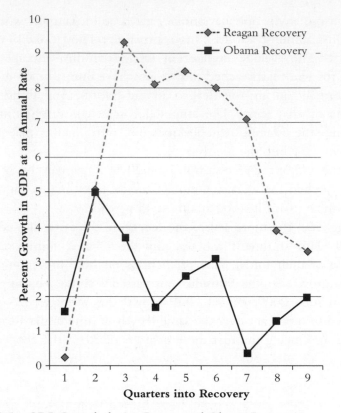

Figure 2.5   GDP Growth during Reagan and Obama Recoveries

slowed down to an incredibly slow annual growth rate of only 1.4 percent, barely keeping pace with the growing population, and meaning
that people's incomes would be stagnant.

Obviously, if more people had been working, it would have
resulted in higher income. So the slow GDP growth we're still seeing
today is tied to our country's continued record high unemployment.

By comparison, the 1973–1975 recession was also long, lasting almost
as long as the 2007–2009 one, and with its unemployment peaking at
9 percent. The aftermath of that severe recession was more akin to the
Reagan recovery than to our current one. Once the recovery started,
noticeable improvements came quickly. For example, there was no increase
in the time people spent looking for a job. And GDP grew, if not as fast as
during the Reagan recovery, much faster than during the current one.

There are many explanations offered by Obama and his supporters for why this has been the worst economic recovery, and we discuss them in Chapter 4. These explanations range from financial crises having a particularly bad negative effect to the earthquake in Japan.

Notes

1. Kate Phillips, "Sunday Breakfast Menu, Jan. 4," *New York Times,* January 3, 2009, http://thecaucus.blogs.nytimes.com/2009/01/03/sunday-breakfast-menu-jan-4/.

   For a similar statement, see also Tom Brokaw, "President-elect Barack Obama," *Meet the Press,* NBC News, December 7, 2008, www.msnbc.msn.com/id/28097635/print/1/displaymode/1098/.

2. Rasmussen Reports, "Rasmussen Consumer Index," Rasmussen Reports, October 26, 2011, www.rasmussenreports.com/public_content/business/indexes/rasmussen_consumer_index/rasmussen_consumer_index.

3. Patrick Caddell and Douglas Schoen, "The Hillary Moment," *Wall Street Journal,* November 21, 2011, http://online.wsj.com/article_email/SB10001424052970203611404577041950781477944-lMyQjAxMTAxMDIwMDEyNDAyWj.html?mod=wsj_share_email.

4. The dates for the beginning and end of recessions is available from the National Bureau of Economic Research, "US Business Cycle Expansions and Contractions," NBER, www.nber.org/cycles/cyclesmain.html.

5. The Department of Labor provides two different sets of labor market statistics: the Establishment Survey and the Household Survey. The Establishment Survey polls 400,000 companies on how many employees they have. The Household Survey questions 60,000 households each month on whether they have jobs and whether someone is looking for one.

   The unemployment rate as well as questions about whether people are leaving the labor force and the length of unemployment are all questions that can be answered only by using the Household Survey data, so instead of switching back and forth between the different data sources, the discussion in the text focuses on the Household Survey data.

   There are a number of technical reasons that the two surveys can yield different numbers. For example, people with more than one job will be counted multiple times in the establishment survey. On the other hand, the self-employed are counted only by the household survey.

   The estimates between the two surveys differ in part because the number of companies in the Establishment Survey does not remain fixed. Old firms die and new ones are born. The Establishment Survey finds out about the company deaths quickly, but it takes longer to learn about births. The current list of firms surveyed excludes firms started over most of the previous two years. What the Establishment Survey shows is total employment in older firms. The Establishment Survey estimate is also much smoother than that for the Household Survey because of the use of regression analysis. It also means that unlike the Household Survey, the Establish Survey numbers are constantly revised in later months.

The two surveys show a similar pattern, though the specific numbers reported do vary. The Establishment Survey shows a larger drop in jobs (6.5 million versus the 5.97 million in the Household Survey), but the increase in jobs after the recession ended is also larger (1 million versus 324,000 in the Household Survey). The general pattern is thus the same, with only a fraction of the jobs lost being recovered.

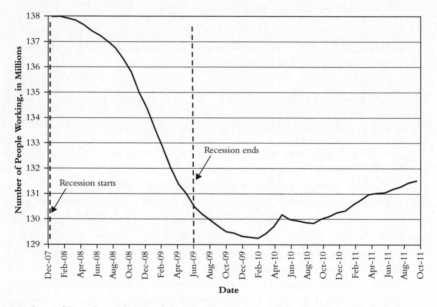

Number of People with Jobs from the Beginning of the Recession to October 2011
SOURCE: Bureau of Labor Statistics Establishment Survey.

6. Reuters, "Obama: U.S. in Worst Crisis Since Depression," Reuters, October 7, 2008, www.reuters.com/article/2008/10/08/usa-politics-debate-economy-idUSN0749084220081008; Staff, "CNN's State of the Union Transcript," *Politico*, January 16, 2009, www.politico.com/news/stories/0109/17543.html; President Barack Obama, "Remarks by the President at a Campaign Event: Pepsi Center, Denver, Colorado,"

The White House, Office of the Press Secretary, October 25, 2011, www.whitehouse.gov/the-press-office/2011/10/25/remarks-president-campaign-event-1. For a sampling of the Obama administration's use of the term *Great Recession*, see http://search.whitehouse.gov/search?affiliate =wh&query=%22great+recession%22&form_id=usasearch_box&submit. x=41&submit.y=9&submit=Search.

7. President Barack Obama, "Remarks by the President in the Rose Garden," The White House, Office of the Press Secretary, November 6, 2009, www.whitehouse.gov/photos-and-video/video/president-obama-speaks-fort-hood-and-job-numbers#transcript.

8. President Barack Obama, "Remarks by the President on the Monthly Jobs Report," The White House, Office of the Press Secretary, July 8, 2011, www.whitehouse.gov/the-press-office/2011/07/08/remarks-president-monthly-jobs-report.

9. John R. Lott Jr., "Goolsbee's Gaffes," *National Review Online,* November 2, 2011, www.nationalreview.com/articles/281919/goolsbee-s-gaffes-john-r-lott-jr?pg=2.

10. This assumption by the Obama administration generated quite a debate among economists in early 2009. Brad DeLong, an economist who worked in the Clinton administration, made the administration's claim quite forcefully when he wrote: "Whether an unexpected fall in production is followed by faster-than-average catch-up growth depends [on] what kind the fall in production is. A fall in production that does not also change the unemployment rate will in all likelihood be permanent. A fall in production that is accompanied by a big rise in the unemployment rate will in all likelihood be reversed." Brad DeLong, "Permanent and Transitory Components of Real GDP," *Grasping Reality with Both Hands* (DeLong's blog), March 3, 2009. See also Paul Krugman, "Roots of Evil (Wonkish)," *New York Times,* March 3, 2009, and Greg Mankiw, "Wanna Bet Some of That Nobel Money?" *Greg Mankiw's Blog,* March 4, 2009, http://greg-mankiw.blogspot.com/2009/03/wanna-bet-some-of-that-nobel-money .html.

Chapter 3

The Stimulus Made Things Worse

What Was Promised

Matt Lauer: At some point will you say, "Wait a minute, we've spent this amount of money. We're not seeing the results. We've got to change course dramatically?" . . .

President Obama: Look, I'm at the start of my administration . . . And . . . and, you know, a year from now, I think people . . . are gonna see that . . . we're starting to make some progress. But there's still gonna be some pain out there. If I don't have this done in three years, then there's gonna be a one-term proposition.

—*Interview on NBC's* Today Show,
February 2, 2009[1]

The overall impact on jobs saved or created is just about what was predicted.

—*Austan Goolsbee, the head of President Obama's
Council of Economic Advisers,
December 3, 2010*[2]

35

E ven before the 2010 midterm elections, with Democrats controlling massive supermajorities in both the House and Senate,
President Obama had passed five stimulus and jobs bills. If you
add up the promises, he boldly promised well over 5.5 million jobs
"created or saved." But reality turned out very differently: There were
2 million fewer people working in September 2011 than when Obama
took office. On top of that, population growth by itself should have
generated more than 3 million new jobs.[3]

President Obama claims that instead of our economy being short
more than 5 million jobs, things would have been even worse without his policies. According to him, we would have lost 10.5 million
jobs without all of his spending. No matter how bad the job numbers
get, Obama points to some hypothetical economic meltdown that was
avoided by his policies. Thus, no evidence whatsoever, no matter how
bad the news, can be used against him.

With the different Stimulus and jobs programs, it is hard to remember all the promises and to keep track of where the money has gone.
There was the massive $825 billion Stimulus that was supposed to cre-
ate or save 4.1 million jobs.[4] The cost was originally supposed to be
$787 billion, but the programs cost more than planned. Then there was
a string of smaller ones: the $38 billion Hiring Incentives to Restore
Employment (HIRE) Act of 2010, which was supposed to create
300,000 jobs, and the $26 billion Public Sector Jobs Bill of 2010 that
was promised to create or save another 300,000 jobs.[5]

And then there was the $42 billion Small Business Jobs Act of
2010, which was supposed to create or save another 500,000 jobs.[6]
Finally, the Disaster Relief and Summer Jobs Act of 2010 contained a
hodgepodge of items, such as $24 billion to help keep teachers, police,
and firefighters employed during the recession and $600 million to
create 300,000 jobs for youth ages 16 to 24.[7]

Even before Obama was sworn into office, Christina Romer, the
first head of his Council of Economic Advisors, and Jared Bernstein,
chief economist and economic policy adviser to Vice President Joseph
Biden, released predictions touting the initial big Stimulus' benefits. On
January 9, 2009, they predicted that the unemployment rate was going
to peak at 7.9 percent during July, August, and September in 2009
and then gradually fall to below 6 percent by April 2012 (Figure 3.1).

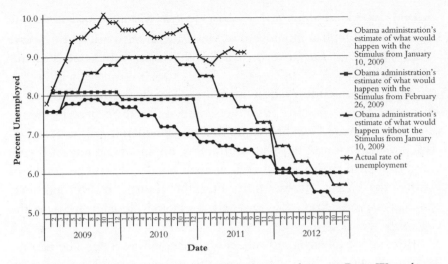

Figure 3.1   Actual versus Obama's Predicted Unemployment Rate: Were the Obama Administration's Forecasts Too Rosy?

Without the Stimulus, the unemployment rate would supposedly rise to 9 percent during most of 2010 and stay above 6 percent through most of 2012. These predictions have been a continual source of embarrassment for the White House, as the unemployment rate shot well past what it was supposed to be without the Stimulus.

Even the mainstream media made the administration defend this prediction. By July 2009, it was obvious that the Obama administration's initial predictions were way off. ABC's *This Week* host George Stephanopoulos asked Vice President Biden how the 9.5 percent unemployment rate in June squared with the administration's prediction that if the Stimulus package was passed, "unemployment will peak at about 8 percent."[8] Biden replied, "We and everyone else misread the economy. The figures we worked off of in January were the consensus figures. . . ."

Biden's answer was quite clear. The economy being much worse than ever predicted wasn't *Obama's* fault—rather, the Bush administration had left us a worse economy than anyone had realized. To Stephanopoulos there were only two alternatives: "either you misread the economy [that the economy was worse than Team Obama realized] or the stimulus package is too slow and too small." And by the day after Stephanopoulos's interview, there was already a headline in the *Wall Street Journal* reporting: "Calls Grow to Increase Stimulus Spending."[9]

The whole administration spun the claim after Biden's interview. Economic adviser Jared Bernstein contended that the 8 percent unemployment estimate "was before we had fourth-quarter results on GDP, which we later found out was contracting on an annual rate of 6 percent, far worse than we expected at that time."[10] Even the president echoed the claim: "It was only after the [fourth]-quarter numbers came in, if you recall, that suddenly everybody looked and said the economy shrank 6%."[11]

But Biden, Obama, and others were factually wrong. The administration never just "worked off" data from January, and the economy was not much worse than they thought. On February 26th, after the 6.2 percent drop in GDP during the fourth quarter of 2008 was publicly released, the administration predicted only an 8.1 percent unemployment rate for 2009 and a 7.9 percent rate in 2010.[12]

There was also plenty of warning before that GDP number was released. In a piece published by the *Wall Street Journal* on December 11, 2008, with the telling headline "Fourth-Quarter GDP: Worse and Worse" the paper estimated a drop in GDP of 6.2 percent at an annual rate for the fourth quarter.[13]

Of course, other advocates of the Stimulus also failed to predict what was going to happen to unemployment rates and GDP growth. Paul Krugman, the *New York Times* columnist who touts his close "genuine contact" with the "smart" economists and others in the Obama administration and the Democratic congressional leadership, has been a staunch advocate of Keynesian policies.[14] The day that President Obama signed the original Stimulus bill into law, Krugman predicted: "I am still guessing that we will peak out at around 9% [unemployment] and that would be late this year."[15] He assured listeners that double-digit unemployment was "not the most likely event." With unemployment peaking at 10.1 percent and still above 9 percent two years after he predicted it would peak, Krugman was wrong on both counts.

Because of the stimulus, the Obama administration predicted a much milder drop in GDP in 2009 and strong economic growth after that (see Figure 3.2). The economy was only supposed to shrink by −1.2 percent in 2009 and then grow by 3.2 percent in 2010 and 4 percent in 2011—leaving the economy up over 6 percent from where it was in 2008.[16] But the actual economy performed much worse each year. Far from growing a robust 4 percent in 2011, the growth was a very anemic 1.4 percent.[17] Over the first three years of the Obama administration, instead of the economy growing by a total of 6 percent, it grew by less than 2 percent.

In March 2009, when Greg Mankiw, the chair of George W. Bush's Council of Economic Advisers, and some conservative economists questioned what they called Obama's "overly optimistic" growth predictions, Paul Krugman questioned their honesty.[18] In a *New York Times* blog post titled the "Roots of Evil," Krugman attacked Mankiw as "more than a bit of deliberate obtuseness" and that "we can expect fast growth."[19] Krugman approvingly cited another liberal economics professor, saying that Mankiw had to know that his arguments were wrong.[20] Mankiw challenged Krugman to a bet over whether

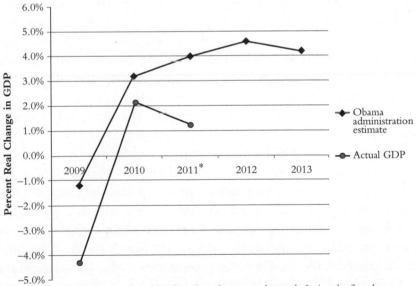

*Estimate for actual GDP growth in 2011 based on the reported growth during the first three quarters of that year.

Figure 3.2 Actual versus Obama's Predicted GDP: Were the Obama Administration's Forecasts Too Rosy?

the Obama prediction was right, but, after all his abusive rhetoric, Krugman never responded.[21] Yet, Krugman must be glad that he never bet his money to back up his heated rhetoric.

It is also hard to believe that the state of the economy took Obama by surprise. He constantly warned of an economic Armageddon during the 2008 campaign and early 2009. At least once in each of the three presidential debates during September and October 2008, Obama claimed that we were in the "worst financial crisis since the Great Depression."[22] It was a constant theme of his campaign, and he made that claim again and again in many different speeches. Right after the election, he warned: "We've got an unprecedented crisis, or at least something that we have not seen since the Great Depression."[23]

The doom-and-gloom mentality continued after taking office. In his first radio address to the nation as president on January 24, Obama started his remarks by saying: "We begin this year and this administration in the midst of an unprecedented crisis that calls for unprecedented action."[24] And during Obama's first national press conference on February 9, he talked about our being in a crisis 12 times and labeled it an "unprecedented crisis."[25] The day after Obama signed his Stimulus bill into law on February 17, the president rehashed that we were in a crisis 24 times, frequently describing in apocalyptic terms that the crisis would drag down the entire economy.[26] The same language was used in his address to a joint session of Congress on February 24, with the word *crisis* mentioned 11 times, covering the "economic crisis, "credit crisis," "housing crisis," and "financial crisis."[27]

But even after the full extent of the poor economic showing during the end of 2008 was clear, the administration's predictions at the end of February were much more optimistic and less accurate than those of most economists. While the administration was expecting an average annual unemployment rate of 8.1 percent for the year, business economists and forecasters surveyed in early March by the *Wall Street Journal* expected the June unemployment rate to be 8.2 percent and the December rate to be at 9.3 percent.[28]

If the administration's January and February forecasts were overly optimistic simply because they didn't know how bad the economy really was in late 2008, why didn't they quickly change their predictions? Instead, time after time, the Obama administration claimed that either success was already here or right around the corner. Some of these boasts started before the original Stimulus was passed, but they continued' on for years. Larry Summers, who then served as Obama's chief economic adviser, promised on January 25, 2009, with unemployment at 7.8 percent, that the economy would start improving "within weeks" of the Stimulus plan being passed.[29] Indeed, Summers touted the "shovel-ready" nature of the jobs program as being "timely, targeted, and temporary."[30] It was supposedly targeted at quickly hiring the unemployed in 90 days or less and lasting until the private sector was able to get back on its feet. Since the Stimulus was signed into law on February 17, 90 days would be by mid-May.[31]

Knowing how bad the economy was by the end of 2011, it is hard to believe that in March 2009, just five weeks after passing the Stimulus, President Obama was perceiving an upswing and started off a press conference by announcing:

> We're beginning to see signs of progress. . . . This [Stimulus] plan's already saved the jobs of teachers and police officers. It's creating construction jobs to rebuild roads and bridges. And yesterday, I met with a man whose company is reopening a factory outside of Pittsburgh that's rehiring workers to build some of the most energy-efficient windows in the world. . . . We've already seen a jump in refinancing of some mortgages, as homeowners take advantage of lower rates.[32]

This newfound optimism over the effects of the Stimulus seemed unaffected by the continued bad economic news. Obama declared later in May that the massive spending program was "already seeing results" and had created or saved almost 150,000 jobs.[33] He talked about how the Stimulus was "laying the foundation for a better economy," and by September, Vice President Biden was declaring: "In my wildest dreams, I never thought it [the Stimulus] would work this well."[34] By April the following year, the unemployment rate still at 9.8 percent, but Biden thought that now, for sure, the economy was just about to boom: "Some time in the next couple of months we're going to be creating between 250,000 jobs a month and 500,000 jobs a month." The administration touted that the summer of 2010 would become known as the "Summer of Recovery."[35]

Of course, each time, they were wrong, and thus most past assertions of the Stimulus working were quickly forgotten. In 2010, Austan Goolsbee gave Fox News viewers a different explanation for why the January and February 2009 economic predictions never panned out: "Let's remember, you're citing the claim that the unemployment rate wouldn't go above 8 percent, but if you remember in that same projection they said that if we didn't pass the Stimulus it would only go to 9 percent, and it was above that before the Stimulus even came into effect."[36] And he was still making this same claim a year and a half later.[37] Yet, despite Mr. Goolsbee's claim, the unemployment rate did not rise above 9 percent until May, two months after Obama's press conference announcing that the Stimulus was already creating jobs. Nor does it explain that the unemployment rate continued to rise, not just above 9 percent, but to 10.1 percent.

Nevertheless, the administration remained undaunted. It still insisted its policies of government spending and deficits worked after more than two years of failure. In May 2011, with unemployment at 9.1 percent, Goolsbee boasted about "the solid pace of employment growth in recent months" and that "the overall trajectory of the economy has improved dramatically over the past two years."[38] The mainstream media did what it could to help. Headlines in the *Los Angeles Times* and the *New York Times* announcing the 9.1 percent unemployment rate somehow made such gloomy numbers out to be good news, trumpeting "solid growth" and "strong growth."[39]

By the end of the summer, in August 2011, the unemployment rate was still at 9.1 percent. It was no longer possible to claim the Stimulus had worked well. Obama claimed that the sluggish economic growth wasn't the fault of his own economic policies; it was the fault of other circumstances that he had no control over. It was either events outside the United States or the irresponsible political behavior of others in Washington. Obama claimed:

In the last few months, the economy has already had to absorb an earthquake in Japan, the economic headwinds coming from Europe, the Arab Spring and the [rise] in oil prices—all of which have been very challenging for the recovery. But these are things we couldn't control. Our economy didn't need Washington to come along with a manufactured crisis to make things worse. That was in our hands. It's pretty likely that the uncertainty surrounding the raising of the debt ceiling—for both businesses and consumers—has been unsettling, and just one more impediment to the full recovery that we need.[40]

There are a couple of problems with his argument. Economic growth had already ground to a halt during the first three months of 2011—with GDP growing by just 0.1 percent. This was well before the Arab Spring, the renewed debt crisis in Greece and other countries, and the July and August 2011 debate over the debt ceiling. And whatever the impact of the March 2011 earthquake, its initial impact during the first quarter in the United States would have been very limited. The president also blamed Republicans for not passing his new legislation when they took over the House of Representatives in January 2011. But with Democratic supermajorities in both the House and Senate for the two previous years, it is pretty hard to blame for the slow growth in the first half of 2011.

In addition, it seems a little hard to blame the Japanese earthquake for our poor unemployment rate when the Japanese unemployment rate fell and ours rose in the five months following the earthquake.[41] Nor is it clear how we can blame "economic headwinds" from Europe when our unemployment rate from January to August 2011 rose while it fell for European countries such as Germany, Italy, and Sweden and stayed the same in France.[42]

Goolsbee, in an interview on Sean Hannity's radio show in late October 2011, justified Obama's references to Japan and the Arab Spring this way: "It is not excuses that he is giving for across the board. The question was: Why did we slow down in 2011 when we were growing and adding millions of jobs in 2010?"[43] But it wasn't just a sudden slowdown in 2011. From December 2009 to December 2010, fewer than a million jobs were added, not "millions."[44] And Goolsbee's argument was quite a change from his comments in June 2011, which was well after these events in March, when he dismissed the previous month's 9.1 percent unemployment rate as an aberration, saying that things were headed in the right direction and that "one month is not a trend."[45]

Unfortunately, this wasn't Goolsbee's only extreme attempt to explain away their failed Stimulus policies. In that same interview, he told Hannity:

> Sean, you need to date the job creation from when the free fall ends. You can't date it from the middle of the free fall, which is what you are doing. The job losses that you are describing were 5 million jobs lost of the 8 million lost in the recession. He comes in at the middle of the free fall. Since the end of the recession, we have added about 3 million jobs.

No matter how you cut it, 3 million jobs have not been added since the recession ended. The recession officially ended in June 2009, and at that time 130.49 million people held jobs according to the Bureau of Labor Statistics' Establishment Survey.[46] The numbers for September 2011 show 131.33 million, an addition of just 840,000 jobs. But with the working-age population having grown by 4.6 million people in the same period, this should be viewed as a miserable failure. Furthermore, out of the 840,000 additional jobs, the vast majority—540,000—were merely "temporary help" service jobs.[47] With just 300,000 permanent jobs added over 27 months, it is understandable why Goolsbee would want to claim 3 million jobs had been added.

It should be pretty obvious: The Stimulus made things worse. Indeed, this is exactly what we predicted on February 3, 2009, when one of us wrote a piece at Fox News declaring: "President Obama and the Democrats' 'stimulus' package will increase the unemployment rate."[48] While the administration was claiming in January and February that unemployment would stop rising once the Stimulus was passed, that prediction was obviously wrong to us then.

The notion that the stimulus package is too slow and too small implies that massive government spending in the various Stimulus packages actually helped the economy. It seems implausible to have unemployment rise above all administration predictions after a trillion-dollar set of packages and believe that something much larger would have helped. But the resources the government spends has to come out of someone else's pocket. Spending almost a trillion dollars on various stimulus projects means moving a lot of resources from the private sector, eliminating the jobs many people currently have.

Did Fearmongering Damage the Economy?

A debate started just weeks after the Stimulus was passed over whether the Obama administration really understood how bad the economy was. On March 13, 2009, at a widely covered address to the Brookings Institution, Larry Summers blamed an unnecessarily fearful public for dragging down the economy, saying that "fear begets fear" and that there was an "excess of fear" about the economy that was unjustifiably pushing down home prices, creating unemployment, and destabilizing the economy.[49]

Summers was right that an "excess of fear" was really harming the economy and that that the downturn had been much sharper than it had to be. Fear did scare consumers into changing their spending decisions. Businesses that would have sold products to consumers had to cut back on employment. But who was responsible for creating that fear?

During the presidential campaign in September 2008, Obama's opponent, John McCain, said: "The fundamentals of our economy are strong, but these are very, very difficult times."[50] But Obama argued that McCain's statement was irresponsible and showed that McCain was out of touch with the traumas facing Americans.[51] "It's not that I think John McCain doesn't care what's going on in the lives of most Americans. I just think he doesn't know. He doesn't get what's happening between the mountain in Sedona where he lives and the corridors of Washington where he works." Joe Biden also countered: "I could walk from here to Lansing, and I wouldn't run into a single person who thought our economy was doing well, unless I ran into John McCain."[52]

Just two days after Summers' warning about "excess" fear, NBC's *Meet the Press* host David Gregory asked Christina Romer if the fundamentals of the economy were sound. She immediately replied: "Well, of course the fundamentals are sound."[53] But the economy seemed worse in March than in September and Gregory wouldn't let the issue drop.

> Gregory: All right, but then what's different between now and then, when the economy was in even better shape than it, it is now, when McCain was saying the fundamentals were strong and then-candidate Obama criticized him?
>
> Romer: I think . . . again, I think what, what we're saying is that the, you know, where we are today is obviously not good. We have a plan in place to get to a good place. I think that's the crucial . . . a fundamentally crucial difference, is to make sure that you have put in place all of the comprehensive programs that'll get us back to those fundamentals.
>
> The other thing I think is so important, the president has actually said in terms of fundamentals, we need to make changes. That's why he's focusing on energy, education, getting the budget deficit under control, precisely because he said . . .
>
> Gregory: Right.
>
> Romer: . . . When we get through this thing, we want to be in a better place.
>
> Gregory: But perhaps Senator McCain was right when he said the fundamentals of the economy were strong, because you have President Obama saying roughly the same thing now?
>
> Romer: I really think you're misinterpreting the president. I think the key thing that the president was saying is we have our eyes on the fundamentals; that is why we're concerned about.
>
> Gregory: Hmm.

Obama was getting the "budget deficit under control"? Even at that time Obama was forecasting trillion-dollar deficits well into the future.

The same day as Romer's comments, George Stephanopoulos remarked to Summers in an interview: "You and the president were also trying to inspire hope, this week, on the economy; some signs of some progress, and of course, that move in the stock market this week."[54] It's hard not to notice that the stock market started recovering the exact same week that the administration stopped its relentless negative drumbeat. On Monday, March 9, the Dow Jones Industrial Average stood at just 6,547 (see Figure 3.3). Exactly a month later, it crossed back over the 8,000 level.

If Obama was scaring people, why did he do it? During the election, the reason was obvious—Obama wanted to win and declaring that things were a disaster certainly helped. It also motivated his big government agenda. He had hoped that the economy would turn around after the Stimulus was signed into law and they could start claiming that the Stimulus was responsible.

As Rahm Emanuel, Obama's first chief of staff, famously announced the Sunday after Obama was elected president: "Rule one:

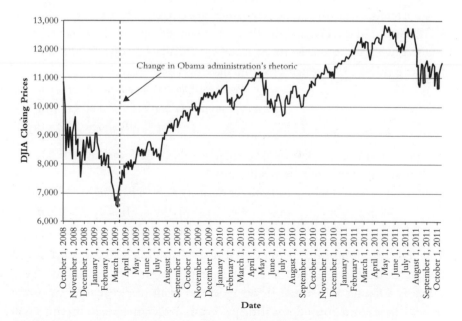

Figure 3.3   Did Fearmongering Affect Stock Prices?

Never allow a crisis to go to waste. They are opportunities to do big things."[55] For example, to push his Stimulus bill, Obama claimed: "We are experiencing an unprecedented economic crisis that has to be dealt with and dealt with rapidly."[56]

Just as Summers's statements imply, Obama has been willing to scare people to get the political programs that he and Democrats have pushed for years. And that has cost us dearly, in unemployment and slow growth and a huge debt.

"Created or Saved" Jobs

Every economist, as I've said, from conservative to liberal, acknowledges that direct government spending on a direct program now is the best way to infuse economic growth and create jobs.[57]

—*Vice President-elect Joe Biden on ABC's* This Week,
December 21, 2008

Now, if you hear some of the critics, they'll say, well, the Recovery Act, I don't know if that's really worked, because we still have high unemployment. But what they fail to understand is that every economist, from the Left and the Right, has said, because of the Recovery Act, what we've started to see is at least a couple of million jobs that have either been created or would have been lost.[58]

—*President Obama's speech to supporters at
a town hall meeting in Nashua, New Hampshire,
February 2, 2010*

Economists on the left and the right say that [the Stimulus] bill has helped saved jobs and averted disaster.[59]

—*President Obama's State of the Union Address,
January 27, 2010*

"Every economist" agrees that the Stimulus was a good idea? Could Obama and Biden even believe this absurd claim themselves? Possibly Obama and Biden never read the *Wall Street Journal* or other op-ed pages and missed the full-page ads by economists in the *New York Times* and elsewhere. But even then, it is hard to understand how they could believe their claim that "every economist" agrees with them about the Stimulus.[60] Tom Sargent, who won the Nobel Prize for economics in 2011, was blunt: "The calculations that I have seen supporting the Stimulus package are back-of-the-envelope ones that ignore what we have learned in the last 60 years of macroeconomic research. . . . [Obama's economic] advisors surely knew that was not an accurate description of the full range of professional opinion."[61]

Back in June 2009, we interviewed several of the economists surveyed by the *Wall Street Journal*.[62] Cary Leahey, an economist and senior managing director with Decision Economics, told us that there were downsides to the Stimulus in the short run: "With transitional moves in government spending [from the Stimulus], there will be dislocations in the economy that will lead to higher unemployment." But he emphasized that he thought those effects would be "short-lived, six to nine months, definitely not more than a year."

Other forecasters saw the administration's claims as the type of exaggerations that could come from just about any administration. Nicholas Perna, president of Perna Associates and a lecturer at Yale University, a supporter of the Stimulus, explained that it was really too early to see improvements from the Stimulus in terms of unemployment or GDP and that the administration's initial claims involved "political considerations" on how to sell the package. He added that "overall, the economy is still clearly declining."

Business economists and forecasters had consistently been expecting the economy to begin showing positive growth in the second half of 2009.[63] But passing the Stimulus appeared to dampen the recovery economists were anticipating.

Take the expected growth in the third quarter (from July to September) of 2009. In January, the forecasters surveyed by the *Wall Street Journal* were expecting GDP during that period to rise by 1.2 percent at an annual rate. Yet, by May, their forecasts were gloomier, and the expected growth had been cut in half, to 0.6 percent. The pattern was similar for predictions covering the entire period from April through December of 2009. Paul Evans, the editor of the *Journal of Money, Credit, and Banking* and an economics professor at Ohio State University, agrees, and told us: "Most likely the economic recovery would have been more rapid at this point without [the Stimulus package]."

Even President Obama's own administration eventually put out numbers acknowledging that the number of jobs created may be a lot less than a couple of million. By August 2011, the administration claimed that somewhere between 560,992 and 3.6 million jobs were "saved or created" by the original $825 billion Stimulus.[64] The lower figure came from a survey of recipients. But even this counting is very weird: If a project receives *any* Stimulus dollars—even if the people worked at that company or organization before and will work there afterward—those jobs are still officially counted as Stimulus-created jobs.[65]

The higher numbers, of several million jobs, are even more speculative. These types of job numbers exist merely within economists' computers and are totally hypothetical, relying on the dubious assumption that there must exist a so-called multiplier effect. The story goes like this: The people with the jobs "saved or created" spend the money, creating more jobs; and the recipients spend the extra money, creating more jobs, and so on. The Obama administration has always assumed that the multiplier is 1.5. That is, for each dollar the government spends, GDP, the value of what our country produces, goes up by $1.50.

But there is a big problem with all of these supposedly new jobs: The resources are taken from someplace to begin with. Whether the government receives the additional money from taxes or by borrowing it, the increased spending by the government, by necessity, implies others have less to spend. Conveniently, to rack up the numbers, the Obama administration counts those who received jobs by government spending but does not subtract those who lost jobs when money was taken away from the private sector. If you are merely moving money from where people would have otherwise been spending it to where the government wants it spent, the multiplier is zero.[66]

Former *Wall Street Journal* reporter Ron Suskind, in his book, *Confidence Men,* provides an inside account of the Obama campaign and administration. According to his account, Austan Goolsbee at least partially understood this point and included it in his briefings to Obama, though it was never included in the administration's public pronouncements. Suskind describes one campaign meeting in late 2007 when Goolsbee explained how subsidies for green jobs could produce "just two million jobs, in all the areas: wind, solar, all renewables," but that the real total would be less than that as "some of that will be offset by expected job losses in the oil sector."[67] Yet, no hint of this type of trade-off has ever been publicly explained by the administration.

When government interferes and causes people to move from one sector to another—say, from oil to wind energy in the preceding example—that also increases unemployment. Workers cannot just instantly move from one job to another. In reality, it takes awhile to find out where the new jobs are, so even if the total number of jobs destroyed is the same as the total numbers of jobs eventually created by government, unemployment increases at least temporarily.

On top of that, the government-created jobs are likely to be temporary and fewer than the number of jobs destroyed elsewhere. The simple reason is that many of these new jobs are artificial and will only exist as long as the government continues heavy subsidies. Take the heavily subsidized so-called green sector, including ethanol, wind power, or solar energy. Few consumers would buy these products because the price would be too high without a high subsidy. But investors realize that subsidies might not continue indefinitely and the companies involved have therefore been reluctant to hire permanent employees.

As if that was not enough, there is another serious flaw with their counting: Obama's Council of Economic Advisers wrongly assumes that all of the Stimulus jobs are filled by the unemployed. But that is clearly wrong. Indeed, most of those getting the new jobs already had a job to begin with. A study by Garett Jones and Daniel Rothschild, economists at George Mason University, shows that 58 percent of workers hired by firms that received Stimulus money were people who were already employed.[68] Stimulus funds had a relatively small impact on hiring: Stimulus funds equal to 10 percent of an organization's annual revenue increased its retraining or hiring of workers by 5 to 6 percent of its workforce. While they couldn't put an exact percentage number on it, much of the hiring involved part-time or temporary jobs.

And whatever jobs might have been created, they did not come cheap. No matter which calculations you use, the bottom line is similar: Any jobs created were exceedingly expensive. Accepting the administration's most optimistic 3.6 million number, it cost $200,000 per job.[69] And if the survey of various recipients is right, the cost per job created soars to over a million dollars.

Part of the reason for that huge cost per job is that the subsidies are temporary. If an investment doesn't make economic sense, why hire a lot of people if you are only going to have let them go as soon as the subsidy ends? In many cases, money was just wasted completely. For instance, at Solyndra, the scandal-plagued solar energy company that got $535 million from the federal government, what had originally been counted as long-term jobs soon disappeared when the company went bankrupt and took the half-billion government loan guarantee with it.

Americans might ask how accurate Obama's claims about jobs "saved or created" are when his administration's numerous predictions about job growth have consistently proven wrong.

States Hit Hardest by Recession Got the Least Stimulus Money

The Stimulus bill "includes help for those hardest hit by our economic crisis," President Obama promised when he signed the bill into law on February 17, 2009. "As a whole, this plan will help poor and working Americans."

But we can analyze data tracking how the Stimulus money was given out across the 50 states and the District of Columbia, and there is a perverse pattern: The states hardest hit by the recession received the least money. States with higher bankruptcy, foreclosure, and unemployment rates got less money. And higher-income states received more. Obama may have claimed that he was motivated to help out those in the toughest shape, but it looks more likely that Democrats were more interested in helping their supporters.

The transfers to the states having the least problems are large. Even after accounting for other factors, each additional $1,000 in a state's per-capita income means that the state, on average, got $86 more per capita in Stimulus funds.[70] With a spread of almost $38,000 in per-person income between the top and bottom states, this has a sizable impact. High-income states got considerably more Stimulus money.

States with higher bankruptcy rates got a lot less, not more, money—roughly $217 less per person for each percentage point increase in the state's bankruptcy rate.[71] States with higher foreclosure rates were treated very similarly, for each one-percentage-point increase in the number of people suffering foreclosures, the state would lose $180 per person.[72]

The spending data come from two reliable sources: the *Wall Street Journal* and the federal government's Recovery.gov website. On August 6, 2009, after the Stimulus had been in effect for almost six months, the *Wall Street Journal* published data on Stimulus spending by state for seven categories of social spending (education, HUD, health, crime fighting, job training, arts, and food and farming) and eight categories of infrastructure spending (transportation, water, energy, military, veterans, government, outdoors, and emergency shelters). The *Journal's* data allow a comparison by each category of government spending. It also provides an easy way of looking at the types of areas in the country that got the money first. Their total accounts for $211 billion out of the $825 billion that was spent on the Stimulus. Out of this money, the amounts vary a lot across the nation, with the very lowest a mere $553 per capita in Florida and the highest at $3,745 per capita in the District of Columbia.

According to Recovery.gov, a total of $268 billion of federal contracts, grants, and loans to states and territories were awarded between February 17, 2009, and June 30, 2011. Unfortunately, this source doesn't provide the same detailed breakdown on where the money went as the *Journal* does. While the variation in payouts across the United States is much greater with the more complete Recovery.gov data, the Recovery.gov and the *Journal* data are almost perfectly correlated with each other, and the bottom line is the same: The money is not going to the states hardest hit by the recession or to the poorest states.[73]

The five accompanying charts (see Figures 3.4 through 3.8) show how Stimulus dollars per capita from the Recovery.gov website vary with the poverty, unemployment, bankruptcy, and foreclosure rates

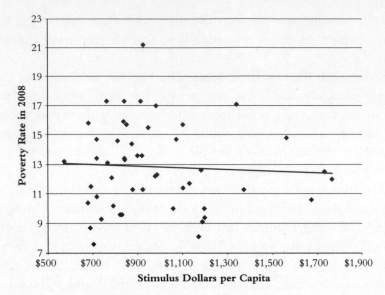

Figure 3.4   Stimulus Dollars per Capita by State and Poverty Rates in 2008, excluding Alaska

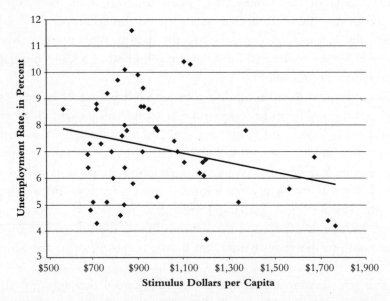

Figure 3.5   Stimulus Dollars per Capita by State and Unemployment Rates (January 2009) in 2008, excluding Alaska

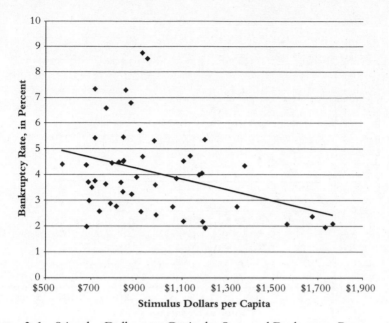

Figure 3.6 Stimulus Dollars per Capita by State and Bankruptcy Rates (4th Quarter 2008), excluding Alaska

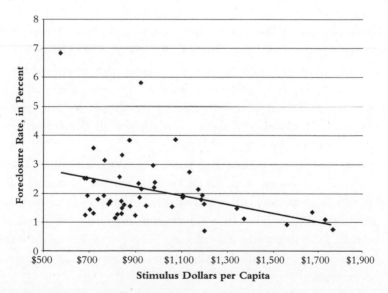

Figure 3.7 Stimulus Dollars per Capita by State and Foreclosure Rate (December 2008), excluding Alaska

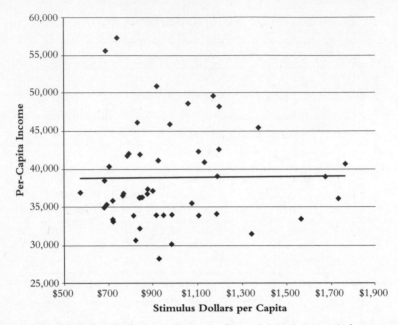

Figure 3.8 Stimulus Dollars per Capita and per Capita Income (4th quarter 2008), excluding Alaska

as well as per capita income for 49 states. Including Alaska doesn't appreciably change these results, but it is such an extreme outlier, getting almost twice as much as North Dakota, the next highest state ($3,248 versus $1,764), that including it obscures the pattern for the other states. The results with Alaska are shown in the appendix. The District of Columbia's final take is simply off the scales, with it receiving $9,313 per person.

A trend line is also included to make comparisons easier. The data for economic conditions were taken from when the Stimulus bill was being passed. For poverty, unemployment, bankruptcy, and foreclosure rates, the trend clearly shows that the states in the worst economic shape got the least federal government money. The graph for income shows that states with more income got slightly more money, but the relationship is very weak.

Even if the Stimulus money isn't going to the states the president promised, a clear pattern does emerge. Two figures show how

Stimulus dollars were awarded to states based on the percentage of a state's congressional and Senate delegations who are Democrats and the percentage of the vote Obama obtained in that state in 2008 (see Figures 3.9 and 3.10). The patterns clearly show that the money went to the places that Democrats represented, and it was much more strongly related to whether Democrats represent the state in Congress than in terms of whether the state voted for Obama.

Obviously all of these measures of economic conditions as well as some other factors could simultaneously play a role in how much money different states received from the federal government. To account for political considerations in how the money was distributed, Obama's share of the vote in a state was also included.[74] Concerns about the Stimulus being used to reward supporters has already been noted in the press.

Politico reported on June 5, 2009, that the "Stimulus tour"—visits by Mr. Obama and other administration officials "across the country to tout the massive spending program or hand out Stimulus cash to grateful local

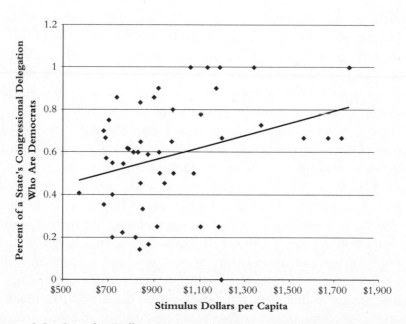

Figure 3.9 Stimulus Dollars per Capita by State and the Percentage of a State's Congressional and Senate Delegation Who Are Democrats in 2009

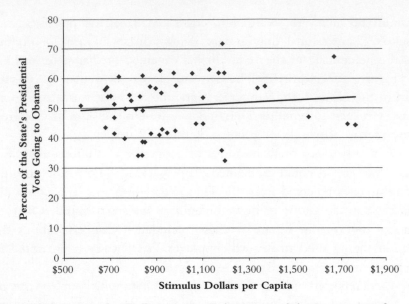

Figure 3.10 Stimulus Dollars per Capita by State and the Percentage of a State's Presidential Vote that Went to Obama in 2008

officials"—overwhelmingly took place in states that voted for Obama: "52 of the 66 events were in states that backed Obama." The other 14 events were in states that Obama lost only narrowly. A July 2009 study released by *USA Today* that looks at the same 49 states shown earlier also finds that counties that voted for Obama received about twice as much Stimulus money per capita as those that voted for McCain.[75]

In our results, Obama's share of the vote accounted for about a quarter of the variation in how the Stimulus money is being allocated. A one-percentage-point increase in Obama's vote share means an additional $31.60 in per-capita spending, but even then the relationship rests on the large amount of money given to the District of Columbia.[76]

Breaking down the data by type of spending shows that money for infrastructure was much more likely than social spending to go to high-income states with low bankruptcy and foreclosure rates. Federal spending on construction and repairs to federal buildings as well as repairs to highways and public transit projects drives much of this perverse relationship between economic distress and infrastructure Stimulus spending.

Back in July 2009, we contacted the chairmen of the Senate and House Appropriation Committees, Senator Dan Inouye, D-Hawaii, and Congressman David Obey, D-Wis., who wrote the Stimulus bill, but neither politician's office was willing to provide any on-the-record comments. "The Stimulus bill is designed to help those who have been hurt by the economic downturn. . . . Do you see disparity out there in where the money is going? Certainly," a Democratic congressional staffer knowledgeable about the process told us. "The people to talk to are in the administration. . . . The administration is deciding where [the money] flows."

An Obama administration official also explained to us that "it is not as simple as looking where the money goes. You could have someone who lives in Maryland and works in Virginia and they are benefited from money given to the Virginia firm even though they live in Maryland." She noted that it didn't really matter who got the money because "giving out money is good for everyone. If you give the money to an old person, they will spend it and that will create more jobs."

She also said that Congress was responsible for deciding where the money would go. "We didn't write the bill. We let Congress write the bill," she said.

Lee Ohanian, an economics professor at UCLA who has extensively studied New Deal policies and depressions, agreed that the spending patterns shown earlier "certainly don't fit what you would think that they would be from the standpoint of government spending as a social safety net. . . . The pattern does seem quite odd. It is certainly not the way the program was advertised."

Even by Keynesian notions, who got the money doesn't make a lot of sense. Democrats gave the most Stimulus money to those states that they represented.

Corrupting Stimulus Money

But the process by which the decision [to give Solyndra a loan guarantee] was made was on the merits. It was straightforward. And of course there were going to be debates internally when you're dealing with something as complicated as this. But I have confidence that the decisions were made based on what would be good for the American economy and the American people and putting people back to work.

                                    —*President Barack Obama, October 6, 2011*[77]

President Obama may advocate "spreading the wealth around" and blame "an ethic of greed" for the economy's problems, but the Obama administration has made a lot of extremely wealthy people a lot wealthier.[78]

Solyndra, of course, sticks out as the number-one example of cronyism under Obama, a case in which half a billion dollars through a taxpayer-subsidized loan was lost through bankruptcy, but it is only a small part of the money handed to politically favored friends of the president. Not surprisingly, George Kaiser, a billionaire and the largest investor in Solyndra, had raised $100,000 for the 2008 Obama campaign long before Solyndra received the massive green energy subsidy.[79] The Obama administration and Kaiser both claimed that Solyndra getting money "was not discussed" with White House officials.[80] Kaiser had met with officials 16 times, but the conversations were claimed to involve only "general policy priorities of the George Kaiser Family Foundation, including early childhood education and poverty, health care policy and energy policy."[81]

But emails finally obtained by the House Energy and Commerce Committee in November 2011 revealed a different story: Such conversations had indeed taken place. One email by Kaiser himself referred to a meeting that took place in February 2009: "Ken and I were visiting with a group of Administration folks in DC who are in charge of the Stimulus process (White House, not DOE) and Solyndra came up. Every one of them responded simultaneously about their thorough knowledge of the Solyndra story, suggesting it was one of their prime poster children."[82]

Despite administration's assurances that only career employees inside the Department of Energy were involved in evaluating whether Solyndra should get a loan, it was discovered that Larry Summers and other top Obama officials "had direct involvement" in advocating the loan.[83] And other emails from Vice President Biden's office revealed a similar, troubling finding: Even within the Department of Energy, it was not just career employees who decided. Instead, the politically appointed Energy Secretary, Steven Chu, was involved in the decision process. One email in late February 2009 mentioned: "It appears things are headed in the right direction and Chu is apparently staying involved in Solyndra's application and continues to talk up the company as a success story."[84]

There were yet more disturbing connections. A green energy adviser for President Obama, David Prend, was offered the job as adviser because he had been a fundraiser during the Obama campaign. According to emails obtained by congressional investigators, Prend was perhaps the first person within the Obama administration to push for the company to get the half-billion-dollar low-interest loan.[85] At the time, a venture capital firm that Prend co-founded owned 7.5 percent of Solyndra. Prend also pushed for Solyndra to get a valuable Navy contract.

Yet another inside administration man involved in the Solyndra case was Steve Spinner. Spinner is described by ABC News as an "elite Obama fundraiser" who helped run energy and environmental policy for the administration and who pushed for the money even though his wife at the time was employed as a lawyer at Solyndra.[86] After the deal went through, his wife's law firm received as much as $2.4 million in federal funds for her work in arranging the half-billion-dollar money transfer.[87]

In the end, despite repeated warnings from the Treasury Department and others, Solyndra received the money in September 2009.[88] In 2008, even before Obama's presidency, credit rating agencies had given Solyndra a low "non-investment grade" rating, determining that the company suffered from a technological risk as well as a financial risk.[89] By March 2010, Solyndra's own auditor, PricewaterhouseCoopers LLP, questioned whether the company was viable: "The Company has suffered recurring losses from operations, negative cash flows since inception" and that there was "substantial doubt about its ability to continue as a going concern."

Indeed, the Obama administration was so determined to help out Solyndra that they very likely broke the Energy Policy Act of 2005 in changing the terms of the loan guarantee.[90] The new rules made it very hard for taxpayers to get any of their money back, but by putting the government far down in priority for creditors, it made it much easier for Solyndra to go and borrow more private money. Unlike the government, in a bankruptcy, private creditors would get something back when Solyndra's assets were sold off.

But the corruption goes even further, with the Obama administration using its influence with Solyndra to hide what was happening to the voters. Obviously, given the half-billion dollars involved, any failure would have been politically embarrassing to the Obama administration. The potential political problems were even more acute since Obama, Biden, and other administration officials had publicly praised Solyndra as the poster child of how a so-called clean-energy initiative should work. Yet, just days before the November 2010 elections, Solyndra notified the Department of Energy that its financial difficulties were going to result in layoffs.[91] Hardly the election eve news the administration wanted for a program that was supposed to create 1,000 jobs. Emails obtained by the House Energy and Commerce Committee from Solyndra's largest investor describe how Department of Energy officials "did push very hard for us to hold our announcement of the consolidation to employees and vendors to November 3rd."[92] Several other emails make it clear that the announcement was postponed for political reasons until after the November 2nd election.

Unfortunately, even though the money lost to Solyndra involved more Stimulus dollars than 35 states got for highways, roads, and bridges,[93] it was hardly the only case in which well-connected, extremely wealthy individuals got government help.[94] Fisker Automotive, which is partly owned by former Vice President Al Gore, whose net worth is over $100 million, is one such example.[95] Fisker got a $529 million loan guarantee.[96] Similarly, a $465 million loan guarantee went to Tesla Motors, whose main owners are billionaire Democrats PayPal's Elon Musk and Google co-founders Larry Page and Sergey Brin.[97] While getting about $335 million in awards and grants and $16 million in loans from the Stimulus, NRG Energy was owned by billionaires with large stakes in the company such as Warren Buffett, Steven Cohen, and Carl Icahn.[98]

"Conflicts of interest" in giving out Stimulus money abound. Jeffrey Immelt headed General Electric at the same time that he headed

Obama's Council on Jobs and served on Obama's Economic Recovery Advisory Board.[99] His company got $128 million in direct contracts and awards from the Stimulus.[100] But that is only a very small part of the money that his company has received from the government. It has invested in solar energy and wind projects that have received $2 billion in federal loan guarantees and, as of the fall of 2011, and they expect to collect another billion dollars in Treasury grants. Also, as the *New York Times* described it: "G.E., for example, lobbied Congress in 2009 to help expand the subsidy programs, and it now profits from every aspect of the boom in renewable-power plant construction."[101] Another member of Obama's jobs council, Lewis Hay III, received nearly $2 billion in loan guarantees for his company, NextEra Energy.[102]

The loans aren't given out randomly. About 75 percent of loans and grants have been given out to companies run by Obama supporters.[103] Pat Stryker, a billionaire who raised $87,000 for Obama's 2008 presidential campaign and $35,000 for his 2012 re-election campaign by June 2011, was a major investor in Abound Solar Manufacturing.[104] The company received a $370 million very-low-interest-rate loan as well as a $5 million grant from the Department of Energy.[105] Or take Michael Froman's case. Mr. Froman, who was a deputy assistant to President Obama and raised $500,000 for his 2008 presidential campaign, was a major investor in Solar Reserve. The company received a $737 million loan from the administration.[106] There are other Obama aides, such as White House deputy chief of staff Nancy Ann DeParle, who have appeared to benefit from these government loans and grants.[107]

Another major category benefiting greatly from the Stimulus has been the unions, in particular the various public employee unions. Besides all the large direct payments for higher salaries and more jobs for public school teachers and other government employees, unions have benefited in other ways. The Obama Department of Transportation has invoked and expanded the Davis–Bacon Act, which established the requirement for paying prevailing wages on public works projects. This act is a Depression–era law that favored unionized companies with higher-wage workers as it protected them from being outbid for contracts.[108] This also meant that lower-wage, low-skilled workers had a harder time winning contracts. Ironically, this favored higher-income workers over lower-income ones, whom President Obama always seems so concerned about.

Take the Small Business Jobs Act that was passed in September 2010. The legislation created a Small Business Lending Fund that lets the Obama administration make $30 billion in investments in "community banks."[109] You won't be surprised to learn that the Obama administration has complete discretion over who gets this money. The targeted tax cuts and subsidies must have been a lobbyist's dream.[110] There is the "bonus depreciation," a tax code provision that provides a 50-percent first-year depreciation. Among the assets eligible are: "single-purpose agricultural (livestock) or horticultural structures," "storage facilities (except buildings and their structural components) used in connection with distributing petroleum or any primary product of petroleum," "sewage disposal services," and "off-the-shelf computer software."

Thus, Obama administration officials and Democratic congressional leaders apparently somehow figured out that an agricultural building that serves just one purpose deserves a deduction. But if it does two or more things, it should not be subsidized. So, a farmer who would have built one building will now build two buildings so that they can get a huge depreciation on both. Why should larger farms, where it may make more sense to have a building that does one function, be the ones to benefit? Of course, this is all nonsensical from an economic point of view. Equally nonsensical are the quick write-offs for certain types of computer software but not others.

Nor have the beneficiaries of the Obama administration been limited to those who got money from the various stimulus or jobs bills. Goldman Sachs was a big supporter of the Dodd-Frank financial market legislation. The legislation prevents many of the giant investment company's former competitors in the banking industry from continuing to offer some services to compete against them.

Huge benefits will also accrue to those companies picked as too big to fail. If the government is going to protect a company from bankruptcy, its cost of borrowing is going to be much lower than the rate that its competitors are going to have to pay. What is not often clear is that when the government uses taxpayer money to shore up specially favored companies, their competitors suffer and are more likely to shrink or even go under. Fannie Mae and Freddie Mac will also be exempt from costly new mortgage regulations imposed on private companies.

Space Aliens Invading as Stimulus

Fareed Zakaria: But even if you were, wouldn't John Maynard Keynes say that if you could employ people to dig a ditch and then fill it up again, that's fine, they're being productively employed, they'll pay taxes, so maybe Boston's Big Dig was just fine, after all.

Paul Krugman: Think about World War II, right? That was actually negative social product spending, and yet it brought us out. . . .

If we discovered that space aliens were planning to attack and we needed a massive buildup to counter the space alien threat and really inflation and budget deficits took secondary place to that, this slump would be over in 18 months. And then if we discovered, oops, we made a mistake, there aren't any aliens, we'd be better off.[111]

—*Paul Krugman,* GPS CNN,
August 12, 2011

Would we really be better off paying workers to dig ditches and then fill them back up? Or, how about paying people to build massive defenses against imaginary space aliens? Krugman also thought that the 9/11 attacks "could even do some economic good" by stimulating the economy because "all of a sudden, we need some new office buildings" and "rebuilding will generate at least some increase in business spending."[112] Unfortunately, this is the cornerstone of Obama's Stimulus program.

The examples also highlight how inconsistently these arguments are used by the president and his defenders. The 9/11 attacks or natural disasters in the United States were supposedly beneficial for the U.S. economy because they increase spending, but the earthquake in Japan was detrimental.

So what really makes the economic pie bigger? There are two sides to this. The supply side: Lower marginal tax rates mean the more that people get to keep from each additional dollar they earn, the harder they will work and the more they will produce.

Obama's approach, the Keynesian view, also often called "the demand-side view" or "the multiplier," is that giving the money to the right people to spend will create wealth. Poorer people are said to spend more of the money that they are given and that will generate more money for others. Democratic House Speaker Nancy Pelosi made this claim many times when she advocated more unemployment insurance benefits: "It injects demand into the economy and is job creating. It creates jobs faster than almost any other initiative you can name. Because, again, it is money that is needed for families to survive and it is spent."[113]

Many others also use this line of reasoning when debating the frequent extensions of unemployment insurance benefits, benefits that are provided to the unemployed for up to 99 weeks. This Keynesian theory also forms the basis for the president's proposed expansion of the earned income tax credit and items such as the college tuition tax credit for relatively lower-income families or the Cash for Clunkers program, which was aimed at poorer people who owned older cars.[114] The notion is that poorer individuals, who are living hand to mouth, will spend all of the money that is given to them. As Krugman notes, the main point is that the money be spent someplace, even if it is on fighting nonexistent alien attacks from outer space.

But this multiplier claim is simply invalid. First, as just noted, the resources have to come from someplace. If you want to increase a country's wealth, it does matter that money be spent in productive ways that people value. Digging ditches and filling them in again leave people no better off. With the "Cash for Clunkers" program, people received $3,500 or $4,500 when buying a new car, but perfectly working cars that may only have been five years old were destroyed and never driven again.[115] When the government makes investments to companies that private lenders won't make, the lower returns or increased riskiness make us poorer.

The problem with asking if government spending increases income is the way that GDP is measured. The government counts money spent to dig ditches and then fill them up as adding as much to income as building a car or something else that people really value. So even if GDP remains unchanged, the country is actually getting poorer, because each dollar isn't going toward something that people value as much. As the late Milton Friedman used to say: "Nobody spends somebody else's money as carefully as he spends his own. Nobody uses somebody else's resources as carefully as he uses his own."

Second, everyone's money is spent one way or another. This claim of some people spending their money while others are saving really assumes that saving is the equivalent of burying one's money in a hole in the backyard. In reality, if you don't spend your money, you are putting it in the bank or you are putting it in stocks or bonds, which means you are giving it to someone else to spend.

Even when a poor person spends his money at the local grocery store, that business is going to either spend it or put it in the bank. Taking money from wealthy people and giving it to poor people doesn't create more spending. It just alters who gets to choose where the money is spent.

President Obama keeps pointing to the tax cuts that were included in the original Stimulus, but his tax cuts actually discourage work for one simple reason: They increase marginal tax rates. In plain English, that means that for every additional dollar someone earns, they get to keep less of that additional dollar. Obama's tax cuts increase marginal tax rates because they are phased out as people make more income. You get the earned income tax credit or the college tuition credit but as you earn more money, those credits are reduced.

There is never a good time for the country to levy increased penalties on the rewards from harder work but surely this is not the time for it, when so many people are already hurting.

Of course, far from stimulating the economy, extended unemployment insurance benefits discourage people from working. People receive the unemployment insurance as well as assistance paying their mortgages and health insurance only as long as they are unemployed. There is a real dollar penalty as soon as they take a job.

The supposed benefits from unemployment insurance get applied to all government spending. In late 2011, when there was a debate over automatic spending cuts that would be triggered from an earlier budget agreement, Obama's defense secretary, Leon Panetta, worried that cutting defense spending by a trillion dollars over 10 years would increase the national unemployment rate by 1 percent—about 1.5 million jobs.[116] His argument depended on a similar multiplier effect to that claimed for unemployment insurance. Even some Republicans have taken to arguing against defense spending cuts because of the impact that they will have on unemployment. Representative Buck McKeon (R-CA), chairman of the House Armed Services Committee, warned that the cut "would kill upwards of 800,000 active duty, civilian, and industrial American jobs."[117]

Disappointingly, many members of the media measure the Stimulus by just counting up the money that is spent. Take the *New York Times*'s David Leonhardt, who writes the paper's "Economix" column. In late 2010, he wrote about the Stimulus in terms of "the amount of money pumped into the ailing economy," not considering the disincentives created against working. Thus, he included an extension of unemployment insurance benefits as among measures "that are more likely to create jobs."[118]

All that said, President Obama did agree to temporarily lower marginal tax rates, that was the one-year, two-percentage point reduction in Social Security taxes during 2011.[119] He then asked for another one-year extension for 2012. Nevertheless, this change did not come close to offsetting the detrimental effect of phasing out different tax credits. The tax rate cuts were also temporary, but the increases in marginal rates are permanent.

Even the Bush tax rates were extended for two years, until January 2013. But temporary gimmicks do not work well in encouraging long-term investments. It takes years before investments begin to pay off, and such a tax cut will be completely irrelevant. Long-term higher tax rates as proposed by Obama are going to have a much bigger impact on investments.

The threat of long-term higher rates in the future do cause people to work harder before the rates go up, but there is no getting around the fact that when the rates do rise, people will be discouraged from working and income will fall. Having people work harder for a short period before taxes rise is more than offset by the undesirable long-term disincentive to working.

Increased marginal tax rates will clearly be bad for the economy. But President Obama just clings on to the old Keynesian arguments that have failed so spectacularly during his administration.

Surrounding himself with economic advisers such as Austan Goolsbee and Larry Summers, Obama's tax policies are unsurprising. Goolsbee's research studied the 1993 increase in the top tax rate from 31 to almost 40 percent. He reached the controversial claim that except for the first year, the increase had almost no impact on how hard people worked.[120] This made him an even stronger defender of these tax increases than former President Bill Clinton, who famously admitted in 1995: "Probably there are people in this room still mad at me at that budget because you think I raised your taxes too much. It might surprise you to know that I think I raised them too much, too."[121] Clinton had good reason to reconsider his tax hikes. Internal Revenue Service data showed that the tax increases raised only one-third as much revenue as the Clinton administration had predicted.[122] Similar to Goolsbee, Summers thinks that federal marginal income tax rates can rise above 50 percent before they pose any problem in regard to altering people's behavior.[123]

Goolsbee was willing to go much further than raising marginal income tax rates in redistributing wealth. In 2008, when asked if he supported a windfall-profits tax on oil companies so that the federal government could "give out $1,000 to each person," Goolsbee answered with an emphatic "yes." He asserted: "They're not plowing the money back into investment, they're taking the money and paying themselves off. . . . There's no question the executives have been doing pretty good. . . . We need to give [people] relief right now, . . .

to put these $1,000 checks into people's hands."[124] He didn't think that reducing profits would have much of a detrimental effect.

But for Obama, tax revenue is a secondary consideration. What matters more to him is redistribution. During the 2008 Democrat primaries, he noted that he might raise capital gains taxes even though doing that would reduce tax revenue because "what I've said is that I would look at raising the capital gains tax for purposes of fairness."[125] Late in the campaign, Obama reiterated this notion of taxes during his famous exchange with Joe Wurzelbacher, better known as "Joe the Plumber." When Joe asked Obama about his new tax proposals, Obama responded: "I think when you spread the wealth around, it's good for everybody."[126]

Wanting to help people is understandable, but there is a trade-off. Higher marginal income tax rates, combined with large government transfers, create a disincentive for people to work hard and make the economic pie smaller. But a smaller pie can mean less for everyone in the long run, even those who get the government handouts.

Obama sees companies as having an obligation to create jobs. But rather than inducing companies through higher profits to hire more people, Obama instead preaches that they should do it for the good of the country, even if it means lower profits. Take his speech in February 2011, when Obama told business people at the U.S. Chamber of Commerce:[127]

> I understand you are under incredible pressure to cut costs and keep your margins up. I understand the significance of your obligations to your shareholders and the pressures that are created by quarterly reports. I get it. But . . . I'm hoping that all of you are thinking what you can do for America. Ask yourselves what you can do to hire more American workers, what you can do to support the American economy and invest in this nation. . . .

It is a point reiterated by Obama's economic advisers, such as Goolsbee, as well as Vice President Biden: that the failure of the economy isn't the government's fault; rather, it rests with the private sector not doing its job.[128]

Notes

1. Matt Lauer, "Obama Sits Down with Matt Lauer," *Today Show,* February 2, 2009, http://today.msnbc.msn.com/id/28975726/ns/today-today_people/t/obama-were-suffering-massive-hangover/.

2. John Harwood, "10 Questions for Austan Goolsbee," *New York Times,* December 3, 2010, http://thecaucus.blogs.nytimes.com/2010/12/03/10-questions-for-austan-goolsbee/.

3. During the time under discussion, the U.S. population grew by 5 million people. If the workforce participation rate had remained the same as it was at the beginning of the period, there would have been 3 million more jobs.

4. The Stimulus had been so large when some of his aides pushed for another round of spending in October 2009, Obama is quoted as saying: "I said it before, I'll say it again. It's not going to happen." Associated Press, "Obama: Stimulus Will Create 4.1 Million Jobs," CNBC, January 10, 2009, http://classic.cnbc.com/id/28590554/.

5. Sam Gustin, "Obama Signs $26 Billion Public Sector Jobs Bill into Law," *Daily Finance,* August 10, 2010, www.dailyfinance.com/2010/08/10/public-sector-jobs-bill-passes-house/?icid=sphere_copyright.

6. Catherine Clifford, "House OKs Small Biz Jobs Bill," CNNMoney.com, September 23, 2010, http://money.cnn.com/2010/09/23/smallbusiness/small_business_legislation_house/index.htm.

7. "Disaster Relief and Summer Jobs Act," Fox News, March 24, 2010, www.foxnews.com/topics/politics/disaster-relief-and-summer-jobs-act.htm. See also "H.R.4899—Disaster Relief and Summer Jobs Act of 2010," OpenCongress.org, www.opencongress.org/bill/111-h4899/show.

8. George Stephanopoulos, "Exclusive: Vice President Joe Biden," *This Week with George Stephanopoulos,* ABC News, July 5, 2009, http://abcnews.go.com/ThisWeek/Politics/Story?id=8002421&page=3.

9. Deborah Solomon, "Calls Grow to Increase Stimulus Spending," *Wall Street Journal,* July 6, 2009, http://online.wsj.com/article/SB124680904844296383.html#mod=loomia?loomia_si=t0:a16:g2:r1:c0.0529546:b26214120.

10. Jared Bernstein, "Press Briefing by Press Secretary Robert Gibbs and the Vice President's Chief Economist, Jared Bernstein," The White House, Office of the Press Secretary, June 8, 2009, www.whitehouse.gov/the_press_office/Briefing-by-Press-Secretary-Robert-Gibbs-with-Jared-Bernstein-the-Vice-Presidents-Chief-Economist-6-8-09/.

11. Chuck Todd, Mark Murray, Domenico Montanaro, and Ali Weinberg, "First Thoughts: Obama on Putin," MSNBC, July 7, 2009, http://firstread.msnbc.msn.com/_news/2009/07/07/4431468-first-thoughts-obama-on-putin.

12. "Notes Projections and the Budget Outlook," White House, February 28, 2009, www.whitehouse.gov/administration/eop/cea/Economic-Projections-and-the-Budget-Outlook/; "A New Era of Responsibility: Renewing America's Promise," Office of Management and Budget, February 26, 2009; see Table S-8, www.whitehouse.gov/sites/default/files/omb/assets/fy2010_new_era/A_New_Era_of_Responsibility2.pdf.

13. WSJ Staff, "Fourth-Quarter GDP: Worse and Worse," *Wall Street Journal,* December 11, 2008, http://blogs.wsj.com/economics/2008/12/11/fourth-quarter-gdp-worse-and-worse/.

14. "Oh, they're good guys and they're smart but just not as forceful as I'd like. . . . I do have genuine contact with both the White House and with congressional leadership," Paul Krugman in his interview with Alison van Tiggelen. Alison van Tiggelen, "Paul Krugman: Transcript—Will Climate Legislation Kill the Economy," *Fresh Dialogues,* December 2, 2009, www.freshdialogues.com/2009/12/09/paul-krugman-transcript-will-climate-legislation-kill-the-economy/.

15. Paul Krugman was actually even more bullish than Summers in regard to how quickly the economy would start benefiting from the Stimulus. On the day that the Stimulus bill was signed by Obama, Krugman told CNBC: "Actually, we are already seeing some positive effects." Paul Krugman, appearing on CNBC on Tuesday, February 17, 2009, www.huffingtonpost.com/2009/02/17/paul-krugman-stimulus-too_n_167721.html.

16. "A New Era of Responsibility: Renewing America's Promise," Office of Management and Budget, February 26, 2009; see Table S-8, www.whitehouse.gov/sites/default/files/omb/assets/fy2010_new_era/A_New_Era_of_Responsibility2.pdf.

17. These numbers were correct as of November 3, 2011. The data are available from the Bureau of Economic Analysis, U.S. Department of Commerce, www.bea.gov/newsreleases/national/gdp/gdpnewsrelease.htm.

18. Greg Mankiw, "Team Obama on the Unit Root Hypothesis," *Greg Mankiw's Blog,* March 3, 2009.

19. Paul Krugman, "Roots of Evil (Wonkish)," *New York Times,* March 3, 2009.

20. Brad DeLong, "Permanent and Transitory Components of Real GDP," *Grasping Reality with Both Hands* (DeLong's blog), March 3, 2009.

21. Greg Mankiw, "Wanna Bet Some of that Nobel Money?" *Greg Mankiw's Blog,* March 4, 2009, http://gregmankiw.blogspot.com/2009/03/wanna-bet-some-of-that-nobel-money.html.

22. "The First McCain–Obama Presidential Debate," Commission on Presidential Debates, September 26, 2008, www.debates.org/index.php?page=2008-debate-transcript; "The Second McCain–Obama Presidential Debate," Commission on Presidential Debates, October 7, 2008, www.debates.org/index.php?page=october-7-2008-debate-transcrip; and "The Third McCain–Obama Presidential Debate," Commission on Presidential Debates, October 15, 2008, www.debates.org/index.php?page=october-15-2008-debate-transcript.

23. Editorial, "Revisionist History on Unemployment," *Washington Times,* June 23, 2010, www.washingtontimes.com/news/2010/jun/23/revisionist-history-on-unemployment/.

24. President Barack Obama, "President Obama Delivers Your Weekly Address," White House blog, January 24, 2009, www.whitehouse.gov/president-obama-delivers-your-weekly-address/.

25. President Barack Obama, "Obama Takes Questions on Economy," CNN Politics, February 9, 2009, www.cnn.com/2009/POLITICS/02/09/obama.conference.transcript/.

26. President Barack Obama, "Transcript: Remarks by President Obama, Home Mortgage Crisis, Mesa, Arizona," White House Press Office, February 18, 2009, www.clipsandcomment.com/2009/02/18/transcript-remarks-by-president-obama-home-mortgage-crisis-mesa-arizona-february-18-2009/.

27. President Barack Obama, "Remarks of President Barack Obama—As Prepared for Delivery, Address to Joint Session of Congress," White House Press Office, February 24, 2009, www.whitehouse.gov/the_press_office/Remarks-of-President-Barack-Obama-Address-to-Joint-Session-of-Congress/.

28. Economic Forecasting Survey, *Wall Street Journal,* http://online.wsj.com/public/resources/documents/info-flash08.html?project=EFORECAST07.

29. "Pelosi Says Job Creation Key to Stimulus Proposals," Fox News, January 25, 2009, www.foxnews.com/politics/president/first100days/2009/01/25/pelosi-job-creation-key-stimulus-proposals/100days/.

30. Sheryl Gay Stolberg, "In a World Not Wholly Cooperative, Obama's Top Economist Makes Do," *New York Times,* February 16, 2009, www.nytimes.com/2009/02/17/us/politics/17summers.html?pagewanted=al); Garrett Jones and Daniel M. Rothschild, "No Such Thing as Shovel Ready: The Supply Side of the Recovery Act," Mercatus Center, George Mason University, September 2011. For a related earlier discussion, see: Lawrence H. Summers, "The State of the U.S. Economy." Presentation at Brookings Institution forum, December 19, 2007, www.brookings.edu/events/2007/1219_us_economy.aspx.

31. Laura Meckler, "Obama Signs Stimulus into Law," *Wall Street Journal,* February 18, 2009, http://online.wsj.com/article/SB123487951033799545.html. Furthermore, Ron Suskind's book reveals that in a private White House meeting in June, Summers predicted "a quick bounce-back" in jobs. See Ron Suskind, *Confidence Men: Wall Street, Washington, and the Education of a President* (New York: Harper, 2011).

32. President Barack Obama, "Transcript: President Obama's Press Conference," *Washington Post,* March 24, 2009, www.washingtonpost.com/wp-dyn/content/article/2009/03/24/AR2009032403036.html; Summers declared even earlier: "Some of the things that the president is doing are starting to have effects." "Larry Summers and Mitch McConnell," *This Week with George Stephanopoulos,* ABC News, March 15, 2009, http://abcnews.go.com/ThisWeek/story?id=7085991&page=3.

33. "Why Is Obama Touting Stimulus after 1.6 Million Jobs Lost?" Fox News, May 28, 2009, http://nation.foxnews.com/politics/2009/05/28/why-obama-touting-stimulus-after-16m-jobs-lost. For a discussion of the Obama administration talking about the "green shoots" of recovery, see Martin Wolf, "Why the 'Green Shoots' of Recovery Could Yet Wither," *Financial Times,* April 21, 2009, www.ft.com/intl/cms/s/0/1ed88b70-2ea9-11de-b7d3-00144feabdc0.html#axzz1aNqnJJfL.

34. Elizabeth Williamson, "Biden on Stimulus: 'Never Thought It Would Work This Well,'" *Wall Street Journal,* September 24, 2009, http://blogs.wsj.com/washwire/2009/09/24/biden-on-stimulus-never-thought-it-would-work-this-well/.

35. Mimi Hall, "Biden Touts 'Summer of Recovery,'" *USA Today,* June 17, 2010, http://content.usatoday.com/communities/theoval/post/2010/06/biden-touts-summer-of-recovery/1.

36. John R. Lott Jr., "Fact Checking Team Obama's Stimulus Claims," Fox News, February 19, 2010, www.foxnews.com/opinion/2010/02/19/john-lott-stimulus-obama-goolsbee-hemmer/.

37. On Sean Hannity's radio show on October 28, 2011, during the third hour, Hannity and Goolsbee had this exchange.

    Hannity: We heard that unemployment wasn't going to go above 8 percent.

    Goolsbee: When they made that 8 percent prediction, that was the same prediction being made by everyone. But you forget the other half of the thing, which is if you did nothing, the rate would go to 8.9 percent, and it was already above that before the first part of the stimulus even went out.

38. Austan Goolsbee, "The Employment Situation in April," Council of Economic Advisers, May 6, 2011, www.whitehouse.gov/blog/2011/05/06/employment-situation-april.

39. Don Lee, "Economy Shows Solid Job Growth for a Third Straight Month," *Los Angeles Times,* May 7, 2011, http://articles.latimes.com/2011/may/07/business/la-fi-april-jobs-report-20110506; Motoko Rich, "Payrolls Show Strong Growth but Jobless Rate Rises," *New York Times,* May 6, 2011, www.nytimes.com/2011/05/07/business/economy/07jobs.html?_r=1.

40. President Barack Obama, "Statement by the President, Rose Garden," The White House, Office of the Press Secretary, August 2, 2011, www.whitehouse.gov/the-press-office/2011/08/02/statement-president.

41. Using the Bureau of Labor Statistics international unemployment rates adjusted to U.S. concepts, the Japanese unemployment rate fell from 4.3 percent in March 2011 to 4.0 percent in August 2011.

42. Using the Bureau of Labor Statistics international unemployment rates adjusted to U.S. concepts, the German, Italian, and Swedish unemployment rates fell from 6.9, 8.2, and 7.7 percent, respectively, in January 2011 to 6.5, 8.0, and 7.3 percent, respectively, in August 2011.

43. Goolsbee was the chair of Obama's Council of Economic Advisers until August 2011, and he had returned back to the University of Chicago Booth School of Business by October 2011.

44. From December 2009 to December 2010, total nonfarm employment using the Establishment Survey of businesses increased by 940,000 and "temporary help" service jobs made up 310,000 of that increase. The Bureau of Labor Statistics numbers are available at www.bls.gov/webapps/legacy/cesbtab1.htm. A third of those were "temporary help" service jobs. The Bureau of Labor Statistics numbers for "temporary help" service jobs are available at www.bls.gov/webapps/legacy/cesbtab1.htm. The unemployment rate was also stuck for virtually the entire year, actually increasing slightly from January to November 2010. The unemployment rate in January 2010 was 9.7 percent and by November 2010, it had gone up to 9.8 percent. The rate then fell to 9.4 percent in December 2010. The Bureau of Labor Statistics numbers are available at www.bls.gov/webapps/legacy/cpsatab1.htm.

45. David Jackson, "Obama Economic Aide: 'One Month Is Not a Trend,'" *USA Today,* June 5, 2011, http://content.usatoday.com/communities/theoval/post/2011/06/obama-economic-aide-one-month-is-not-a-trend/1. Goolsbee also made virtually identical comments on Christiane Amanpour's Sunday program *This Week* when he told her: "Don't bank too much of any one month's jobs report." James Sunshine, "Austan Goolsbee:

Don't Worry About Recent Lack of Job Creation," Huffington Post, June 6, 2011, www.huffingtonpost.com/2011/06/06/goolsbee-on-jobs-numbers_n_871742.html.

46. The Bureau of Labor Statistics numbers are available at www.bls.gov/webapps/legacy/cesbtab1.htm.

47. The Bureau of Labor Statistics numbers for "temporary help" service jobs are available at www.bls.gov/webapps/legacy/cesbtab1.htm.

48. John Lott Jr., "Obama's Stimulus Package Will Increase Unemployment," Fox News, February 3, 2009, www.foxnews.com/story/0,2933,487425,00.html.

49. Lawrence Summers, "Responding to an Historic Economic Crisis: The Obama Program," Address at the Brookings Institution, March 13, 2009, www.brookings.edu/~/media/Files/events/2009/0313_summers/20090313_summers.pdf.

50. John Bentley, "McCain Says 'Fundamentals' of U.S. Economy Are Strong," CBS News, September 15, 2008, www.cbsnews.com/8301-502443_162-4450366-502443.html.

51. Associated Press, "White House: Economy Still Has 'Strong' Underpinnings," *USA Today,* March 15, 2009, www.usatoday.com/news/washington/2009-03-15-dem-economy_N.htm.

52. *Daily Mail* Reporter, "McCain Calls U.S. Economy 'Fundamentally Sound' on Same Day Lehman Brothers Declared Bankrupt," *Daily Mail* (UK), September 16, 2008, www.dailymail.co.uk/news/article-1056475/McCain-calls-U-S-economy-fundamentally-sound-day-Lehman-Brothers-declared-bankrupt.html.

53. David Gregory, "*Meet the Press* transcript for March 15, 2009," *Meet the Press,* NBC News, March 15, 2009, www.msnbc.msn.com/id/29705720/ns/meet_the_press/t/meet-press-transcript-march/#.Tphjp-seI0M.

54. "Larry Summers and Mitch McConnell," *This Week with George Stephanopoulos,* ABC News, March 15, 2009, (http://abcnews.go.com/ThisWeek/story?id=7085991&page=3).

55. Jeff Zeleny, "Obama Weighs Quick Undoing of Bush Policy," *New York Times,* November 9, 2008 www.nytimes.com/2008/11/10/us/politics/10obama.html?ref=politics.

56. "Obama Sees Stimulus Package by Mid-February,"MSNBC.com news services, January 23, 2009, www.msnbc.msn.com/id/28811470#.TpicsuseI0M.

57. "*This Week* Transcript: VP-Elect Joe Biden," ABC News, December 21, 2008, http://abcnews.go.com/ThisWeek/story?id=6499340&page=3.

58. President Barack Obama, "Remarks by the President in Town Hall Meeting in Nashua, New Hampshire," The White House, Office of the Press Secretary, February 2, 2010, www.whitehouse.gov/the-press-office/ remarks-president-town-hall-meeting-nashua-new-hampshire.

59. President Barack Obama, "State of the Union Address," *Washington Post*, January 27, 2010, http://voices.washingtonpost.com/44/2010/01/obama-on-jobs-in-state-of-the.html. Obama has backed down from these claims over time, though they are still misleading. By October 2011, he was making it sound as if all independent economists supported his economic plan: "This jobs bill can help guard against another downturn here in America. This is what independent economists have said. Not just politicians. Not just people in my administration. Independent experts who do this for a living have said that this jobs bill will have a significant effect for our economy and middle-class families all across America." Jamie Klatell, "Obama: Economists Back My Jobs Plan," *The Hill,* October 8, 2011, http://thehill .com/video/administration/186347-obama-economists-back-my-jobs-plan-gop-should-explain-opposition.

60. There was also an ad placed in the *New York Times* on January 28, 2009, with the names of 259 economists who opposed Obama's Stimulus bill (www. cato.org/special/stimulus09/cato_stimulus.pdf). Greg Mankiw also put together a short list of 11 very prominent economists who also opposed the bill (http://gregmankiw.blogspot.com/2009/01/is-joe-biden-disingenuous-or.html).

61. Art Rolnick, "Modern Macroeconomics Under Attack," *The Region,* September 2010, https://files.nyu.edu/ts43/public/personal/sargent_Mpls_ interview.pdf.

62. John R. Lott Jr., "Is the Stimulus Working?" Fox News, June 2, 2009, http://johnrlott.tripod.com/op-eds/FoxNewsIsStimWorking060209.html.

63. Economic Forecasting Survey, *Wall Street Journal,* http://online.wsj.com/ public/resources/documents/info-flash08.html?project=EFORECAST07.

64. CBO, "Estimated Impact of the American Recovery and Reinvestment Act on Employment and Economic Output from April 2011 through June 2011," Congressional Budget Office, August 2011, www.cbo.gov/ ftpdocs/123xx/doc12385/08-24-ARRA.pdf.

65. "In other words, if the project is being funded with stimulus dollars— even if the person worked at that company or organization before and will work the same place afterwards—that's a stimulus job." Kristina Wong, "Farewell 'Saved or Created': Obama Administration Changes the Counting of Stimulus Jobs," ABC News, *Political Punch,* January 11, 2010, http://abcnews.go.com/blogs/politics/2010/01/farewell-saved-or

-created-obama-administration-changes-the-counting-of-stimulus-jobs/. See also William McGurn, "The Media Fall for Phony 'Jobs' Claims," *Wall Street Journal,* June 10, 2009, http://online.wsj.com/article/SB124451592762396883.html.

66. Robert Barro, "Government Spending Is No Free Lunch," *Wall Street Journal,* January 22, 2009, http://online.wsj.com/article/SB123258618204604599.html.

67. Suskind, *Confidence Men,* 18.

68. Garrett Jones and Daniel M. Rothschild, "Did Stimulus Dollars Hire the Unemployed? Answers to Questions about the American Recovery and Reinvestment Act," Mercatus Center, George Mason University, September 2011.

69. About 85 percent of the Stimulus's budgetary impact was born by June 2011, so that implies about $700 out of $825 billion. CBO, "Estimated Impact of the American Recovery and Reinvestment Act on Employment and Economic Output from April 2011 through June 2011," Congressional Budget Office, August 2011, www.cbo.gov/ftpdocs/123xx/doc12385/08-24-ARRA.pdf.

70. Using Office of Labor Statistics data, the regression result using the Recovery.gov data was (absolute t-statistic in parentheses):

    Per-Capita Stimulus Dollars Awarded = 0.0858 (4.16); Per-Capita Income in the 4th Quarter of 2008−2205 (2.66);

    adj-R2 = 0.2458; F statistic = 17.30; Number of Observations = 51.

71. Using Office of Labor Statistics data, the regression result using the Recovery.gov data was (absolute t-statistic in parentheses):

    Per-Capita Stimulus Dollars Awarded = −217.4 (2.25); Bankruptcy Rate in 1st quarter 2009 + 2050 (4.88);

    adj-R2 = 0.0750; F statistic = 5.05; Number of Observations = 51.

72. Using Office of Labor Statistics data, the regression result using the Recovery.gov data was (absolute t-statistic in parentheses):

    Per-Capita Stimulus Dollars Awarded = −179.79 (1.19); Foreclosures in 4th quarter 2008 + 1556.4 (4.35);

    adj-R2 = 0.0281; F statistic = 1.42; Number of Observations = 51.

73. The correlation coefficient between the Recovery.gov and the *Wall Street Journal* data is 0.979.

74. This was calculated as a share of the two-person vote (Obama's vote share = (Obama's vote/(Obama's vote + McCain's vote))).

75. Brad Heath, "Billions in Aid Go to Areas that Backed Obama in '08," *USA Today,* July 9, 2009, www.usatoday.com/news/washington/2009-07-08-redblue_N.htm.

76. Using Office of Labor Statistics data, the regression result using the Recovery.gov data was (absolute t-statistic in parentheses):

   Stimulus Dollars Awarded = 0.0802 (3.25); Per-Capita Income in the 4th Quarter of 2008 + 31.60 (1.93); Percent of the Vote for Obama in 2008 + 180.6 (3.51); Poverty Rate in 2008−110.7 (1.16); Bankruptcy Rate in 1st quarter 2009−155.94 (1.12); Foreclosures in 4th quarter 2008 + 5.80 (0.06); Unemployment Rate in January 2009−5199.96 (4.06);

   adj-R2= 0.4434; F statistic = 7.64; Number of Observations = 51.

77. President Barack Obama, "President Obama's News Conference on the American Jobs Act," The White House Press Office, October 6, 2011, www.whitehouse.gov/photos-and-video/video/2011/10/06/president-obama-s-news-conference-american-jobs-act#transcript.

78. Michael Dobbs, "Obama's Redistribution 'Bombshell,'" *Washington Post,* October 27, 2008 (http://voices.washingtonpost.com/fact-checker/2008/10/obamas_redistribution_bombshel.html); Jeanne Cummings, "Obama Blames 'Ethic of Greed' for Economy," *Politico*, March 27, 2008, www.politico.com/news/stories/0308/9238.html.

79. Matthew Mosk and Ronnie Greene, "Obama Fundraiser Pushed Solyndra Deal from Inside," ABC News, October 7, 2011, http://abcnews.go.com/Blotter/obama-fundraiser-pushed-solyndra-deal-inside/story?id=14691618.

80. Matthew Mosk, "Obama: Solyndra Got Loan 'On the Merits,'" ABC News, October 6, 2011, http://abcnews.go.com/Blotter/white-house-donor-george-kaiser-lobby-solyndra/story?id=14676071.

81. Ibid.

82. Philip Klein, "Emails Show Obama Donor Discussed Solyndra with WH," *Washington Examiner,* November 9, 2011, http://campaign2012.washingtonexaminer.com/blogs/beltway-confidential/emails-show-obama-donor-discussed-solyndra-wh.

83. Besides Larry Summers, Valerie Jarrett and Ron Klain were directly involved in getting the money to Solyndra through; see Mosk, "Obama: Solyndra Got Loan 'On the Merits.'"

84. Chad Pergram, "Solyndra Emails Claim Biden Team 'About Had an Orgasm' About Energy Loans to Firm," Fox News, November 9, 2011,

www.foxnews.com/politics/2011/11/09/solyndra-emails-claim-bidens-staff-about-had-orgasm-about-energy-loans-to-firm.

85. Chris Stirewalt, "Another Inside Man for Solyndra at the White House," Fox News, October 14, 2011, www.foxnews.com/politics/2011/10/14/another-inside-man-for-solyndra-at-white-house/.

86. Ibid.; Matthew Mosk and Ronnie Greene, "Obama Fundraiser Pushed Solyndra Deal from Inside," ABC News, October 7, 2011, http://abc-news.go.com/Blotter/obama-fundraiser-pushed-solyndra-deal-inside/story?id=14691618.

87. Mosk and Greene, "Obama Fundraiser Pushed Solyndra Deal from Inside."

88. Roberta Rampton, "Solyndra Probe to Hear from Energy's Chu on November 17," Reuters, October 27, 2011, www.reuters.com/article/2011/10/28/us-solyndra-chu-idUSTRE79R06320111028.

89. Ronnie Greene, "Recurring Red Flags Failed to Slow Obama Administration's Race to Help Solyndra," iWatchNews, September 13, 2011, www.iwatchnews.org/2011/09/13/6434/recurring-red-flags-failed-slow-obama-administrations-race-help-solyndra.

90. Darren Samuelson, "Say DOE Broke the Law on Solyndra—So What?" Politico, October 21, 2011, www.politico.com/news/stories/1011/66592.html.

91. Carol Leonning and Joe Stephens, "Solyndra: Energy Dept. Pushed Firm to Keep Layoffs Quiet Until after Midterms," Washington Post, November 15, 2011, www.washingtonpost.com/politics/solyndra-department-of-energy-pushed-hard-for-company-not-to-announce-layoffs-until-after-2010-mid-term-elections/2011/11/15/gIQA2AriON_story.html.

92. Internal Memorandum, "Hearing on 'The Solyndra Failure: Views from DOE Secretary Chu,'" Committee on Energy and Commerce, U.S. House of Representatives, November 15, 2011, http://Republicans.EnergyCommerce.house.gov/Media/file/Hearings/Oversight/111511/Memo.pdf.

93. Neil Cavuto, "Report: Solyndra Execs Will Not Testify at Hearing," Fox News, September 20, 2011, www.foxnews.com/on-air/your-world-cavuto/2011/09/21/report-solyndra-execs-will-not-testify-hearing.

94. Beyond the list in the text, speculation abounds about other multi-billionaires who have benefited from Obama administration favors. LightSquared is a company seeking to establish a new wireless broadband network, but the portion of the broadcast spectrum it is using could interfere with GPS systems that are vital for everything from air traffic control to the military. The company is owned by Philip Falcone, who

has donated money primarily to Democrats. George Soros is also believed to have a financial interest in the company and has funded four organizations that have helped lobby on the company's behalf. Controversy erupted when four-star Air Force General William Shelton told Congress that the White House had pressured him to change his testimony so that it was more favorable to LightSquared. Discussions of the potential harms from the LightSquared system is available here: "The Difference Engine: Off the Radar," *The Economist,* August 4, 2011, and "Soros Surfaces on the Edge of White House Controversy Involving LightSquared," Fox News, September 23, 2011, www.foxnews.com/politics/2011/09/23/soros-surfaces-on-edge-white-house-controversy/. The Fox News piece also contains information on General Shelton's testimony. Information on Falcone's campaign contributions is available at http://query.nictusa.com/cgi-bin/qind/.

95. Ellen McGirt, "Al Gore's $100 Million Makeover," *Fast Company,* July 1, 2007, www.fastcompany.com/magazine/117/features-gore.html.

96. Matthew Mosk, Brian Ross, and Ronnie Greene, "Car Company Gets U.S. Loan, Builds Cars in Finland," ABC News, October 20, 2011, http://abcnews.go.com/Blotter/car-company-us-loan-builds-cars-finland/story?id=14770875.

97. Chuck Squatriglia, "Feds Lend Tesla $465 Million to Build Electric Car," CNN, June 23, 2009, http://articles.cnn.com/2009-06-23/tech/tesla.electric.cars_1_fuel-efficient-tesla-model-s-sedan?_s=PM:TECH.

98. The numbers on the amount given to NRG are from Recovery.org as of November 12, 2011, www.recovery.gov/Pages/TextViewProjSummary.aspx?data=recipientAwardsList&AwardType=CGL&RecipName=NRG; "Energy Holdings of Billionaires," *Seeking Alpha,* August 29, 2010, http://seekingalpha.com/article/222770-energy-holdings-of-billionaires. Robert Holmes, "10 Stocks Billionaire Steven Cohen Is Buying," *The Street,* August 16, 2010, www.thestreet.com/story/11221080/5/10-stocks-billionaire-steven-cohen-is-buying.html; "Icahn Bets on NRG and Anadarko, Dumps Blockbuster," *Financial Post,* August 16, 2010, www.bullfax.com/?q=node-icahn-bets-nrg-and-anadarko-dumps-blockbuster.

99. "Jeffrey Immelt Net Worth," Celebrity Net Worth, last checked on November 11, 2011, www.celebritynetworth.com/richest-businessmen/ceos/jeffrey-immelt-net-worth/#.

100. Information available at Recovery.gov on November 10, 2011 www.recovery.gov/Pages/TextViewProjSummary.aspx?data=recipientAwardsList&AwardType=CGL&RecipName=general%20electric&PageNumber=2.

101. Eric Lipton and Clifford Krauss, "A Gold Rush of Subsidies in Clean Energy Search," *New York Times,* November 11, 2011, www.nytimes

.com/2011/11/12/business/energy-environment/a-cornucopia-of-help-for-renewable-energy.html.

102. Judson Berger, "Jobs Panel Member Whose Solar Firm Won Loan Guarantees Raises 'Conflict of Interest' Concerns," Fox News, November 1, 2011, www.foxnews.com/politics/2011/11/01/jobs-panel-member-whose-solar-firm-won-2b-loan-raises-conflict-interest/.

103. Fox News, "Solyndra Case Reveals Gateway between Administration Loans, Obama Allies," FoxNews.com, November 16, 2011, www.foxnews.com/politics/2011/11/16/solyndra-case-reveals-gateway-between-admin-istration-loans-obama-allies/.

104. Information on Pat Stryker's donation history is available at http://fundrace .huffingtonpost.com/neighbors.php?type=name&lname=Stryker&fname =Pat. She is from Fort Collins, Colorado.

105. See the information available at www.recovery.gov/Pages/TextView ProjSummary.aspx?data=recipientAwardsList&AwardType=CGL&Recip Name=Abound%20Solar.

106. Fox News, "Solyndra Case Reveals Gateway between Administration Loans, Obama Allies," FoxNews.com, November 16, 2011, www.foxnews.com/politics/2011/11/16/solyndra-case-reveals-gateway-between-administration-loans-obama-allies/.

107. Ibid.

108. Congressional Budget Office, "Modifying the Davis–Bacon Act: Implications for the Labor Market and the Federal Budget," the Congressional Budget Office, July 1983, xii, www.cbo.gov/ftpdocs/50xx/doc5030/doc12-Entire.pdf.

109. John Tozzi, "What We Don't Know about Small Business Lending," *Business Week,* June 22, 2010, www.businessweek.com/smallbiz/content/jun2010/sb20100621_999226.htm.

110. Robb Mandelbaum, "What's in the Senate Small-Business Jobs Bill for You," *New York Times,* July 1, 2010, http://boss.blogs.nytimes.com/2010/07/01/whats-in-the-senate-small-business-jobs-bill-for-you/.

111. Fareed Zakaria, "Watch GPS: Krugman Calls for Space Aliens to Fix U.S. Economy?" CNN World, August 12, 2011, http://globalpublicsquare .blogs.cnn.com/2011/08/12/gps-this-sunday-krugman-calls-for-space-aliens-to-fix-u-s-economy/.

112. Paul Krugman, "Reckonings; After the Horror," *New York Times,* September 14, 2001, www.nytimes.com/2001/09/14/opinion/reckonings-after-the-horror.html.

113. Mary Kate Cary, "Why Pelosi, Democrats Are Wrong on Unemployment Extension," *U.S. News,* July 2, 2010, www.usnews.com/opinion/

blogs/mary-kate-cary/2010/07/02/Why-Pelosi-Democrats-Are-Wrong-on-Unemployment-Extension.

114. Lynn Neary, "Why One Economist Pushed Cash For Clunkers," National Public Radio, August 11, 2009, www.npr.org/templates/story/story.php?storyId=111781653. In an interview with Neary, liberal economics professor Alan Blinder states: "One of its objectives was to assist poor people who tend to own the clunkers."

115. John Lott Jr., "Cash for Clunkers Falls Flat," Fox News, August 3, 2009, www.foxnews.com/opinion/2009/08/03/john-lott-cash-clunkers/.

116. Rick Maze, "GOP Lawmakers Dig in Against Defense Cuts," *Army Times,* October 10, 2011, www.armytimes.com/news/2011/10/military-gop-lawmakers-dig-in-against-defense-cuts-101011w/.

117. Buck McKeon, "Why Defense Cuts Don't Make Sense," *Wall Street Journal,* October 14, 2011, http://online.wsj.com/article/SB10001424052970203914304576628882195814642.html.

118. David Leonhardt, "So Much for Momentum," *New York Times,* December 3, 2010, http://economix.blogs.nytimes.com/2010/12/03/so-much-for-momentum/.

119. Richard Wolf, "Obama Announces Tentative Deal to Extend Bush Tax Cuts," *USA Today,* December 6, 2010, www.usatoday.com/communities/theoval/post/2010/12/obama-addresses-possible-deal-on-bush-tax-cuts/1.

120. Austan Goolsbee, "What Happened When You Tax the Rich? Evidence from Executive Compensation," *Journal of Political Economy* 108, no. 2 (2000): 352–378, www.ssc.wisc.edu/~scholz/Teaching_742/Goolsbee_Rich.pdf.

121. Todd S. Purdum, "Clinton Angers Friend and Foe in Tax Remark," *New York Times,* October 19, 1995, www.nytimes.com/1995/10/19/us/clinton-angers-friend-and-foe-in-tax-remark.html.

122. This shows how far off even Goolsbee's short-run estimates were. Martin Feldstein, "What the '93 Tax Increases Really Did," *Wall Street Journal,* October 26, 1995.

123. Editorial, "The Compleat Summers," *Wall Street Journal,* November 25, 2008, http://online.wsj.com/article/SB122757308122854859.html.

124. The economic problems with Goolsbee's discussion in this interview are many. Goolsbee justifies the higher profits tax on oil companies because the companies have gotten subsidies in the past. There may be a fairness argument here, but just because a company may have invested too much a couple of decades ago doesn't mean that you should want them to invest too little now. Taxing just U.S. oil company profits will cause more production to be shifted to companies based in other countries. It will just

make America more dependent on foreign oil production. With a world market for oil, the tax will also probably have very little effect on the price that consumers pay for gas. "Obama's Emergency Economic Plan," CNBC, August 6, 2008 (a windfall profits tax on oil companies).

125. "Transcript: Obama and Clinton Debate," ABC News, April 16, 2008, 18, http://abcnews.go.com/Politics/DemocraticDebate/story?id=4670271 &page=18.

126. Natalie Gewargis, "Spread the Wealth?" ABC News, *Political Punch,* October 14, 2008, http://abcnews.go.com/blogs/politics/2008/10/spread-the-weal/.

127. President Barack Obama, "Remarks by the President to the Chamber of Commerce," The White House, Office of the Press Secretary, February 7, 2011, www.whitehouse.gov/the-press-office/2011/02/07/remarks-president-chamber-commerce.

128. A year after Obama's first Stimulus bill was passed, Austan Goolsbee told Fox News: "The private sector needs to do the rest." John Lott Jr., "Fact Checking Team Obama's Stimulus Claims," Fox News, February 19, 2010, www.foxnews.com/opinion/2010/02/19/john-lott-stimulus-obama-goolsbee-hemmer/. For the exact same phrase by Vice President Joe Biden, see Mike Memoli, "Biden: 'No Possibility' of Restoring Lost Jobs," *Chicago Tribune,* June 25, 2010.

Chapter 4

Would the Economy Have Been in Worse Shape without the Stimulus?

A s mentioned, however bad things get, Obama keeps defending his policies by arguing that without his Stimulus the economy would have been even worse. Yet, he is hardly alone. In October 2011, Nancy Pelosi claimed:

> Without the Recovery Act and accompanying federal interventions, whether from the Fed, or Cash for Clunkers, or other initiatives, the unemployment rate last year at the time of the election [November 2010] would have been fourteen and a half percent, not nine and a half percent.[1]

These claims are questionable for a number of reasons. It is hard to put much weight on these claims of jobs being created, especially since Obama and his economics team repeatedly get their economic predictions so completely wrong. How many times can you predict a "Recovery Summer," with massive job growth, and have people believe that you understand what creates jobs? Also, during the 2008 election, Mr. Obama repeatedly blamed our economic problems on the big government spending, big deficit policies. He was indeed right back then. But Obama never really offered an explanation for why his policies differed so dramatically from what he campaigned for.

If the Stimulus was so successful, shouldn't this recovery compare well to previous recoveries? But, as we have already seen in Chapter 2, while the recession might not have set records for being the worst, the recovery surely has been the most anemic in over six decades. Finally, shouldn't the U.S. economy have fared better than other countries after it was adopted?

Obama's Own Words

If a massive Keynesian stimulus—an 18 percent increase in federal government spending from 2008 to 2009 and over $4 trillion in deficits for the first three years of his administration—was the key to making the economy better, you wouldn't have heard candidate Obama making that claim during the 2008 presidential campaign.

In his first year in office, Obama and the Democratically controlled Congress increased government spending by almost as much as Republicans did during the four fiscal years from 2004 to 2007 when Bush was president and Republicans controlled both houses of Congress ($535 versus $569 billion). And the deficit during each of Obama's first three years in office was bigger than the deficits for those four fiscal years combined ($1.4 trillion for Obama's first year versus $1.1 trillion for the fiscal 2004 to 2007 budgets taken together).

As a candidate, Obama claimed that one cause of the economic crisis was the large deficits the country was running, and he promised that he would fix things by cutting government spending. During the third presidential debate, less than three weeks before the election, Obama promised to rein in the budget deficit. When debate moderator Bob Schieffer asked Obama what he was going to do about the deficit, Obama promised to cut it: "But there is no doubt that we've been living beyond our means and we're going to have to make some adjustments. Now, what I've done throughout this campaign is to propose a net spending cut."[2]

Or take the second presidential debate, on October 7th,[3] when Obama assured the 63 million Americans watching:

> I understand your frustration and your cynicism, because while you've been carrying out your responsibilities—most of the people here, you've got a family budget. If less money is coming in, you end up making cuts. Maybe you don't go out to dinner as much. Maybe you put off buying a new car.
>
> That's not what happens in Washington. . . . When George Bush came into office, we had surpluses. And now we have half-a-trillion-dollar deficit annually. . . .
>
> So we're going to have to make some investments, but we've also got to make spending cuts. And what I've proposed, you'll hear Senator McCain say, well, he's proposing a whole bunch of new spending, but actually I'm cutting more than I'm spending so that it will be a net spending cut.[4]

So much for his promises. After Obama racked up the largest inflation-adjusted increases ever in government spending and the largest deficits (even larger than the worst part of World War II), it is hard to remember that his constant theme during the presidential debates was "net spending cut."[5]

His complete reversal happened immediately after winning the presidency. Just one week later, Obama went from campaigning on cutting government spending before the election on November 4th to talking about up to a $500 billion stimulus.[6] Two weeks after the election, Larry Summers told the Associated Press that the amount should be between $500 billion and $700 billion.[7] Of course, what turned out to be an $825 billion bill that passed in February was much higher still. So what changed?

Did he learn something immediately after the election about the economy? Before the election, Obama was already regularly claiming that the economy was in the worst financial crisis since the Depression; no particularly new data seem to have surfaced in the weeks right after the election. The only economics number released soon after the election was the November 7th unemployment report, showing that the unemployment rate had risen from 6.6 to 6.8 percent. Not good, but hardly a crisis by itself and definitely not worse than Obama's previous description of the economy.

Even if some new surprising information had indeed been released, how do go from arguing that you should cut spending when you are in the worst financial crisis since the Depression to claiming that you should massively increase it if you can claim that things have gotten a little worse?

By the beginning of January, still weeks before his inauguration, Obama was warning Americans that we will be facing trillion-dollar deficits "for years to come."[8] There was no hint of these policies on November 4th.

The most obvious explanation for the big switch in Obama's position is that he always wanted a much bigger government, but he knew that Americans wouldn't vote for him if he openly campaigned on it.

Comparing Our Experience to Other Countries

If Obama's policies worked so well, we should expect our experience to compare well with other countries that chose to follow other policies. That turns out not to be the case.

Our next-door neighbor, Canada, provides an interesting comparison. As our economies are so interconnected, it is natural that when U.S. industries—from autos to cell phones—suffer, similar Canadian industries suffer also. Canada is our largest trading partner, and when American consumers cut down on buying products, many of those products not purchased are Canadian-made.

Before proceeding, we should note that there are lots of differences in how countries calculate their unemployment rates. Canada treats people as unemployed if they have engaged in any job search during the previous month, no matter how superficial. By contrast, the United States only labels people unemployed if they are out of work and are actively searching—meaning that they have to actually apply to jobs and go through all the necessary interviews.[9] Fortunately, the U.S. Bureau of Labor Statistics has recalculated Canadian unemployment rates so that their measure is comparable to the U.S. rate. The Canadian and U.S. unemployment rates have been remarkably similar from 1976 until the beginning of 2009, never differing by more than 1.3 percentage points and usually by much less than one percentage point.[10] All that changed after President Obama's Stimulus passed in February 2009.

Originally, the recession had hit Canada hard, just as it did in the United States. In December 2008, Canadians were within three percentage points as likely to rate their economy as "bad" as Americans did, and Canadians were at least as pessimistic about the future.[11] Canadian and the U.S. unemployment rates increased in lockstep from August 2008 up until six months later in February 2009, when the Stimulus was passed in the United States. During those six months, the U.S. unemployment rate rose by 2.1 percentage points, from 6.1 to 8.2 percent, the Canadian by 1.9 percent from 5.1 to 7.0 percent. Figure 4.1 illustrates how the unemployment rate shot up so similarly during this time.

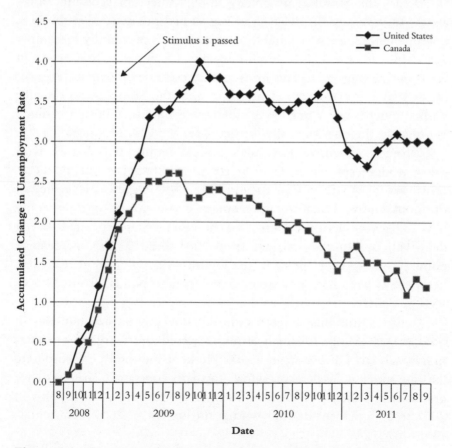

Figure 4.1   Comparing the Accumulated Change in U.S. and Canadian Unemployment Rates Since September 2008

But immediately after President Obama passed his Stimulus, the picture changed. Canada greatly outperformed the United States in creating jobs—supposedly the whole point of the Stimulus. U.S. unemployment continued shooting up to 10.1 percent by October 2009 and continued to stay very high, remaining at least at 9.5 percent for the next 14 months. In sharp contrast, Canadian unemployment peaked at 7.7 percent in July and August 2009 and has kept on falling ever since. While our unemployment rate by September 2011 was stuck at 9.1 percent, Canada's had fallen to 6.3 percent. Put another way, while the U.S. rate had increased by 1.3 percentage points since Obama became president, Canadian unemployment had actually fallen below its January 2009 level.

Before the Stimulus in January 2009, American economic forecasters surveyed by the *Wall Street Journal* had predicted that the U.S. unemployment rate was going to increase by 0.8 percent by December 2009. Instead, the U.S. rate climbed by 2.1 percent. In Canada, it went up by 1 percent. The irony is that the unemployment changes in the two countries were identical up until the Stimulus. So Canada, with a much smaller and quite different Stimulus, followed a much better path, the one originally predicted for the U.S. economy.

Obama's expensive Keynesian policies contrasted sharply with the Canadian approach. True, as frequently happens during recessions, revenues fell in Canada and their deficit grew. Nevertheless, the conservative Canadian government chose not to introduce any new big government programs. For the United States, our federal net debt will rise as a share of GDP from 2008 to 2012 by 33 percentage points, from 48 to 81 percent (see Figure 4.2). By contrast, Canada's net debt will rise by just over 13 percentage points, from 22.4 to 35.8 percent.[12]

Canada's stimulus differed radically not just in size but also in how it was set up. Obama's Stimulus raised the marginal tax rates individuals face, discouraging work. He kept the total U.S. corporate tax rate stuck at 39 percent, while, in sharp contrast, Canadians have gradually cut their *total corporate* income tax rate from 34 percent in 2007 to 27.6 percent in 2011, with a further cut to 26 percent scheduled for 2012.

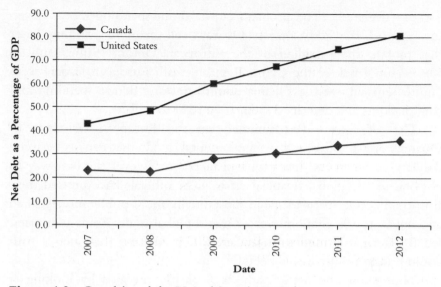

Figure 4.2   Canada's and the United States' Net Debt

What a difference a few years has made in Canadian and American perceptions about where their respective economies are headed. By October 2011, Canadians were no longer as upset about their current conditions or as pessimistic about the future as Americans. Sixty-three percent of Canadians were then viewing their economy as "in good or very good shape."[13] For Americans, only 9 percent viewed theirs as "good or excellent."[14]

Of course, there are other differences between the Canadian and U.S. economies. The United States in particular was burdened by regulations that forced mortgage companies to make loans that they expected to lose money on. But it is hard to see how those other differences would cause the sudden change in fortunes right at the very moment the Stimulus was passed.

It is not just Canada where people are faring better. Despite strong political pressure from Obama for Europe to spend about $225 billion more on fiscal Stimuli, other countries, too, decided against following his lead.[15] In March 2009, with German chancellor Angela Merkel nodding in agreement at French president Nicolas Sarkozy's side,

Sarkozy declared: "The problem is not about spending more." Even the British Labor Party rejected Obama's call for more spending. Later that month, the president of the European Union, Prime Minister Mirek Topolanek of the Czech Republic, said European leaders were "quite alarmed" at the Obama administration's deficit spending and bank bailouts and described them as "a road to hell."[16]

The *Washington Post* summed up the European resistance to Obama's pressure this way: a "fundamental divide that persists between the United States and many European countries over the best way to respond to the global financial crisis. U.S. officials have pressed their European counterparts to spend substantially more public money in an attempt to revive economic growth and global trade. Some countries, led by Germany, have strongly resisted, predicting that such a path could lead to unsustainable debts. . . ."[17]

They chose the better path, as is clearly revealed by looking at their unemployment numbers. Besides Canada, the U.S. Bureau of Labor Statistics has recalculated the unemployment rates for eight other foreign countries—Australia, Japan, France, Germany, Italy, the Netherlands, Sweden, and the United Kingdom—so that they are comparable to ours. The United States had more of a Stimulus as a percentage of our GDP than any of these countries, almost three times the average percentage spent by them,[18] but none did as consistently poorly as the United States has since the beginning of 2009.

Germany, which faced most of the Obama administration's anger, really stands out. Just as with Canada, Germany's unemployment rate was following a relatively similar pattern with ours until right after the Stimulus was passed (see Figure 4.3). Our unemployment rate kept rising, but theirs leveled off and started to fall. Germany's unemployment rate is now a percentage point below what it was when Obama passed the Stimulus. If the whole point of Germany spending more money was to help pull the rest of the world out of recession, they obviously have done a better job of doing that by refusing to follow Obama's Keynesian advice.

Some might want to forget their predictions about Germany. Paul Krugman criticized the reduction in German government spending in June 2010 as a "huge mistake," and said that "budget cuts will hurt your economy and reduce revenues [by reducing

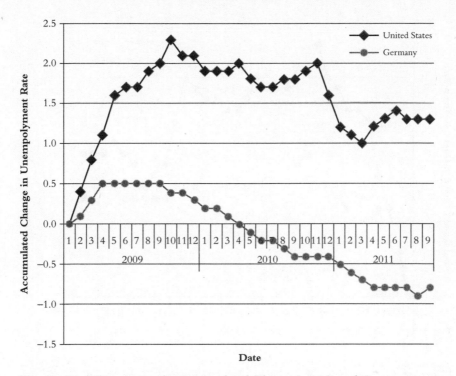

Figure 4.3   Comparing the Accumulated Change in U.S. and German Unemployment Rates (January 2009 to September 2011)

economic growth]."[19] By August 2010, he was saying that it was still too early to evaluate the policy.[20] Yet, more than a year later, Germany's unemployment rate continued falling, dropping by 0.7 percentage points between June 2010 and August 2011. And as of June 2011, German GDP over the previous year had grown at 2.7 percent, appreciably better than our own anemic 1.6 percent. Germany accomplished the lower unemployment and higher growth rates without burdening its children with the higher debt that Obama and Krugman advocated.

French unemployment was also rising along with ours during the beginning of 2009, but as soon as the United States adopted the Stimulus, the unemployment rates between France and the United States began to diverge (see Figure 4.4). Finally, the remaining six countries are shown in Figure 4.5. Sweden experienced a similar increase in unemployment to the United States, but has since done

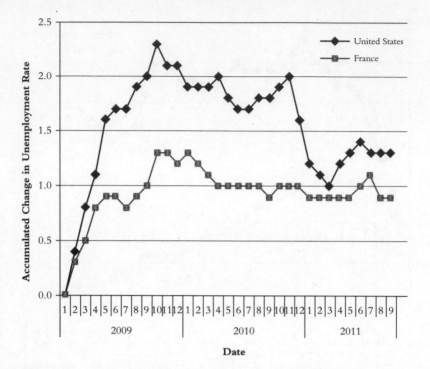

Figure 4.4   Comparing the Accumulated Change in U.S. and French Unemployment Rates (January 2009 to September 2011)

much better. The Netherlands is the only country that had seen as big of an increase in unemployment as the United States through August 2011.

Did States Getting the Most Stimulus Money Create the Most Jobs?

[S]tates that got more money per person did better on jobs. . . . *Of course,* more federal spending in a given state or county creates more jobs. And the burden of proof should always have been on stimulus critics to explain why this doesn't mean that stimulus spending creates jobs at the national level, too.[21]

—*Paul Krugman,* New York Times,
February 25, 2011

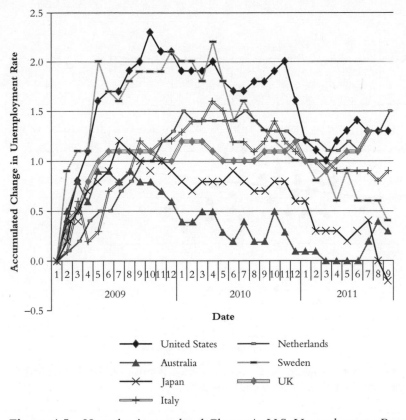

Figure 4.5 How the Accumulated Change in U.S. Unemployment Rates Compares to that in Other Countries (January 2009 to September 2011)

Taking resources from the rest of the country and giving it to a particular state will also transfer jobs. The more the favored states get, the more jobs they will gain. But despite what Krugman claims, that is not the same thing as saying that increasing federal government spending increases the number of jobs at the *national* level. Indeed, the federal government can end up, on net, destroying jobs at the same time that it moves jobs from those states that don't get much money to those that get a lot.[22]

About 85 percent of the Stimulus had been given out by June 2011.[23] Consider the Recovery.gov data, presented earlier in Chapter 3. At first glance, the percentage of the population that is working seems to be increasing slightly with the amount of per capita spending (see the trend line in Figure 4.6). Given that the average state received about

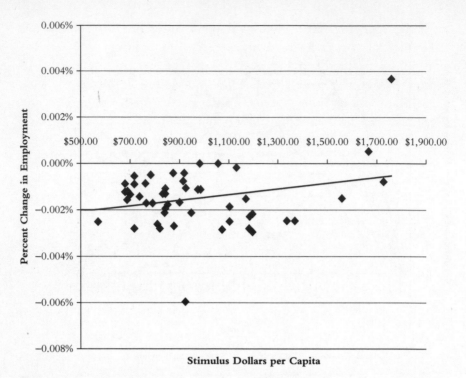

Figure 4.6 The Change in the Percentage of the Population that Is Employed by a State between February 2009 and June 2011

$1,021 in Stimulus per person (a total of $6.37 billion for the state), that average Stimulus would be associated with 78 jobs—a cost of about $82 million per job.[24]

However, this conclusion is rather naive, as the results really hinge on just one outlier, North Dakota. That state's unusualness can be easily seen by looking at Figure 4.6. Thus, it happened to be that North Dakota received the second most Stimulus dollars per person in the entire United States and, at the same time, experienced a massive oil boom. Oil production in North Dakota more than doubled from the beginning of 2009 to the middle of 2011.[25]

About 10,000 of the 28,000 new jobs in North Dakota were directly related to the increased oil production, and that does not include the generation of jobs in the railroads to transport the oil or other related activities such as housing.[26] With news headlines such as "North Dakota Oil Boom Creates Camps of Men" (*New York Times*) and "Riding the North Dakota Oil Boom" (*Wall Street Journal*), no one is going to seriously argue that the Stimulus is responsible for North Dakota enjoying by far the lowest unemployment rate in the country.[27] Its rate was a mere 3.5 percent in October 2011, far lower than the runner-up, Nebraska, with 4.2 percent, and the national average at 9 percent.[28]

If there is something unusual occurring for one or two states that don't seem to have anything to do with the Stimulus, the obvious response is to see if the pattern is still observed when those unusual observations are removed. So does the pattern still hold for the states without North Dakota? No. Removing just this one outlying state, North Dakota, eliminates any relationship whatsoever between Stimulus dollars and job creation (see Figure 4.7).[29]

So Krugman got it wrong again. The Stimulus didn't create more jobs in the states that got more money.[30] This is a very important result. The question is: Why wasn't there a benefit? It could be that there were many strings attached to the projects. For example, with all the pressure to hire union workers, the Stimulus may have

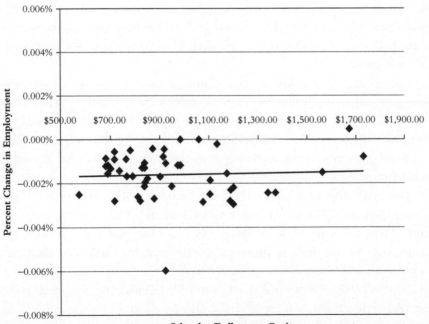

Figure 4.7 The Change in the Percentage of the Population that Is Employed by a State between February 2009 and June 2011 (trend line after removing North Dakota)

caused states to switch from lower-cost projects that they were going to pay for themselves to higher-cost ones that the federal government picked up some of the cost for. The fact that the Stimulus increased unemployment and somehow managed not to create more jobs in the states that got the most federal money just shows how incredibly inefficiently the government spent the money.

Did the Financial Crisis Cause Long-Term Unemployment?

[The economy] is not growing quite as fast as we would like, because after a financial crisis, typically there's a bigger drag on the economy for a longer period of time.[31]

— *Obama at his Facebook Town Hall in Palo Alto, California, April 21, 2011*

A couple of academics, Carmen Reinhart and Ken Rogoff, argue that financial crises tend to exacerbate recessions and slow down recoveries. Not surprisingly, Obama and others have picked up on this claim.[32] If true, it would largely absolve Obama for the bad economy. But is it correct?

No, it isn't. For example, this claim doesn't explain why the sudden gap in unemployment rates between the United States and Canada and the other countries we have just discussed appeared so dramatically after Obama's Stimulus was passed. At the very least, the increased gap right at that time suggests the opposite, that the Stimulus made things worse.

But may the United States have faced higher and longer-term unemployment because of the financial crisis? The information we have allows us to look more closely at that issue. Of the nine foreign countries that we have consistent unemployment data for, Reinhart and Rogoff identify four as suffering from a financial crisis (Germany, Japan, the Netherlands, and the United Kingdom) and five that were not (Australia, Canada, France, Italy, and Sweden).[33] Despite claims to the contrary, after January 2009, the unemployment rate in the countries with financial crises actually increased *less* than in those that avoided such a crisis (0.66 versus 0.86 percentage points) (see Figure 4.8). The difference is extremely statistically significant.[34] The evidence only

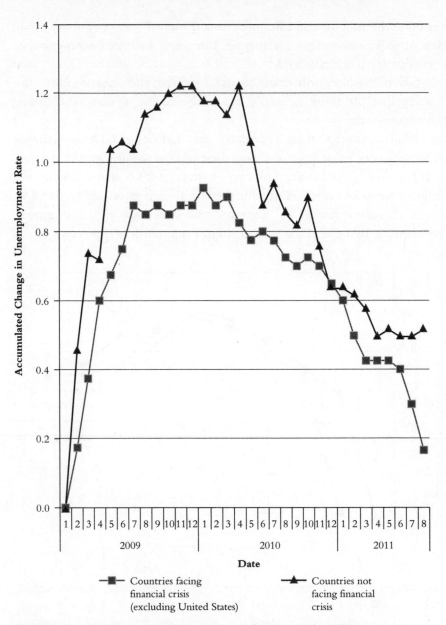

Figure 4.8   Did Countries Facing Financial Crises Endure Worse Unemployment Problems?

supports the Reinhart and Rogoff claim if each different country's own definition of unemployment is used, but using such incomparable data seems pretty hard to defend.[35]

Given the attention given to the Reinhart and Rogoff claim, this finding that the result is simply a consequence is of using the wrong data noteworthy.

While countries facing a financial crisis had slower GDP growth, the difference wasn't that large nor were their recoveries substantially delayed. It is really only during the first two quarters of 2009 that countries not facing a financial crisis had much different growth rates (see Figure 4.9). From the third quarter of 2009 on, the difference in GDP growth between the two sets of states averaged just one-tenth of 1 percent.

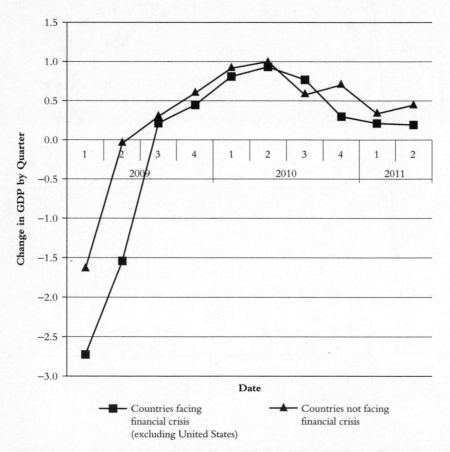

Figure 4.9 Did Countries Facing Financial Crises Endure Slower Growth During Their Recoveries?

Didn't the Stimulus Slow Job Losses?

I think it is important to put [job losses] in context, because they are, I think, still part of this overall trend towards greatly moderating job losses. I mean, I'll give you one statistic. In the first quarter of 2009, when we first came in, we were losing on average 691,000 jobs per month. With these new numbers in the fourth quarter, we were losing 69,000 jobs.[36]

— *Obama's Council of Economic Advisers chief Christina Romer on ABC News'* This Week with George Stephanopoulos,

January 10, 2010

Many graphs have appeared in the media illustrating Ms. Romer's claim that the job market started to improve (or stopped getting worse) a few months after the Stimulus was passed. Figure 4.10 covers the time that she refers to, and since July 2009, there has indeed been a

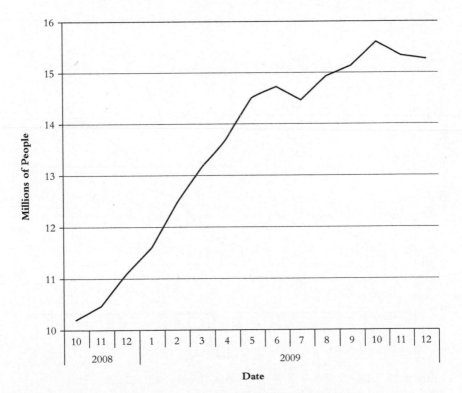

Figure 4.10   The Number of Working-Age Unemployed
SOURCE: Bureau of Labor Statistics Household Survey.

significant decline in the number of Americans who have become unemployed.

While people stop being unemployed when they get a job, they can also stop being unemployed, by government definition, in a less desirable way—they give up looking for work. This second reason for why people stop being unemployed is largely ignored. Few graphs show the number of people who have given up looking for work. People are no longer counted as unemployed if they have not actively looked for work during the previous four weeks. And there are many reasons why people don't work (for example, women staying at home to take care of children, or illness). But the question is how the number not working has changed. Figure 4.11 shows how the number of working-age adults who have left the labor force has changed over the last year. At about the same time that the increase in unemployment began to slow, there was a similar increase in the

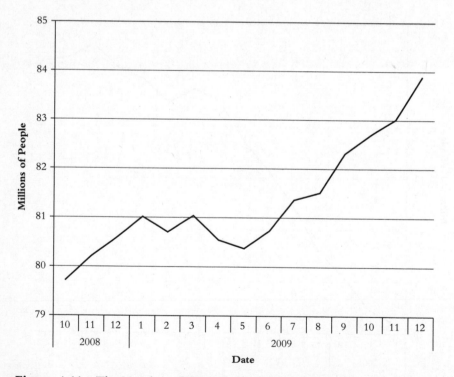

Figure 4.11   The Number of Working-Age People Not in Labor Force
SOURCE: Bureau of Labor Statistics Household Survey.

number of people who stopped looking for work. This suggests that the improvement in the unemployment numbers really just represented a shift in the number of people who have given up.

So is any improvement in the number unemployed just being offset by the number of people who have given up looking for work? Indeed, that is exactly what Figure 4.12 shows, and the result is a virtually straight, upward line. During a period of economic expansion as the number unemployed fell and more people entered the labor force, this graph would show a downward sloping line. But this figure indicates that any change in the number of new people being unemployed is completely offset by people leaving the labor force.

These charts make it very hard to argue that the Stimulus had any noticeable beneficial impact on moderating the number of unemployed.

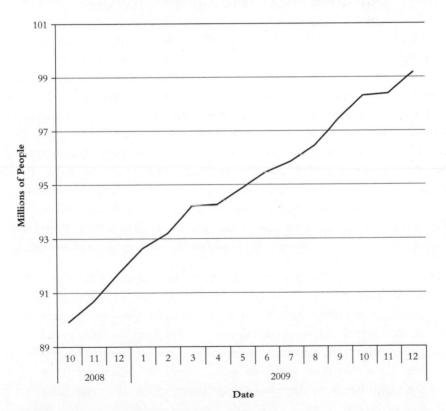

Figure 4.12   Unemployed + Not in Labor Force
SOURCE: Bureau of Labor Statistics Household Survey.

We asked the White House about these numbers and they were unwilling to respond to these findings on the record. However, off the record, one senior White House official strenuously objected to both the data used here as well as what those data mean. "The payroll survey is better than the household survey for tracking the impact of stimulus on employment/unemployment," the official emailed us off the record.[37] It is a strange answer since the payroll survey fails to provide any information on the number of people unemployed or who is looking for work. It only surveys employers, who tell the government the number of people working for each company. The Household Survey provides the only measure of the number unemployed.

So What Went Wrong? The Excuses

Besides blaming everything from the earthquake in Japan and the problems in Europe, the primary explanation for the weak economy is that government just didn't do enough. Supposedly, if only government spending had kept growing and government jobs hadn't faced "huge" cutbacks, the economy would have recovered. But only in Washington, DC or publications such as the *New York Times* would the tiny cuts in the large growth of government spending be considered "austerity."[38] We have already talked about the economics behind these ideas, but the claims that weak government spending and employment can explain the weak economy are simply false. Much of the intellectual firepower for the Keynesian position has come from Paul Krugman's *New York Times* columns, so it is worth a few minutes to look at his explanation.

> So as I said, the big government expansion everyone talks about never happened. . . . And federal aid to state and local governments wasn't enough to make up for plunging tax receipts in the face of the economic slump. . . . [T]here's a widespread perception that government spending has surged, when it hasn't—is that there has been a disinformation campaign from the right, based on the usual combination of fact-free assertions and cooked numbers.
>
> Paul Krugman, "Hey, Small Spender,"
> *New York Times,* October 10, 2010

It is true that local government spending has declined since 2009, but even that is only after large increases in spending during the two previous years. Federal and state government have grown dramatically. While the private sector has faced deep cuts, total government spending has grown by 12 percent since 2008 and 20 percent since 2007, the year immediately before the recession started. All levels of government spending increased. As can be seen in Table 4.1, even after adjusting for inflation, total government spending has gone up.[39]

There is only one year when total government spending declined, from 2009 to 2010. And even then, it was still much higher than just a couple of years earlier. Only by picking this comparison between just 2009 and 2010 can Krugman make his claim that government spending hasn't surged. But government spending surged when the recession hit and has stayed high throughout. The economy may have gone nowhere in 2011, but total government spending, lead by the federal government, still grew from its already very high levels by $135 billion.

Table 4.1 Soaring Government Spending (in trillions of dollars)

Fiscal Year	Federal	State	Local	Total
2000	$1.789	$0.946	$0.986	$3.721
2001	$1.863	$1.016	$1.059	$3.938
2002	$2.011	$1.088	$1.129	$4.229
2003	$2.160	$1.127	$1.183	$4.470
2004	$2.293	$1.181	$1.246	$4.720
2005	$2.472	$1.266	$1.297	$5.035
2006	$2.655	$1.343	$1.373	$5.372
2007	$2.729	$1.425	$1.486	$5.640
2008	$2.983	$1.478	$1.577	$6.038
2009	$3.518	$1.547	$1.589	$6.654
2010	$3.456	$1.624*	$1.572*	$6.652*
2011	$3.600*	$1.608*	$1.580*	$6.787*
Percentage change from 2008 to 2011	21%	9%	0.1%	12%

*Estimate

Sources: Federal data from *Monthly Budget Review,* Congressional Budget Office Analysis, October 7, 2011, and Council of Economic Advisers, *Economic Report of the President,* White House, 2011. State data from State Expenditure Report, National Association of State Budget Officers, Fiscal Years 2001 to 2010. Local data from USGovernmentSpending.com

Look, in particular, at actual government purchases of goods and services. . . . When the recession officially ended, spending was rising at an annual rate of around $60 billion. [N]ow it's declining at an annual rate of $60 billion [in 2011]. That difference is around 1 percent of GDP, and maybe 1.5 percent once you take the multiplier into account. That makes the turn toward austerity a major factor in our growth slowdown.[40]

—Paul Krugman, "The Austerity Economy,"
New York Times, September 3, 2011

Again, Krugman is cherry picking to make Obama look frugal. He excludes transfer payments and only considers direct spending, implying that government transfer payments no longer count as stimulative government spending. Yet, just a year earlier in 2010, Krugman was singing the praises of transfer payments as stimulus. When writing pieces in favor of longer unemployment insurance benefits, he claimed that transfer payments were "a highly cost-effective form of economic stimulus. And unlike, say, large infrastructure projects, aid to the unemployed creates jobs quickly—while allowing that aid to lapse, which is what is happening right now, is a recipe for even weaker job growth, not in the distant future but over the next few months."[41] So, in 2010, the threat of reduced transfer payments posed a real threat to economic growth, but now they don't count. Transfer payments are important except when they don't give him the right results.

It's very clear that private sector jobs have been doing just fine; it's the public sector jobs where we've lost huge numbers, and that's what this legislation [Obama's sixth Stimulus bill] is all about.

—Senate Majority Leader Harry Reid (D-NV),
October 19, 2011

The drop in state and local government workers, rather than federal workers, since the recession started may be what concerns Senator Reid, but it is only a third of the percentage drop in private sector employment over the same time (5.4 versus 1.8 percent). Governments, despite these mounting debts, have resisted cutting jobs.

Since the beginning of 2008, the only group of workers who are "doing just fine" are those working for the federal government, where total employment has increased by 11 percent since the start of the recession. Federal employment grew consistently from the beginning of the recession up through the beginning of 2010. The huge temporary spike then occurred because of the hiring for the federal 2010 census. Both private sector and state and local government employment have fallen, but while private sector employment has recovered slightly from the 7.5 percent drop it originally suffered, in the fall of 2011, it was still down 5.4 percent. In contrast, state and local government employment has only fallen by less than 2 percent.

More money for government jobs means less for other activities. Why drain resources that would have gone to others to invest and spend?

Our Government Was Already Very Big

Even before the Obama administration, the federal government was very large. Less than a hundred years ago, the federal government exceeded only about 3 percent of GDP during wars, and would quickly return to that level of spending as soon as the war had ended. The federal government has grown dramatically since the 1920s.

But our government is not just much larger than before, it has also grown compared to governments in other countries. How much money does it take for governments of sovereign nations to do their job? To take care of the poor and those who need help and are in trouble? Different countries obviously have different answers. Countries run by social democratic or socialist parties will spend lavishly on cradle-to-grave social systems. On the other hand, citizens in nonsocialist countries have more choice over how to spend their money. When Americans think of countries with really big governments, they probably think of Sweden, France, or Finland. Most of Europe is thought to have much larger governments than the United States.

Unfortunately, this isn't true anymore. Even after adjusting for differences in the cost of living and taking into account how many people live in the country, total U.S. government spending—at all levels of government—accounts for more real resources per capita than 95 percent of the countries in the world. In fact, 166 out of 175 countries have governments that spend less money than the United States. Our

government spends 276 percent more than is spent by the average
government of another country around the world. That comes out to
about $17,400 per person living in the United States—almost $70,000
for a family of four. See Table 4.2.

Sweden's famous welfare state spends only about 8.6 percent more
per capita than the United States—probably a much smaller difference than most would have guessed. France spends virtually the same

Table 4.2 Per Capita Government Expenditures after Accounting for Price
Differences for the Top 50 Countries, 2009

Country	Per Capita Government Expenditures	Country	Per Capita Government Expenditures
Luxembourg	$29,285	Kuwait	$10,846
Qatar	$25,964	New Zealand	$10,730
Norway	$21,787	Seychelles	$10,601
Austria	$18,942	Czech Republic	$10,394
Sweden	$18,865	Malta	$10,063
Denmark	$18,730	Portugal	$10,006
The Netherlands	$17,793	Oman	$9,738
France	$17,648	United Arab Emirates	$9,648
United States	$17,370	Hungary	$9,218
Belgium	$17,235	Bahrain	$8,997
Finland	$16,301	Korea, South	$8,032
Iceland	$15,828	Saudi Arabia	$7,624
United Kingdom	$15,473	Poland	$7,573
Germany	$15,125	Kiribati	$7,535
Canada	$14,971	Croatia	$7,508
Ireland	$14,080	Slovakia	$7,353
Italy	$14,030	Barbados	$7,251
Switzerland	$13,829	Estonia	$6,408
Greece	$13,577	The Bahamas	$6,289
Israel	$13,118	Trinidad and Tobago	$6,213
Cyprus	$12,826	Singapore	$6,179
Australia	$12,757	Hong Kong	$6,173
Slovenia	$12,094	Belarus	$5,943
Japan	$11,814	Lithuania	$5,515
Spain	$11,456	Russia	$5,504

Government spending as a percentage of GDP (www.heritage.org/index/Ranking.aspx)
Real GDP per capita. Purchasing Power Parity (http://en.wikipedia.org/wiki/
list_of_countries_by_GDP_(PPP)_per_capita)

amount as the United States, just 1.6 percent more. Meanwhile, Finland spends 6 percent less. Countries such as Germany, Italy, and the United Kingdom don't even come close to the United States. And our neighbor Canada spends 14 percent less per capita than the United States does. Japan spends 32 percent less.

Two of the eight countries where governments spend more than our government likely do so because the government owns the country's oil wealth (Qatar and Norway).

Looking at government spending alone isn't a perfect way to compare countries. For example, while the Swedish government rewards parents with a check for each additional child a family has, the United States uses the tax credits and the tax code to accomplish the same goal. That would make the federal government's expenditures look relatively smaller, even though the end result is the same.

Americans spend more on national defense than most other countries, but the differences in defense expenditures are relatively minor so that comparing nondefense government expenditures doesn't make that much difference. Our total per capita non-defense government expenditures still exceed that of 93 percent of other countries.

With the new trillion-dollar health law signed by President Obama, the United States' total spending and rank is guaranteed to go up further.

The federal government has control over more resources per capita than virtually every other country in the world. The government decides from whom the money is taken, who gets it, and how that money can be spent. Of course, the money also pays for the enforcement of all the regulations and laws that tell us what to do and not do. That is a huge amount of government control over people's lives. Think about just how much more freedom the average family of four would have if they, not the government, got to determine how that $70,000 was spent.

The Hangover

Amid all the debt hysteria, it's worth taking a look at the actual arithmetic here—because what this arithmetic says is that the size of the deficit in the next year or two hardly matters for the U.S.

fiscal position—and in fact the size over the next decade is barely significant.[42]

— *Paul Krugman,* New York Times,
February 25, 2011

The $825 billion Stimulus and other jobs bills have clearly racked up a hefty debt that will have to be paid by future generations. Despite the high price tag, it has—just like so many other government programs and regulations—failed to improve the economy.

True, we can blame previous policies, especially George W. Bush's policies, for some of our debt problems, but the increase under Obama is worlds apart in magnitude. Publicly held U.S. federal debt of $3.4 trillion by the end of 2000, shortly before Bush became president, and by the end of his tenure after eight years, in 2008, rose to $5.8 trillion.[43] According to the Congressional Budget Office, the policies adopted at the end of Bush's administration were going to create roughly another $455 billion in debt in 2009.[44]

No doubt, this already constituted a very serious problem. To fathom the extent of the debt, imagine a family of four. During 2000 to 2009, the family's share of the publicly held national debt rose from $63,000 to almost $87,000 (all in 2011 dollars).

Nevertheless, this increase is minor when compared to what Obama has done as president. In just three short years, the Obama administration has raised publicly held U.S. debt to almost $11 trillion (as of October 2011). For the average family, that means their share of the federal debt went from $87,000 to $140,000. If Obama remains president for a second term, assuming no new pet projects or other changes, each family's share of the debt would balloon, reaching a whopping $186,000 by October 2016. And that is undoubtedly a low estimate, as it comes from the Obama administration itself for the 2012 budget. As we have seen, the administration is well known for being overly optimistic, hoping for unrealistically high future economic growth, lowered unemployment, and Obamacare's low costs.

To put it differently, by 2016, after two terms, President Obama will most likely have overseen an increase of $100,000 in the share of the national debt facing the average family of four. That is amazingly fast and it is four times faster than the debt accumulated under President G. W. Bush. Obviously, this cannot keep going on, or we will approach the Greek crisis.

Americans really need to ask themselves a question: Have people really noticed their lives so greatly improved by the increased government spending that it is worth all this new debt? For example, cutting back the 2012 budget to what was spent in 2008 would leave the deficit at a few hundred billion dollars, instead of more than $1.1 trillion.

Another way of thinking about what we get from government spending is to look at President Bill Clinton's last budget, which was approved in 2000. If federal government spending after President Clinton's last budget had simply grown enough just to keep up with inflation and the growth in population, the 2012 budget would be running more than a $70 billion surplus.[45] In his State of the Union address to the nation that year, Clinton was quite clear. He didn't view government as being too small or that Americans were seriously hurting because there weren't enough government programs to help them. Instead, Clinton told the country: "My fellow Americans, the state of our union is the strongest it has ever been."[46] But President Obama wants to spend about $1.2 trillion more after adjusting for inflation and population growth than Bill Clinton would have provided. Has all that additional government spending really made us that much better off?

If we don't rein in these deficits now, our finances risk spinning completely out of control. The problem isn't just the massive debt that we have already accumulated, but the promises that our government has made. In the next 15 years, as the baby boomers retire and Social Security and Medicare costs soar, there will be few new workers to pick up the additional costs. Those promised payments to older Americans and the taxes on workers that will be necessary to fund them already risk what economists Larry Kotlikoff and Scott Burns call *The Coming Generational Storm*.[47] The International Monetary Fund warns that Obamacare will dramatically add to these unfunded promises.[48] The massive debt that we are accumulating will make it even more difficult to keep these already difficult to pay for promises.

Notes

1. "Pelosi: Unemployment Rate Would Have Hit 14.5% Without 2009 Stimulus," Fox News, October 6, 2011, http://nation.foxnews.com/nancy-pelosi/2011/10/06/pelosi-unemployment-rate-would-have-hit-145-without-2009-stimulus.

2. "Complete Final Debate Transcript: John McCain and Barack Obama," *Los Angeles Times,* October 15, 2008, http://latimesblogs.latimes.com/washington/2008/10/debate-transcri.html.

3. "The Second Presidential Debate," *New York Times,* October 7, 2008, http://elections.nytimes.com/2008/president/debates/transcripts/second-presidential-debate.html.

4. "63.2 Million Watched McCain and Obama's Second Debate," Nielsen-wire, October 8, 2008, http://blog.nielsen.com/nielsenwire/media_entertainment/632-million-watched-mccain-and-obamas-second-debate/.

5. The federal deficit reached $54.6 billion dollars in 1943. After adjusting for inflation, that would have been $669 billion in 2009. Yet, the actual 2009 federal deficit was $1.41 trillion, more than twice as large. As to the increase in government spending, during World War II, federal government spending increased by $43.4 billion in 1943, the equivalent of $532.5 billion in 2009. Still, this increase was slightly less than the $535 billion in spending during Obama's first year. Office of Management and Budget, "Fiscal Year 2012 Historical Tables, Budget of the U.S. Government," Executive Office of the President of the United States, www.whitehouse.gov/sites/default/files/omb/budget/fy2012/assets/hist.pdf.

6. "Obama's aides have begun working on a plan to spend up to $500 billion in new funds if the economy continues to worsen. That's well over the roughly $300 billion House Speaker Nancy Pelosi (D-Calif.) had initially considered for a new package—a figure that had been viewed as the outside limit until now." Jane Sasseen, "How Obama Will Stoke the Economy," *Business Week,* November 12, 2008, www.businessweek.com/magazine/content/08_47/b4109026234142.htm.

7. Martin Crutsinger, "Obama Aides Cite Need for Big Stimulus Program," *Boston Globe,* November 17, 2008, www.boston.com/business/articles/2008/11/17/obama_aides_cite_need_for_big_stimulus_program/.

8. "Obama Predicts 'Trillion-Dollar Deficits for Years to Come,'" Fox News, January 6, 2009, www.foxnews.com/politics/2009/01/06/congress-convenes-confront-economic-crisis-obama-response/.

9. W. Craig Riddell, "Why Is Canada's Unemployment Rate Persistently Higher than that in the US?" Centre for the Study of Living Standards,

2003, 3, www.csls.ca/events/cea2003/riddell–cea2003.pdf. See also "Job Search," National Longitudinal Survey, Bureau of Labor Statistics, U.S. Department of Labor, www.nlsinfo.org/nlsy97/nlsdocs/nlsy97/topicalguide/jobsearch.html.

10. W. Craig Riddell, "Why Is Canada's Unemployment Rate Persistently Higher than that in the US?" Centre for the Study of Living Standards, 2003, www.csls.ca/events/cea2003/riddell–cea2003.pdf.

11. An Angus-Reid Survey conducted during December 17 to 18, 2008, found that 56 percent of Canadians thought that their economy was "bad." Forty-nine percent of Canadians thought that the economy was going to get worse. A Gallup survey from December 18 to 20, 2008, found that 57 percent of Americans described their economy as "poor." Another Gallup survey found that in 2009, 35 percent thought that the economy was getting worse. "Canadians Head to 2009 with Gloomy Forecast for the National Economy," Angus Reid Strategies, December 30, 2008, www.angus-reid.com/wp-content/uploads/archived-pdf/2008.12.30_EcoIndex.pdf; "Gallup Daily: U.S. Economic Conditions," Gallup, www.gallup.com/poll/110821/Gallup-Daily-US-Economic-Conditions.aspx; "In U.S., 6 in 10 Do Not Expect Economy to Improve Soon," Gallup, www.gallup.com/poll/149576/not-expect-economy-improve-soon.aspx.

12. For a discussion of Canada's debt and deficits over the last few decades, see David R. Henderson, "Canada's Budget Triumph," Mercatus Center, George Mason University, August 2010, http://mercatus.org/sites/default/files/publication/Canada's%20Budget%20Triumph.WP_.pdf.

13. "Three-in-Five Canadians Satisfied with Country's Economic Conditions," Angus Reid Public Opinion, October 19, 2011, www.angus-reid.com/polls/44091/three-in-five-canadians-satisfied-with-countrys-economic-conditions/.

14. "Gallup Daily: U.S. Economic Conditions," Gallup, www.gallup.com/poll/110821/Gallup-Daily-US-Economic-Conditions.aspx.

15. William L. Watts, "Clash over Stimulus Spending Clouds G20 Outlook," Market Watch, *Wall Street Journal,* March 13, 2009, www.marketwatch.com/story/clash-over-stimulus-spending-clouds-g20.

16. "The U.S. Treasury secretary talks about permanent action and we at our [EU summit] were quite alarmed by that. He talks about an extensive U.S. stimulus campaign. All of these steps are the road to hell," Mirek Topolanek, the Czech prime minister, warned. Ian Traynor, "Obama's Rescue Plan Is 'Road to Hell,' claims EU president," *The Guardian* (United Kingdom), March 25, 2009.

17. Craig Whitlock, "European Union President Criticizes Obama's Economic Policies," *Washington Post,* March 26, 2009, www.washingtonpost.com/wp-dyn/content/article/2009/03/25/AR2009032502074.html.

18. For the 2008 to 2010 period, stimuli as a percentage of GDP by country were: Australia, 4.6; Japan, 2.0; France, 0.6; Germany, 3.0; Italy, 0; the Netherlands, 1.5; Sweden, 2.8; the United Kingdom, 1.4; and the United States, 5.6. See Table 3.1 on page 110 of the "OECD Economic Outlook," Interim Report, March 2009, www.iier.org/i/uploadedfiles/publication/real/1300670938_010309EconomicOutlookOECD4B.pdf.

19. Paul Krugman, "That '30s Feeling," *New York Times,* June 17, 2010, www.nytimes.com/2010/06/18/opinion/18krugman.html.

20. Paul Krugman, "What about Germany?" *New York Times,* August 24, 2010, http://krugman.blogs.nytimes.com/2010/08/24/what-about-germany/.

21. Paul Krugman, "Small Is Beautiful," *New York Times,* February 25, 2011, http://krugman.blogs.nytimes.com/2011/02/25/small-is-beautiful/. Krugman is referencing a paper by two Dartmouth College economics professors, James Feyrer and Bruce Sacerdote ("Did the Stimulus Stimulate? Real-Time Estimates of the Effects of the American Re-adjustment and Recovery Act," National Bureau of Economic Research Working Paper 16759, http://nasbo.org/LinkClick.aspx?fileticket=H6sHQ5MhK5o%3D&tabid=81).

22. The Feyrer and Sacerdote estimates do not consider the distinction between the benefits that individual states might get from receiving more money and that, in the aggregate, the Stimulus can reduce employment. They just look at whether the states getting more Stimulus money end up with relatively more employment. The negative intercept coefficients that they have for their state-level regressions in their Table 3 (columns 1 to 3) are certainly consistent with the Stimulus destroying jobs in the aggregate. Indeed, the intercept is so negative that only Alaska has a net increase in employment as a percent of the population.

In this section, we follow Feyrer and Sacerdote and look at the percentage of the population employed. Normally, we would have reported the percentage of the working-age population that is employed, but the results do not depend on the ratio used, and there is some benefit for being consistent with what supporters of the Stimulus have done.

23. About 85 percent of the Stimulus's budgetary impact was born by June 2011, which implies about $700 out of $825 billion. Congressional Budget Office, "Estimated Impact of the American Recovery and Reinvestment Act on Employment and Economic Output from April 2011 Through June 2011," Congressional Budget Office, August 2011, www.cbo.gov/ftpdocs/123xx/doc12385/08-24-ARRA.pdf.

24. Including Alaska reduces the estimated number of jobs associated with the Stimulus to 53, $120 million per job.

25. Mark J. Perry, "North Dakota's Booming Oil Economy," *Carpe Diem,* June 30, 2011, http://mjperry.blogspot.com/2011/06/north-dakotas-booming-oil-economy.html. For a set of numbers that roughly confirm those shown by Perry, see the various issues of the Bureau of Labor Statistics Table 6 "Employees on Nonfarm Payrolls by State and Selected Industry Sector, Not Seasonally Adjusted," www.bls.gov/news.release/laus.t06.htm.

26. A. G. Sulzberger, "Oil Rigs Bring Camps of Men to the Prairie," *New York Times,* November 25, 2011, www.nytimes.com/2011/11/26/us/north-dakota-oil-boom-creates-camps-of-men.html?pagewanted=all; Mark Peters and Ben LeFebvre, "Riding the Dakota Oil Boom," *Wall Street Journal,* November 2, 2011, http://online.wsj.com/article/SB10001424052970203 70750457701046393423498.html.

27. Sulzberger, "Oil Rigs Bring Camps of Men to the Prairie"; Mark Peters and Ben LeFebvre, "Riding the Dakota Oil Boom," *Wall Street Journal,* November 2, 2011, http://online.wsj.com/article/SB10001424052970203 70750457701046393423498.html.

28. Unemployment Rates for States, Bureau of Labor Statistics, October 2011, www.bls.gov/web/laus/laumstrk.htm.

29. Weighted least squares actually implies a negative (though statistically insignificant) relationship between stimulus dollars and unemployment. Feyrer and Sacerdote use weighted least squares for their county-level data, but do not report such estimates for their state-level data.

   Using Office of Labor Statistics data, the regression result for all states (including Alaska) using the Recovery.gov data was (absolute t-statistic in parentheses):

   Per Capita Stimulus Dollars Awarded = 8.36 e-09 (1.96); Percent of
   the population that is employed
   between February 2009 and June
   2011 − .000023 (4.96);

   adj-R^2 = 0.0551; F statistic = 3.86; Number of Observations = 50

   Using Office of Labor Statistics data, the regression result for all states except North Dakota using the Recovery.gov data was (absolute t-statistic in parentheses):

   Per Capita Stimulus Dollars Awarded = 4.24 e-09 (1.13); Percent of the population that is employed between February
   2009 and June 2011 − .00002 (4.93);

   adj-R^2 = 0.0057; F statistic = 1.28; Number of Observations = 49

Using weighted least squares, the regression result for all states using the Recovery.gov data was (absolute *t*-statistic in parentheses):

Per Capita Stimulus Dollars Awarded = −.00037 (0.57); Percent of the population that is employed between February 2009 and June 2011 − .8956 (1.55);

adj-R2 = −0.0139; F statistic = 0.33; Number of Observations = 50

The average state received Stimulus dollars per person of $1,020 and the average change in the percentage of the population that is employed is −.0015 percentage points.

30. As Krugman explained, "If stimulus funds were directed to states with especially severe unemployment problems, you might find a spurious negative correlation between stimulus and unemployment. What you need to get around this is some variable that is correlated with stimulus but not affected by the job changes. . . ." We have already seen the Stimulus money was related to unemployment, but it went the other way: The states with the higher unemployment rates got less money. Fortunately, more heavily Democrat congressional and Senate delegations got more money, and while Democrats got more Stimulus money, there is no independent reason why states with more heavily Democrat delegations should have experienced faster job growth. Feyrer and Sacerdote use the mean seniority of a state's House delegation, and one can quibble with that on multiple grounds (for example, Republicans were cut out of the process, so it isn't clear why their seniority matters, and their measure completely ignores the Senate). But the bottom line is that this quibbling doesn't matter since weighting the results by state population eliminates the relationship that they say exists.

Using an instrumental variables (2SLS) regression for all states using the Recovery.gov data and where the instrument was the percentage of the congressional and Senate delegation that are Democrats produced this result for the IV stage (absolute t-statistic in parentheses):

Per Capita Stimulus Dollars Awarded = 9.18 e-9 (0.73); Percent of the population that is employed between February 2009 and June 2011 − .00011 (0.84);

adj-R2 = ; *F* statistic = 0.53; Number of Observations = 50

31. President Barack Obama, "The President's Facebook Town Hall: Budgets, Values, Engagement," The White House, Office of the Press Secretary, April 21, 2011, http://m.whitehouse.gov/the-press-office/2011/04/20/remarks-president-facebook-town-hall.

32. Even if Reinhart and Rogoff are correct that financial crises are associated with deeper and longer-term contractions, there is the issue of causation. They clearly note (2968–2970): "One should be careful not to interpret this first pass at our long historical data set as definitive evidence of the causal effects of banking crises; there is a relatively new area in which much further work is yet to be done." In other words, is it the crisis per se that causes the problems or how the crisis is usually dealt with? It isn't too surprising that the greater the financial collapse, the greater the new regulations, and the more those new regulations retard future growth. See Carmen M. Reinhart and Kenneth Rogoff, *This Time Is Different: Eight Centuries of Financial Folly* (Princeton, NJ: Princeton University Press, 2009).

33. The entire list of countries facing a financial crisis was: Iceland, Spain, the United States, Belgium, Ireland, Hungary, the United Kingdom, the Netherlands, Austria, Germany, and Japan (see, for example, Figure 15.1). Carmen M. Reinhart and Kenneth Rogoff, *This Time Is Different: Eight Centuries of Financial Folly* (Princeton, NJ: Princeton University Press, 2009).

34. The t-test for a two-tailed test equals 9.5 and is statistically significant at greater than the .00001 level.

35. If you use the Bureau of Labor Statistics unemployment adjusted data for the period from January 2009 to August 2011, the countries not facing financial crises had an average increase in unemployment of .87 percentage points. If you include the United States among the countries with financial crises, their average increase was 0.849. If you take the unadjusted data, the relationship is reversed (it is now consistent with the Reinhart and Rogoff story). For countries not facing financial crises, the average increase in unemployment is .815 percentage points. If you include the United States among the countries with financial crises, that average increase was 0.868.

36. George Stephanopoulos, "Christina Romer on the Economy," *This Week with George Stephanopoulos,* ABC News, January 10, 2010, www.realclearpolitics. com/printpage/?url=www.realclearpolitics.com/articles/2010/01/10/ christina_romer_on_the_economy_on_this_week_99850.html.

37. John Lott Jr., "What Obama's Not Going to Tell You About Jobs," Fox News, January 27, 2010, www.foxnews.com/opinion/2010/01/27/ john-lott-obama-state-union-economy-jobs-unemployment/.

38. "We will leave it to the historians to figure out how both political parties, and many Americans, became convinced that austerity is the road to recovery." Unsigned editorial, "Meanwhile, Back in the Economy," *New York Times,* July 30, 2011. See also numerous op-eds by Paul Krugman, including, "The Hijacked Crisis," *New York Times,* August 11, 2011, www.nytimes .com/2011/08/12/opinion/the-hijacked-crisis.html?ref=paulkrugman.

39. Krugman doesn't adjust his numbers for either inflation or population growth, but even if one does that, he still isn't correct that there was a drop in total government spending.

Year	Government Spending in Trillions of 2000 Dollars (Adjusted for Inflation)			
	Federal	State	Local	Total
2000	$1.789	$0.946	$0.986	$3.721
2001	$1.812	$0.988	$1.030	$3.831
2002	$1.926	$1.042	$1.081	$4.049
2003	$2.022	$1.055	$1.107	$4.184
2004	$2.090	$1.077	$1.135	$4.301
2005	$2.179	$1.116	$1.143	$4.438
2006	$2.268	$1.147	$1.173	$4.588
2007	$2.267	$1.184	$1.234	$4.685
2008	$2.387	$1.183	$1.262	$4.832
2009	$2.827	$1.243	$1.277	$5.347
2010	$2.734	$1.284	$1.243	$5.261
2011	$2.764	$1.235	$1.213	$5.212
Percentage change from 2007 to 2011	22%	4%	1%	11%
Percentage change from 2008 to 2011	16%	4%	−4%	8%

*Estimate

Sources: Federal data from *Monthly Budget Review,* Congressional Budget Office Analysis, October 7, 2011, and Council of Economic Advisers, *Economic Report of the President,* White House, 2011.
State: State Expenditure Report, National Association of State Budget Officers, Fiscal Years 2001 to 2010.
Local: USGovernmentSpending.com
www.usinflationcalculator.com/inflation/historical-inflation-rates/
www.census.gov/popest/data/intercensal/state/state2010.html.

40. Paul Krugman, "The Austerity Economy," *New York Times,* September 3, 2011, http://krugman.blogs.nytimes.com/2011/09/03/the-austerity-economy/?scp=1&sq=%22austerity%20economy%22&st=Search.

41. Paul Krugman, "Punishing the Jobless," *New York Times,* July 4, 2010, www.nytimes.com/2010/07/05/opinion/05krugman.html?ref=paulkrugman.

42. Paul Krugman, "The Arithmetic of Near-term Deficits and Debt," *New York Times,* August 6, 2011, http://krugman.blogs.nytimes.com/2011/08/06/the-arithmetic-of-near-term-deficits-and-debt/.

Krugman has viciously lashed out at those who think that Americans should be concerned about the deficits. In 2010, he wrote: "This conventional wisdom isn't based on either evidence or careful analysis. Instead, it rests on what we might charitably call sheer speculation, and less charitably call figments of the policy elite's imagination—specifically, on belief in what I've come to think of as the invisible bond vigilante and the confidence fairy." Paul Krugman, "Myths of Austerity," *New York Times,* July 1, 2010, www.nytimes.com/2010/07/02/opinion/02krugman.html?src=me.

Yet there are economists who have extensively studied this debt problem and don't view it as a figment of our imaginations.

43. The information on publicly held federal debt is from the Obama's administration's Office of Management and Budget. Office of Management and Budget, "Fiscal Year 2012 Historical Tables, Budget of the U.S. Government," Executive Office of the President of the United States, www.whitehouse.gov/sites/default/files/omb/budget/fy2012/assets/hist.pdf.

44. Most likely the increase in the outstanding publicly held debt would have been quite a bit less than $455 billion because over the next year the Federal Reserve printed up a lot of money and used it to buy outstanding government bonds. The Federal Reserve did that so as to prevent deflation from occurring, but in the process it took government debt out of circulation. For a very public discussion on the expected deficit over the next year when even Obama recognized that it would be about this size, see "The Third McCain-Obama Presidential Debate," Commission on Presidential Debates, October 15, 2008, www.debates.org/index.php?page=october-15-2008-debate-transcript.

45. John Lott Jr., "Paul Ryan Is Right About the Budget—Americans Cannot Afford Another Decade of Massive Government Spending," Fox News, April 5, 2011, www.foxnews.com/opinion/2011/04/05/paul-ryan-right-budget-americans-afford-decade-massive-government-spending/.

46. President Bill Clinton, "State of the Union Address," U.S. Government Info, January 27, 2000, http://usgovinfo.about.com/library/ref/blsoufull.htm.

47. Lawrence J. Kotlikoff and Scott Burns, *The Coming Generational Storm,* (Cambridge, MA: MIT Press, Revised edition, 2005).

48. Lawrence J. Kotlikoff, "U.S. Is Bankrupt and We Don't Even Know It," Bloomberg, August 10, 2010, www.bloomberg.com/news/2010-08-11/u-s-is-bankrupt-and-we-don-t-even-know-commentary-by-laurence-kotlikoff.html. John R. Lott, Jr., "Believe It or Not, the U.S. Is In Worse Financial Shape Than Greece," Fox News, August 19, 2010, www.foxnews.com/opinion/2010/08/19/john-lott-imf-obama-government-greece-debt-fiscal-gap-debt-gdp.

Chapter 5

Regulatory Thuggery

What I find is a lot of business people can be supportive of new regulations and new standards, but particularly in a fragile time, they don't like to have too many things changing at once.[1]

— *Bill Clinton, former Democrat president,*
September 20, 2011

"You're headed for a one-term presidency," [Steve] Jobs told Obama at the outset. To prevent that, he said, the administration needed to be a lot more business-friendly. He described how easy it was to build a factory in China, and said that it was almost impossible to do so these days in America, largely because of regulations and unnecessary costs.[2]

— *Walter Isaacson, biographer of Steve Jobs,*
2011

And I'm saying it bluntly, that this administration is the greatest wet blanket to business and progress and job creation in my lifetime. . . . Well, my customers and the companies that provide the vitality for the hospitality and restaurant industry, in the United States of America, they are frightened of this administration. And it makes you slow down and not invest your money. . . . I am a Democratic businessman and I support Harry Reid.[3]

— *Steve Wynn, CEO of Wynn Resorts,*
July 18, 2011

E ven before the 2008 election, Mr. Obama's views toward business were clear: The problems that the country faces were due
to unbridled capitalism and greed and the federal government
needed to step in to fix it. According to Obama, deregulation, even
under Democratic President Bill Clinton's administration, produced an
"'anything goes' environment that helped foster devastating dislocations
in our economy."[4] The proper government regulations can prevent the
"chaotic, unforgiving" nature of capitalism.[5] For telecommunications,
electricity, banking, and accounting, he blamed the failures on markets
being out of control, with not enough government regulations to rein
in "an ethic of greed, corner cutting, insider dealing, things that have
always threatened the long-term stability of our economic system."[6]
Perhaps it isn't too surprising that Obama won't listen to Democratic
businessmen such as Steve Jobs or Steve Wynn. Even fellow Democrat
Clinton's advice on going a little more slowly on all the new regulations
is ignored.

Gradually realizing his views were not shared with the general public,
a year and a half after getting into office, the White House would occa-
sionally try convincing Americans that President Obama doesn't hate business. The president claimed: "It's very hard to find evidence of anything
that we've done that is designed to squash business as opposed to promote
business."[7] His administration's economists, primarily Austan Goolsbee,
argued that Obama was actually *pro-business*.[8] Other Democrats joined
in. For example, former Clinton labor secretary Robert Reich, declared:
"[The Obama] administration has been one of the most business-friendly
in history."[9]

Yet Obama, during his presidency, regularly calls Wall Street executives "fat cats,"[10] bondholders "speculators,"[11] and accuses doctors who
zealously test patients of being "driven from a business mentality."[12] He
regularly blames private companies rather than the government for the
financial crisis.[13] Indeed, the only blame he gives to the federal government is that there wasn't enough regulation. Even liberal New York
City mayor Michael Bloomberg warned: "[Obama's] bashing of Wall
Street is something that should worry everybody."[14]

But Bloomberg's warning did little to dampen Obama's rhetoric.
Despite a former pollster for Bill Clinton finding that Occupy Wall
Street demonstrators showing their "deep commitment to radical

left-wing policies" and "support for radical redistribution of wealth,"[15] Obama kept expressing his sympathy for the protesters.[16] A White House spokesman went so far as indicating that Occupy Wall Street represents the "interests of 99 percent of Americans."[17]

Obama conjured up a greatly exaggerated picture of a health insurance industry concentrated into only a few hands so as to justify government intervention. And he lashed out against doctors numerous times, accusing them of preferring to amputate a foot rather than "treat [diabetes] as effectively as it could" because they can earn more money.[18] Or that if a patient has "a bad sore throat," if they have allergies, the doctors will think to themselves: "I make a lot more money if I take this kid's tonsils out."[19]

Businessmen as Bad Guys

But does Obama really understand how the market operates? Take his claim during the health care debate that private insurance costs more than government insurance simply because private companies have to add on profits to the expenses of providing the service.[20] It ignores that costs, including administrative costs, are driven down by the incentive for higher profits. That is the reason why very few goods or services are sold by nonprofit companies despite huge tax subsidies—profits motivate companies to find ways produce better-quality products at a lower cost. Obama thinks that the experts are in Washington and that they can figure out better ways to run things than the greedy investors who have their money at stake.

With all of Obama's bashing of speculators, it is clear that he doesn't understand what speculators do. In April 2011 at a community college in northern Virginia, with gasoline prices nearing $4 per gallon, the president explained the high price of gas this way:

> And I know that if you've got a limited budget and you just watch that hard-earned money going away to oil companies that will once again probably make record profits this quarter, it's pretty frustrating. . . . There's enough oil out there for world demand. The problem is, is that oil is sold on these world

markets, and speculators and people make various bets, and they say, you know what, we think that maybe there's a 20 percent chance that something might happen in the Middle East that might disrupt oil supply, so we're going to bet that oil is going to go up real high. And that spikes up prices significantly. . . .[21]

Sure, with the high oil prices, energy companies were making a lot of money. Just a couple of weeks after his speech, ExxonMobil, the largest company in the United States, reported quarterly profits of $10 billion, earning about 9 cents per dollar in revenue. Royal Dutch Shell, Europe's biggest oil company, earned 8 cents, and ConocoPhillips pulled in 5 cents. But what is wrong with that? The prospect of high profits is precisely the lure needed to encourage and allow further investments in producing energy. That is how oil supplies are increased, and that is what will put downward pressure on future prices.

What Obama identified as being a problem is actually the way that markets are supposed to work. Oil prices spiked in 2011 when riots erupted in the Middle East during the Arab Spring. Governments in Tunisia, Egypt, Libya, and Yemen fell. The constant shootings of demonstrators had been going on for months in Syria when this chapter was written. This violence reduced oil production and caused fear of future reductions in supplies.

But what would happen if riots had also broken out in Saudi Arabia, which accounted for about 12 percent of world oil production?[22] Prices would soar. Speculators make profits by buying oil when the price is low and selling it when the price is high. Buying oil now to set it aside in case disaster strikes and supplies are interrupted protects consumers— because if disaster strikes, the stored supplies will be released and the shortage will be partly alleviated. Storing oil for such a time will prevent what would have been even higher prices. Higher prices today also encourage more conservation, thus making even more oil available if disaster strikes. If speculators didn't do that and Saudi shipments are halted, the much bigger increase in oil prices would surely cause much worse problems than the current rise in prices. Speculators make money by smoothing out the changes in prices over time.

Speculators are taking these risks with their own money. If Saudi Arabia and other Middle Eastern oil countries keep producing, speculators will be out of luck, paying a lot for the oil they stored and ending up selling it for less. Obama surely wasn't going to shed tears over the money the speculators lost. Yet, if production ended up being cut and the stored oil keeps prices from skyrocketing, would the president have thanked the speculators for a job well done? Absolutely not. Indeed, President Obama called for the Department of Justice to investigate "any illegal activity by traders and speculators."[23]

Ever More Regulations and Their Burden

President Obama boasts that he has done more than any past president in reducing government regulation. At a press conference in June 2011, when asked if regulations might "chill job growth," he reprimanded businesses for always complaining (emphasis added):

> Keep in mind that the business community is always complaining about regulations. When unemployment is at 3 percent and they're making record profits, they're going to still complain about regulations because, frankly, they want to be able to do whatever they think is going to maximize their profits. . . . But what I have done—and this is *unprecedented, by the way, no administration has done this before*—is I've said to each agency, don't just look at current regulations—or don't just look at future regulations, regulations that we're proposing, let's go backwards and look at regulations that are already on the books, and if they don't make sense, let's get rid of them. . . .[24]

Even the fact check watchdog PolitiFact, a rather liberal organization, rated Obama's assertion that his administration was doing an "unprecedented" review of existing regulations as a complete lie: "We rate Obama's statement Pants On Fire." As they conclude: "Lots of presidents have done that."

With Paul Krugman's genuine ties to the Obama administration, it was not too surprising that he echoed Obama's claims: "But aren't business people complaining about the burden of taxes and regulations? Yes, but no more than usual."[25] Krugman's evidence? A survey of small businesses by the National Federation of Independent Business, which represents hundreds of thousands of small businesses, asks: "What is the single most important problem your business faces?" During the Obama administration, small business owners have gotten more upset about "poor sales," "taxes," and "regulations." Krugman neglects to mention that taxes and regulations together are the biggest concern for 35 percent of businesses, while poor sales are the biggest for 30 percent. So taxes and regulations are bigger problems for business than poor sales. Surely that says something about how bad taxes and regulations are.

Ironically, there is a simpler way of figuring out how the National Federation of Independent Business views the new regulations: ask them. The week before Krugman's article, the association released a survey of its members showing that 90 percent thought that "federal over-regulation hampers their ability to function and grow as a business" and about half found it "extremely challenging" to keep up with new federal regulations.[26] Also, two days before Krugman's article, the association's executive director, Roger Geiger, wrote a column complaining: "Small businesses across America are being caught under a deluge of federal regulations, which are not only expensive to comply with but hinder job growth and raise prices for consumers."[27] His piece went on to note that as of September 2011 there were a record "4,226 federal regulations in the pipeline" and that since 2005 there was a 60 percent increase in the regulations "defined as 'major' or 'economically significant'— costing the economy $100 million or more."

The U.S. Chamber of Commerce survey of small and medium-size business CEOs found only 13 percent wanted "a helping hand" from government, and 80 percent wanted government to "get out of the way."[28] Among the top challenges facing small business, "loss of revenue" came in fifth as a concern, well behind over-regulation, the Obama health care bill, and America's growing debt.

The annual average number of regulations is higher during Obama's first three years in office than during either George W. Bush's or Bill Clinton's administrations, but the dramatic increase has occurred in what are called "economically significant" regulations, those which the government thinks will cost businesses $100 million or more each year (see Figure 5.1).[29] There was about a 40 percent increase in those significant regulations compared to the last term of the Bush administration and

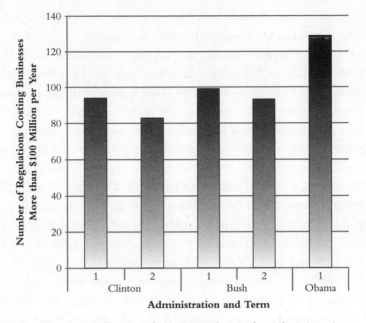

Figure 5.1 "Economically Significant" Regulations by Administration

fifty-five percent more than Clinton's last four years. Just 75 of those new regulations under Obama will cost companies an average of $38 billion a year over the coming decade.[30]

These costs aren't just theoretical ones borne by some greedy shareholders. Americans will feel them in the pocketbook. Even Obama's National Highway Traffic Safety Administration and Environmental Protection Agency estimate that his regulations will add an average of $2,000 to the price of the average car.[31]

Because these regulations have such a large impact, many organizations have measured the changes. From 1995 to 2011, the *Wall Street Journal* and the Heritage Foundation have tracked protection of property rights, regulations on investments, financial market regulations, regulation of business, and the tax rates that businesses and individuals face. Does the government encourage investment by protecting private property rights and the degree to which its government enforces those laws?[32] How onerous are regulations on investments and financial markets.[33] For general business regulations, do regulations make it harder to start, operate, and close a business?[34]

While the United States' ranking has slipped across the board, some areas have deteriorated dramatically over the past few years. Our rank in terms of business regulations has slipped the least, falling from tenth in 2008 to thirteenth in 2011. But the other changes have been dramatic, particularly when one considers how short a period of time is involved. Over the same time period, rankings on investment and financial regulations have plummeted from eleventh to twenty-eighth and from eighth to eighteenth, respectively. Property rights in the United States are also much less secure relative to other countries than they used to be, with the U.S. rank falling from fifth to seventeenth. Our tax system is particularly dysfunctional, going from 48th in rank in 1995 to 139th in 2011. The Bush administration briefly stalled this fall, leaving our ranking at the end of his term the same as it was when he came into office, but the trend has returned during Obama's time in office.

The World Economic Forum may not agree with the conservative Heritage Foundation on much, but they do agree that the United States has become less competitive. When the forum began reporting its current index in 2004, the United States was ranked for five years as having the world's most competitive economy, slipping to second in 2009. In 2010, we slipped to fourth. In 2011, we fell to fifth. The Cato Institute's Economic Freedom of the World Index was started in 2009 and is thus more limited in evaluating the Obama administration than the other rankings. Still, their overall U.S. ranking declined from seventh in 2008 to tenth in 2009. Similar declines occurred in our regulations of credit, labor, and business and there was a very large drop in our ranking in protecting property rights.[35]

The task for dismissing claims that Obama is antibusiness often fell to Austan Goolsbee. Goolsbee told the *Wall Street Journal* in late 2010 that Obama isn't antibusiness since he *"pushed through 16 tax cuts to assist small businesses and proposed additional incentives."*[36]

The statement regarding small business is revealing. Obama obviously considers it to be the role of the government rather than the private investors who should decide what size businesses should invest the most. But even for small business, the tax deductions and government loans in the bill are *targeted for firms that behave the way the government wants them to.* And Obama wants the deductions balanced off by higher marginal tax rates.

Goolsbee explained away the angry sentiment of businessmen toward the administration by blaming the bad economy: "When the unemployment rate is 9.6 percent, and when you're coming out of the deepest hole in anybody's lifetime, you knew that there were going to be a lot of people generally upset and not feeling good about where they are. . . ." Nevertheless, despite even harder times in the early 1980s, no one viewed President Ronald Reagan as antibusiness.

Businessmen such as Steve Wynn apparently were under a delusion regarding their fears of new regulations. Before the big battle over the debt ceiling increase during July and August 2011, Goolsbee said that the "wet blanket" scaring businesses was not regulation, but uncertainty over the level of government spending:

> I do think it's important we remove this wet blanket of uncertainty that is permeating the private sector where they don't know that the government—there are people actively advocating that the government declare it's not going to pay its bills.

Yet, obviously, uncertainty over government spending wasn't the problem. The economy started slowing down during the first quarter of 2010, when it grew by just 0.1 percent, seven months before there was any real discussion over the debt ceiling being increased. And the economy remained slow even after the $2.1 trillion increase in the debt ceiling was passed.

It will be years before we see the full regulatory impact of all the laws that were passed during Obama's first two years in office. Even after new laws are passed, it takes time for government agencies to actually turn a law into new regulations. One six-page-long section of Obamacare (Patient Protection and Affordable Care Act) has turned into 429 pages of dense regulations released in 2011 created by the Department of Health and Human Services.[37] In other cases, a single paragraph of the bill will probably end up producing hundreds or more pages of rules. Obamacare created 159 new agencies, commissions, panels, and other governmental bodies. The Dodd-Frank financial regulatory reform has 447 new rules that are either required or suggested.[38] Some of the other new regulatory laws include "sweeping restrictions on credit-card issuers" and the Helping Families Save Their Homes Act to make foreclosures more difficult and prevent "predatory lending practices."[39]

The barrage of recently developed regulations often involves interpreting existing laws. During the summer of 2009, there was a seemingly trivial example of the Obama administration's regulatory mindset. The Food and Drug Administration (FDA) surprisingly threatened to ban the sale of Cheerios, the top-selling breakfast cereal in the United States.[40] Two claims on the Cheerios box created the ruckus: "Cheerios is clinically proven to reduce cholesterol 4 percent in 6 weeks" and "Cheerios can help reduce the risk of coronary heart disease, by lowering the 'bad' cholesterol."[41] Susan Cruzan, with the FDA's press office, told us that the FDA wasn't objecting to the fact that clinical studies do in fact find what General Mills claims they do. "This is a food product and they do have a health claim. . . . [General Mills] could say 'heart disease,' but they are being specific and saying 'coronary heart disease,'" she claimed. Unless the claims were removed, the Obama administration would classify Cheerios as a new drug and it couldn't be sold until it had gone through the proper FDA safety testing.

Take one proposed regulation that was revealed in late November 2011. The Obama administration wanted to ban many children under 18 from doing chores on their family farms.[42] And don't even think of letting them try helping out on their grandparents' or neighbors' farms.

On a more major scale, the EPA unleashed an "unprecedented wave of rules," pushing regulations that even internal administration critics thought would endanger the security and reliability of the U.S. electric power supply. The Federal Energy Regulatory Commission chairman, Jon Wellinghoff, a Democratic political appointee, told Alaska Republican senator Lisa Murkowski that the administration's air quality regulations to deal with carbon emissions would eliminate as much as 8 percent of U.S. electricity generation.[43] Under pressure from Democrats and the EPA, Wellinghoff disavowed the calculations that he had provided Murkowski, but was unwilling to supply any new estimates.

Socialist Takeovers

Ironically, on September 29, 2010, the very same day that the government announced it was taking a 92 percent ownership stake in AIG, Mr. Goolsbee declared it "totally bogus" to say that the president "is a socialist."[44] Despite Obama wanting government ownership of GM and many financial institutions or pushing for government-run health insurance, he might not be a pure socialist. Still, President Obama thinks that government, not consumers and private businesses, should ultimately run the economy.

But Obama's animosity against the private sector goes well beyond disapproving of profits. He holds little respect for property rights. When President Obama failed to persuade firms to follow his wishes, he did not hesitate to use threats of financial destruction. What Obama fails to recognize is that these threats scare not only the firms he threatens, but also investors around the world who won't view investments in the United States as being as safe as they used to be.

Cliff Asness, the co-founder of the $20 billion hedge fund AQR Capital Management, laid bare one of the attacks in May 2009:

> The President screaming that the hedge funds are looking for an unjustified taxpayer-funded bailout is the big lie writ large. Find me a hedge fund that has been bailed out. Find me a hedge fund, even a failed one, that has asked for one. In fact, it was only because hedge funds have not taken government funds that they could stand up to this bullying. The TARP recipients had no choice but to go along.[45]

This was just the latest in a string of intimidating tactics, starting with threatening costly public audits to get compliance. Then there were the threats of firing CEOs who had the audacity to oppose government plans. The very latest is threats to use "the full force of the White House Press Corps [to] destroy [the firm Perella Weinberg's] reputation" if it resisted the government stealing their money, according to Thomas Lauria, who previously represented the firm.[46] ABC News's Jake Tapper reports that Mr. Steven Rattner, Obama's car czar, made the threat.[47]

The White House had pushed hard to nationalize the automobile companies. While bondholders and the government have loaned similar amounts each to GM and Chrysler, the White House feels that the government should get 70 percent ownership of GM and the creditors about 10 percent. If a company were worth less than what creditors had lent it, the creditors would normally get 100 percent, not 10 percent, of the company. The *Wall Street Journal* quoted one anonymous Chrysler debt holder calling the government's proposal "ugly" and promised to fight it.[48]

The unions also got stock and other benefits that should be going to the creditors. For GM, that amounted to $6.5 billion in preferred stock paying a 9 percent dividend, $2.5 billion in debt, 17.5 percent of the new company and future warrants allowing purchase of another 2.5 percent.[49] The United Auto Workers was originally going to get 39 percent of GM stock, but it decided that GM's future was simply too risky.[50] In Chrysler's case, the UAW ended up owning 63.5 percent.[51]

The *Wall Street Journal*'s Holman Jenkins summarized the fight this way: "[GM bondholders] have been intransigent precisely because they calculate the UAW is too important to Democratic electoral politics for Mr. Obama to risk losing control of the reorganization process to a bankruptcy judge. The GM bailout has become a political operation run out of the White House."[52]

Quite a deal for the unions, given that bankruptcy would have normally meant that the unions wouldn't have gotten all these payouts and their labor contracts also would have been invalidated. Instead, as the *Washington Post* noted, for workers already at GM, "Union concessions were 'painful' only by the peculiar standards of Big Three labor relations: At a time when some American workers are facing stiff pay cuts, UAW workers gave up their customary paid holiday on Easter Monday and their right to overtime pay after less than 40 hours per week. They still get health benefits that are far better than those received by many American families upon whose tax money GM jobs now depend. Ditto for UAW hourly wages. . . . Cumbersome UAW work rules have only been tweaked."[53]

Austan Goolsbee, who also served on Obama's Auto Task Force, had quite a different spin from the *Washington Post,* telling PBS's *NewsHour* that it was the greedy bondholders who were demanding special treatment: "I think there has been an element, especially on the part of the bondholders, of feeling like, well, ultimately the government will just keep bailing us out, so we don't actually have to bite the bullet and make these sacrifices. And the president made clear that's not going to be the case."[54] In a later interview with Reuters Television,

Goolsbee talked of the shared sacrifice, saying that "bondholders are going to have to take some haircut."[55]

Most of the financial institutions holding these bonds went along with Obama's nationalization of the car companies for a simple reason—the government has already nationalized them and they do the government's bidding. As ABC News and the *Wall Street Journal* note: JPMorgan Chase, Citigroup, Morgan Stanley, and Goldman Sachs have been given up to $100 billion by the government.[56] The irony is that the feds gave these financial institutions money because they were hemorrhaging financially and now the government orders these same institutions to throw away money and take losses that no private company would voluntarily do.[57]

The government only obtained ownership of many financial institutions through threats of imposing unnecessary costly public audits and either threatening to replace or actually replacing disobedient CEOs and boards of directors with political cronies willing to do Obama's bidding.[58]

Yet, there are financial institutions that the government still has not gotten control over, and they are fighting this wave of nationalization. So how does the Obama administration control these financial institutions that have avoided being forced to take government bailouts? Why, of course, their standard method: threats.

Not surprisingly, as the financial institutions did not cave in, President Obama then followed through on his promise and attacked these creditors. During his announcement of Chrysler's filing for bankruptcy, he warned, "While many stakeholders made sacrifices and worked constructively, I have to tell you some did not."[59] Despite the financial institutions offering to give up 50 percent of their bonds' value, Obama claimed: "They were hoping that everybody else would make sacrifices, and they would have to make none." The *New York Times* and other media have joined in on this attack.[60]

There were other consequences of the president singling out these creditors and falsely claiming that bankruptcy means companies close their doors and send their employees home.[61] That very rarely happens for Chapter 11 bankruptcies and it wasn't going to happen here, but Obama's assertion that "one million American jobs" would have been lost assumed that all of GM's and Chrysler's jobs, as well as all the jobs of their parts-supplier employees and car-dealer employees, would have been lost.[62] It is understandable that a lot of people were really scared. The *Detroit News* reported that creditors *received death threats* and that the threats have been turned over to the FBI.[63]

Yet, the president's inflammatory rhetoric is even more outrageous because his economic advisers had told him that these claims were false. Steve Rattner describes in his book, *Overhaul*, discussions in April 2009 when Austan Goolsbee told Obama that even the complete liquidation of Chrysler would mean the loss of 25,000 to 60,000 jobs, significant, but "a far cry from the 300,000" Obama's later speeches continually relied on in making his million-job claim.[64]

In many ways, Rattner seemed the perfect person to handle all the political payoffs as well as serve as an enforcer in the auto bailouts. In April 2009, the *Wall Street Journal* reported that during his tenure with the Obama administration, Rattner's former private equity firm, Quadrangle Group, was the target of a long-running pay-to-play investigation.[65] After Rattner left office, his partners at Quadrangle publicly attacked him for his "unethical behavior" in paying bribes to get government contracts.[66] Rattner was eventually forced to pay $10 million in restitution in a deal with the New York Attorney General's office as well as repay $6.2 million to the Securities and Exchange Commission and agree to a two-year ban from the securities industry.[67]

Of course, the administration denies that it has threatened Chrysler's creditors, though without threats, it is hard to explain why bondholders caved and agreed to accept what amounted to pennies on the dollar when they were entitled to so much more.

Some creditors, such as Perella Weinberg Partners, gave in to the president's threats over Chrysler. But breaking contracts through thuggish threats makes investment riskier and increases the costs as much as any big tax increase. Driving investment overseas is not the way to make America wealthier.[68]

To Obama, it might be a simple matter of "fairness" that bondholders suffer bigger financial losses and that their money be given to unions and the government. But in the long term, making bonds riskier means that companies won't be lent as much money as they used to.

The Obama administration has also tried to fix the housing crisis by repeatedly trying to force mortgage lenders to agree to large write-offs—to forgive parts of loans. The argument is that if homeowners don't owe as much money, they are less likely to default.[69] But if the reduced risk from default really offset lenders' costs from writing off portions of their loans, no one would need to force lenders to make the write-offs. Obama might make existing borrowers who get the write-offs very happy, but what about anyone who wants a new loan? Why would lenders want to lend money for mortgages if a year from now they face government pressure to write off $50,000 or $100,000 of the mortgage?

Companies learn the hard way not to cross the Obama administration. The U.S. Department of Justice has been investigating Standard & Poor's (S&P) improper rating of dozens of mortgage securities before the financial crisis, but the New York Times reported that after Standard & Poor's downgraded the U.S. credit rating in August 2011, Democrats have "questioned the agency's secretive process, its credibility and the competence of its analysts, claiming to have found an error in its debt calculations."[70] The government is now investigating S&P for not foreseeing a financial crisis that the government itself didn't foresee. But if S&P doesn't rate bonds and other assets properly, people won't pay them very much for their ratings. The market will punish S&P for any mistakes that it makes.

Goolsbee also learned how to punish the president's political adversaries. The battle between the Koch bothers and President Obama hasn't gotten as much coverage as that between George Soros and Republicans, but it is about as bitter. A New Yorker headline gives one side of the "The billionaire brothers who are waging a war against Obama."[71] Goolsbee entered the fray at an August 27, 2010, press briefing where he let slip that he knew that Koch Industries, a multibillion-dollar energy business run by the libertarian Koch brothers, had paid no income taxes. "[W]e have a series of entities that do not pay corporate income tax, some of which are really giant firms. You know, Koch Industries is a multibillion-dollar business," Mr. Goolsbee told reporters during an on-the-record background briefing on corporate taxes.

Koch Industries is a privately held company and therefore their tax returns and tax payments are not normally publicly available. This recalls shades of Richard Nixon's abuse of the Internal Revenue Service to collect information on his enemies, and there were serious questions of how Mr. Goolsbee obtained this information. At first, the White House sent Politico an email explaining that the information was publicly available and referenced testimony to the President's Economic Recovery Advisory Board and Koch's own website.[72] But they were just dead wrong. How much taxes Koch Industries pays appears in neither place.

The Obama administration then switched to a second line of defense: that Mr. Goolsbee simply misspoke, that he didn't mean to say what he said, and that it was merely a coincidence that he had just happened to guess their tax information.[73] But it was quite a lucky guess. The IRS's Inspector General promised to look into whether Goolsbee had illegally gotten confidential tax information,[74] but a report was never released, and with Democrats in control of both the Senate and House at the time, there was no congressional pressure on the Obama administration to release the report.[75]

The power to regulate also means the power to destroy, and can be used to pressure companies in areas far outside the activities that are regulated. Ford Motor Company, the one car company that didn't take any money from the government bailout, briefly ran an ad in 2011 in which a real customer named Chris had a simple message: "I wasn't going to buy another car that was bailed out by our government. I was going to buy from a manufacturer that's standing on their own: win, lose, or draw. That's what America is about, . . . taking the chance to succeed and understanding when you fail that you gotta pick yourself up and go back to work. Ford is that company for me." The *Detroit News* reported:

> But the Obama administration didn't care for the free market message and . . . the White House contacted Ford to discuss the ad and the company has now pulled the popular spot. . . . such inquiries from the White House represent coercion. . . . The most obvious reason [for the White House concern] relates to the president's re-election bid. [76]

With the impact of government destroying property rights and attempts to force writedowns, is anyone surprised that bondholders and mortgage lenders have been reluctant to lend money? If potential homeowners can't borrow money to buy houses, fewer houses will be purchased and the price of houses will fall. But to President Obama, the solution wasn't to back away from these regulations. Instead, in December 2009, he called the CEOs of America's 12 largest financial institutions to the White House's Diplomatic Reception Room and threatened them with regulatory retaliation if they persisted in lobbying against the Dodd-Frank financial regulation bill, and then paraded the CEOs in front of television cameras at an Obama press conference.[77]

While making the thinly veiled threat that he really didn't want "to dictate to them [how to run their companies] or micromanage their compensation practices," the president told the press that had gathered:

> Now, I should note that around the table all the financial industry executives said they supported financial regulatory reform. The problem is there's a big gap between what I'm hearing here in the White House and the activities of lobbyists on behalf of these institutions or associations of which they're a member up on Capitol Hill. I urged them to close that gap, and they assured me that they would make every effort to do so.[78]

One executive after another acknowledged their mistake and said that he always meant to support Mr. Obama's regulatory takeover. They had all, every single one of them, simply miscommunicated their desires to their lobbyists. No one ever tried explaining the implausible coincidence that all of these CEOs similarly miscommunicated such instructions. It was an unprecedented display of power and public humiliation whereby regulatory threats stopped financial institutions from lobbying against legislation against regulations that directly affected them.

The battle to pass Obamacare was filled with similar stories. When the health care battle heated up during September 2009, Democrats had no problem imposing all sorts of regulatory costs on one of their major opponents, the private insurance industry.[79] Private insurance companies were given less than three weeks to supply the government with detailed compensation data for board members and top executives as well as a "table listing all conferences, retreats or other events held outside company facilities from January 1, 2007, to the present that were paid for, reimbursed or subsidized in whole or in part by your company."[80] For employees or officers making more than $500,000 a year, the companies were mandated to provide detailed "salary, bonus, options, and pension" information.

These demands were made at the same time that President Obama was attacking insurance companies for "making record profits,"[81] though the profits were really hardly record breaking.[82] Democratic House Speaker Nancy Pelosi labeled insurance companies as "villains."[83] No similar blanket demands were made of other health care industries, such as the pharmaceutical industry, which was putting in up to $150 million to promote passing Obamacare on the promise that their interests would be protected in the final bill.[84]

Still, regulatory power was clearly abused. The *Wall Street Journal* editorialized about a couple of particularly egregious cases in which the Obama administration forced two CEOs for small pharmaceutical companies to be removed from office.[85] The government didn't argue that these CEOs had done anything themselves but asserted the odd charge that "marketing to doctors common among drug companies amounted to fraud against Medicare and Medicaid." It was only after the CEOs agreed to a plea deal that the government "unearthed a dusty provision in the Social Security Act" and demanded that the CEOs be fired from their jobs. Their real crime seems to have been their opposition to Obamacare.

Regulations are not only enforced to punish opponents, they also seem to be used to reward supporters. By August 19, 2011, Health and Human Services Secretary Kathleen Sebelius had granted 1,472 waivers for those who had wanted to be exempt at least temporarily from Obamacare.[86] Waivers provided exemptions for up to three years. But even though unions strongly backed the new law, 50 percent of waivers were granted to organizations with unionized employees.[87] Hardly a number that is proportional to the only 6.9 percent of private sector workers who are unionized.

Or take the case of the pharmaceutical firm Siga Technologies, a firm where a controlling share is owned by billionaire Democratic donor Ronald Perelman. In May 2011, the Obama administration granted the company a highly unusual $433 million no-bid contract to supply a treatment that can't be tested on humans.[88] The drug was being designed to treat unvaccinated troops exposed to a smallpox biological weapon from Russia, the only other country besides the United States that has a sample of the virus that was eradicated worldwide in 1978. Critics pointed out that since we already have a vaccine, even if such a biological weapon were developed, there is little benefit to developing a drug that can't be tested because doing so would require infecting people with the deadly smallpox virus. The existing vaccine costs only $3 per dose and can successfully treat people when given up to four days after exposure.

But with all the Obama administration's attacks on greedy pharmaceutical companies, one of the most surprising aspects of this contract was that Siga successfully removed the government's lead negotiator when he objected to the company making an incredible 180 percent profit margin. The *Los Angeles Times* reported that the chief medical officer for Health and Human Services' biodefense preparedness unit called the profit margin "outrageous" and said that no government contracting officer "would sign a 3-digit profit percentage." But political appointees overruled him and replaced the negotiator.

A Case Study: Obama and the Push for Health Care Regulation

Consumers do better when there is choice and competition. Unfortunately, in 34 states, 75 percent of the insurance market is controlled by five or fewer companies. In Alabama, almost 90 percent is controlled by just one company. Without competition, the price of insurance goes up and the quality goes down . . . an additional step we can take to keep insurance companies honest is by making a not-for-profit public option available in the insurance exchange. . . .

—*President Barack Obama,*
Address to Congress on health care,
September 9, 2009

As we have already mentioned, demonizing greedy insurance companies and doctors has been a frequent staple of Obama's speeches. During Obama's first year and a half as president, passing Obamacare was the president's number-one goal. It is hard to conceive of a more far-reaching piece of legislation. The 2,560-page Obamacare legislation created massive new regulation involving 159 new agencies, commissions, panels, and other bodies.[89] Indeed, there are so many new regulations that the Obama administration can't even keep up. By November 2011, the administration had missed deadlines for 60 percent of the new regulations they were supposed to file.[90] Some of those deadlines have been missed by more than seven months.

Businesses have been very worried about the costs of the new regulations. Thirty percent of employers are thinking of completely dropping health insurance coverage and many others are likely to change their plans. So much for Obama's frequent promise:

> If you like your health care plan, you keep your health care plan. Nobody is going to force you to leave your health care plan. If you like your doctor, you keep seeing your doctor. I don't want government bureaucrats meddling in your health care.[91]

The administration was willing to go overboard to attack his critics so as to get his signature legislation passed. Many of the supposed facts pushed during the debate were shaped more by what the polls *said*, as detailed carefully in Ron Suskind's book, *Confidence Men*. According to Suskind, President Obama relied heavily on opinion polls to shape his lashings out at insurance companies: "New polling showed that, unlike the debacle of the 1990s, the principal villain in the 2000s was no longer seen as government bureaucracy, but rather insurance profiteering."[92] Joel Benenson, Obama's head pollster, told the Economic Club of Canada in early 2009 how the goal was to get people to "think the insurance companies have been the villains here, not the government."[93]

Even worse, insider accounts by Suskind's book and former Obama adviser Peter Dreier show how the picking of insurance companies as a villain evolved.[94] During the spring of 2009, the health care reform debate started with a "grand bargain" between the health insurance companies and Obama. In exchange for agreeing to more regulations, health insurance companies would get to cover more people at taxpayer expense. The deal initially prevented Obama from attacking insurance companies as an obstacle to Obamacare, but parts of the agreement—including an insurance mandate, taxing some premiums, diverting Medicare funds—alienated not just conservatives but also, importantly, parts of Obama's own base. As Suskind notes, "Once the White House abandoned that [grand bargain]—its strongest bipartisan stance—the insurers became a convenient scapegoat."[95] The insurance companies facing "some combination of fear or bribery" had agreed to give Obama what he wanted, but when Obama changed the deal and decided to move further left politically, they became the villains.[96]

As Obama's quote shown at the beginning of this section illustrates, he consistently pushed claims in the health care debate shown in their internal polls to match people's prejudices. These claims were often at odds with what the facts were. Thus, the president worked to reinforce the following beliefs: (1) that there is little competition among those providing health insurance and (2) that it is important to take the profit motive out of providing health insurance. But both are myths based on a misinterpretation of the data. In reality, nonprofit insurers are so abundant that the largest insurer in virtually every state is a nonprofit.

Nevertheless, his carefully crafted speeches went over well. Take his warnings from the end of August 2009: "Insurance companies and their allies don't like this idea [government-provided health insurance], or any that would promote greater competition."[97] Even some Republicans accepted these arguments. "There is a serious problem with the lack of competition among insurers," said Republican senator Olympia Snowe of Maine.[98] "The impact on the consumer is significant."

The administration pointed to a 2008 study by the American Medical Association to support their claims about the high concentration in the health insurance market (see Table 5.1).[99] That study supposedly showed that one or two health insurance providers dominated the market in most states. This fact, in turn, would strongly suggest implying that the providers could be exploiting a monopoly-like situation to generate excessive profits.

Table 5.1   States with Most Concentrated Full Insurance Market for 15 Most Concentrated States

State	Name of Company with Largest Share of Full Insurance Market (nonprofit firms marked in bold italics)	Market Share of Full Insurance Market for the Largest Firm	Name of Company with Second-Largest Share of Full Insurance Market (nonprofit firms marked in bold italics)	Market Share of Full Insurance Market for Second-Largest Firm	Market Share of Full Insurance Market for the Two Largest Firms
Hawaii	*Blue Cross Blue Shield HI*	78%	Kaiser Permanente	20%	98%
Rhode Island	*Blue Cross Blue Shield RI*	79%	United Health Group Inc.	16%	95%
Alaska	*Premera Blue Cross*	60%	Aetna Inc.	35%	95%
Vermont	*Blue Cross Blue Shield VT*	77%	CIGNA Corp.	13%	90%
Alabama	*Blue Cross Blue Shield AL*	83%	Health Choice	5%	88%
Maine	WellPoint Inc.	78%	Aetna Inc.	10%	88%
Montana	*Blue Cross Blue Shield MT*	75%	New West Health Services	10%	85%
Wyoming	*Blue Cross Blue Shield WY*	70%	United Health Group Inc.	15%	85%
Arkansas	*Blue Cross Blue Shield AR*	75%	United Health Group Inc.	6%	81%
Iowa	*Wellmark Blue Cross Blue Shield*	71%	United Health Group Inc.	9%	80%
Missouri	WellPoint Inc.	68%	United Health Group Inc.	11%	79%
Minnesota	*Blue Cross Blue Shield MN*	50%	Medica	26%	76%
South Carolina	*Blue Cross Blue Shield SC*	66%	CIGNA Corp.	9%	75%
Indiana	WellPoint Inc.	60%	M*Plan (Health Care Group)	15%	75%

The problem with these AMA numbers is that they only cover less than half of the health insurance market. The numbers leave out the fact that for most people it is their employer, not the insurance companies, that pays for any bad health outcomes. The firm does so out of the company's own pocket. The companies do what is called *self-insure* or *self-fund* their plans, and that occurs for around 55 percent of employees, according to the federal government's Agency for Healthcare Research and Quality, a part of the Department of Health and Human Services.[100]

Take Maine, which is Senator Snowe's home state. According to the AMA, the two largest insurance companies appear to control 88 percent of the market, with WellPoint Inc. making up most of that—78 percent. But, again, these numbers only deal with privately insured patients who are insured by insurance companies. Slightly more than half of the privately insured in Maine (52.1 percent) get their insurance through their employers, who self-insure. These employers merely hire other companies to handle the paperwork. WellPoint Inc. thus really provides primary, or full, insurance to the 78 percent of the market not covered by self-insurers. Doing the math gives: 78 percent $\times$ (1 − 52.1%) = 37.1 percent. That is only a little more than a third of the total market in Maine. The second largest insurance company, Aetna, has only 4.8 percent of the total market.

It is not just Maine. We can look at the 43 states for which the AMA compiled data ranking them by those with the market share held by the two largest insurance companies (see Figure 5.2). The pattern is fairly similar. On average, over 53 percent of people with insurance in those states get their insurance from companies that self-insure. For Alabama, instead of the "almost 90 percent is controlled by just one company," as the president claims, the correct number is just 36 percent. And the second-largest company has just 2.1 percent of the market.[101]

Even with the "almost 90 percent" number, it is worth noting that the president rounded that up from the actual share in the full insurance market of 83 percent. The president just wasn't happy to claim that the largest insurance company in Alabama had an 83 percent share when the right number was 36 percent, but he had to go further and raise it to "almost 90 percent." On top of that, in his attacks on for-profit insurance companies, he couldn't even acknowledge that Alabama's largest insurer was a nonprofit company.

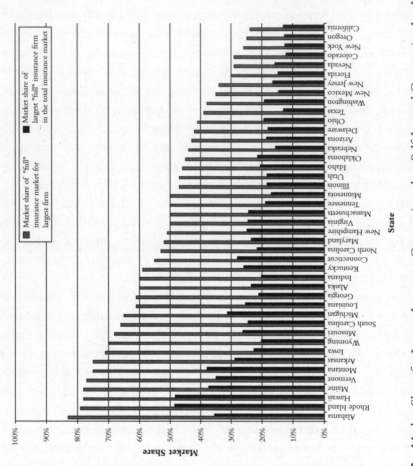

Figure 5.2 Market Share for Largest Insurance Companies when Self-Insured Companies Are Included

Obviously, 37 percent is a lot less concentrated than 78 percent, but the 52.1 percent covered by self-insurers is extremely competitive. Thousands of employers in Maine are self-insurers, and they compete for workers not only on the basis of the salary they pay, but also on the benefits they offer.

So what about President Obama's claim that in the 34 most concentrated states 75 percent of the insurance market is controlled by five or fewer companies? Given that self-insured firms cover 57 percent of people insured in those states, the correct total market share for the five largest firms' control is 32 percent, not 75 percent. Despite repeated requests, the administration wouldn't respond to our question of how their figures would be affected by including those insured by their own companies.[102]

Ernie Clevenger, publisher of *My Health Guide* (a self-insurance industry newsletter), told us that he estimates that there are about 900 third-party administrators (TPAs)—companies that are hired by self-insured businesses to handle their employees' policies. Unlike primary or full-service insurance companies, these TPAs can compete across state lines.

Given all the attacks on profit-making insurance companies, what is possibly more surprising is that by far the dominant players in the full-insurance market are nonprofits. Indeed, one of the motives of the government insurance option is to take profits out of the picture.[103]

Yet, in 29 of the 43 states, the dominant company in the full-insurance market is a nonprofit company. In state after state, Blue Cross and Blue Shield hold the largest market share. On average, the largest nonprofit holds more than half of the full market share in those 29 states.

Demonizing insurance companies helped pass the massive Obamacare regulations. But in the process, President Obama managed to paint what is actually a very competitive market as instead controlled by a few greedy for-profit insurance companies. Never mind that thousands of companies in each state had their own insurance company and that the largest insurance company in each state was usually a nonprofit. It just shows how far President Obama was willing to go to get the new regulations that he wanted.

Notes

1. Jim Meyers and Christopher Ruddy, "Ex-President Clinton to Newsmax: Raising Taxes Won't Work," *Newsmax*, September 20, 2011, www.newsmax .com/Headline/bill-clinton-obama-taxes/2011/09/20/id/ 411720?s=al&promo_code=D170-1.

2. Walter Isaacson, *Steve Jobs* (New York: Simon & Schuster, 2011).

3. "Wynn Slams Obama on Business: 'Responsible for Fear in America,'" Real Clear Politics Video, July 18, 2011, www.realclearpolitics.com/ video/2011/07/18/wynn_slams_obama_on_business_responsible_for_this_ fear_in_america.html.

4. Congressional Quarterly Transcripts, "Obama Remarks on Economy," *Washington Post*, March 27, 2008, www.washingtonpost.com/wp-dyn/ content/article/2008/03/27/AR2008032701631.html.

5. Ibid.

6. Ibid.

7. CNBC Transcript: CNBC Broadcasts, "Investing in America: A CNBC Town Hall Event with President Obama," September 20, 2010 (www .cnbc.com/id/39211696/CNBC_EXCLUSIVE_CNBC_TRANSCRIPT_ CNBC_BROADCASTS_INVESTING_IN_AMERICA_A_CNBC_ TOWN_HALL_EVENT_WITH_PRESIDENT_OBAMA_TODAY_ MONDAY_SEPTEMBER_20TH_AT_12PM_ET).

8. Sudeep Reddy, "Big Interview: Goolsbee Defends Obama Record on Business," *Wall Street Journal*, October 1, 2010, http://blogs.wsj.com/ economics/2010/10/01/big-interview-goolsbee-defends-obama-record- on-business/; Larry Kudlow, "An Interview with Austan Goolsbee," *National Review,* August 18, 2011, www.nationalreview.com/kudlows- money-politics/274931/interview-austan-goolsbee.

9. Carrie Budoff Brown, "President Obama at War with Himself over Wall Street," Politico, October 21, 2011, www.politico.com/news/stories/1011/ 66514.html.

10. Brian Montopoli, "Obama versus the 'Fat Cats,'" CBS News, December 13, 2009, www.cbsnews.com/8301-503544_162-5975318-503544.html?tag= contentMain;contentBody.

11. Editorial, "About those 'Speculators,'" *Wall Street Journal*, May 21, 2009, http://online.wsj.com/article/SB124286497706641485.html.

12. President Barack Obama, "Remarks by the President in Town Hall Meeting on Health Care," The White House, Office of the Press Secretary, June 11, 2009, www.whitehouse.gov/the_press_office/Remarks-by-the-President- in-Town-Hall-Meeting-on-Health-Care-in-Green-Bay-Wisconsin/.

13. President Barack Obama, "Obama's Speech on Overhauling Financial Regulation," *New York Times*, April 22, 2010, www.nytimes.com/2010/04/23/business/economy/23prexy-text.html?pagewanted=all.

14. Sara Kugler, "NYC Mayor Defends Wall Street before Obama's Visit," Associated Press, April 21, 2010, www.breitbart.com/article.php?id=D9F7LQ7O1&show_article=1.

15. Douglas Schoen, "Polling the Occupy Wall Street Crowd," *Wall Street Journal*, October 18, 2011, http://online.wsj.com/article/SB100014240529 70204479504576637082965745362.html?mod=WSJ_hp_mostpop_read.

16. Doyle McManus, "Pre-Occupied: Obama Finds Sympathy Loves Company," *Sydney Morning Herald*, October 22, 2011 (www.smh.com.au/business/world-business/preoccupied-obama-finds-sympathy-loves-company-20111021-1mcee.html); Carrie Budoff Brown, "President Obama at War with Himself over Wall Street," Politico, October 21, 2011, www.politico.com/news/stories/1011/66514.html.

17. Zeke Miller, "White House Draws Closer to Occupy Wall Street, Says Obama Is Fighting for the Interests of the 99%," *Business Insider*, October 16, 2011, http://articles.businessinsider.com/2011-10-16/politics/30285591_1_house-spokesman-josh-earnest-president-barack-obama-class-warrior.

18. One of the times that President Obama made this claim was at the Portsmouth High School in Portsmouth, New Hampshire, on August 11, 2009. Obama claimed: "Take the example of something like diabetes, one of—a disease that's skyrocketing, partly because of obesity, partly because it's not treated as effectively as it could be. Right now, if we paid a family—if a family care physician works with his or her patient to help them lose weight, modify diet, monitors whether they're taking their medications in a timely fashion, they might get reimbursed a pittance. But if that same diabetic ends up getting their foot amputated, that's $30,000, $40,000, $50,000—immediately the surgeon is reimbursed. Well, why not make sure that we're also reimbursing the care that prevents the amputation, right?" The problem that Obama never addresses is: Why would insurance companies or hospitals have an incentive to give doctors the wrong payment scheme? Why would the government have a better incentive than those who have their own money at risk or who are getting the care to get these compensation payments right? President Barack Obama, "Remarks by the President in Health Insurance Reform Town Hall," The White House, Office of the Press Secretary, August 11, 2009, www.whitehouse.gov/the_press_office/Remarks-by-the-President-at-Town-Hall-on-Health-Insurance-Reform-in-Portsmouth-New-Hampshire/.

19. President Barack Obama, "News Conference by the President, July 22, 2009," The White House, Office of the Press Secretary, July 23, 2009, www.whitehouse.gov/the_press_office/News-Conference-by-the-President-July-22-2009.

20. President Barack Obama, "Remarks by the President in the Organizing for American National Health Care Forum," The White House, Office of the Press Secretary, August 20, 2009, www.whitehouse.gov/the-press-office/ remarks-president-organizating-america-national-health-care-forum.

21. President Barack Obama, "Remarks by the President at a Town Hall in Annandale, Virginia," The White House, Office of the Press Secretary, April 19, 2011, www.whitehouse.gov/the-press-office/2011/04/19/remarks-president-town-hall-annandale-virginia.

22. International Energy Statistics, U.S. Energy Information Agency, www.eia .gov/cfapps/ipdbproject/iedindex3.cfm?tid=5&pid=53&aid=1&cid= regions&syid=1980&eyid=2010&unit=TBPD.

23. Richard Wolf, "Obama on Rising Gas Prices: 'No Silver Bullet,'" *USA Today*, April 23, 2011, http://content.usatoday.com/communities/theoval/ post/2011/04/obama-on-rising-gas-prices-no-silver-bullet/1.

24. Press Conference by the President, "Transcript of Obama News Conference," *Wall Street Journal*, June 29, 2011, http://blogs.wsj.com/washwire/ 2011/06/29/transcript-of-obama-news-conference/.

25. Paul Krugman, "Phony Fear Factor," *New York Times,* September 29, 2011, www.nytimes.com/2011/09/30/opinion/krugman-phony-fear-factor.html?_r=1. See also Lawrence Mishel, "Regulatory Uncertainty: A Phony Explanation for Our Jobs Problem," Economic Policy Institute, Briefing Paper No. 330, September 27, 2011, http://w3.epi-data.org/ temp2011/EPIBriefingPaper330b.pdf. "I do have genuine contact with both the White House and with congressional leadership," Paul Krugman in his interview with Alison van Tiggelen; see Alison van Tiggelen, "Paul Krugman: Transcript—Will Climate Legislation Kill the Economy," *Fresh Dialogues,* December 2, 2009, www.freshdialogues.com/2009/12/09/ paul-krugman-transcript-will-climate-legislation-kill-the-economy/.

26. National Federation of Independent Business, "Members Show Overwhelming Opposition to Federal Regulations," National Federation of Independent Business, September, 2011, www.nfib.com/nfib-in-my-state/ nfib-in-my-state-content?cmsid=58245.

27. Geiger is the executive director of the National Federation of Independent Business. Roger R. Geiger, "Small Business Struggles under Thumb of Regulators," Cincinnati.com, September 27, 2011, http://news.cincinnati .com/article/20110928/EDIT02/109280336/Guest-Column-Regulators-hinder-small-businesses?odyssey=mod%7Cnewswell%7Ctext%7CFRONTP AGE%7Cs.

28. The previous quarter's survey results were fairly similar, so even though these survey data came out right after the column, he could have used the Chamber of Commerce's previous survey. U.S. Chamber of Commerce,

"Q3 Small Business Outlook Survey," Harris Interactive, October 12, 2011, www.uschambersmallbusinessnation.com/uploads/US%20Chamber%20Small%20Business%20Survey%20Q3%20Report.pdf. Still another survey done by Gallup in October 2011 found that the biggest concern of small businesses was "complying with government regulation." Joshua Altman, "Democrat Criticizes Obama for '4,200 pages' of pending regulations," *The Hill,* November 22, 2011, http://thehill.com/video/in-the-news/195091-dem-criticizes-obama-admin-for-4200-pages-of-pending-regulations.

29. See www.reginfo.gov/public/do/eoHistReviewSearch.

30. Byron York, "New Report Cites 'Regulatory Tsunami' under Obama," *Washington Examiner,* September 13, 2011, http://campaign2012.washington-examiner.com/blogs/beltway-confidential/new-report-cites-regulatory-tsunami-under-obama.

31. C. J. Ciaramella, "Obama Regulations Adding $2K to Cost of Cars," Fox News, November 17, 2011, http://nation.foxnews.com/government-regulations/2011/11/17/obama-regulations-adding-2k-cost-cars.

32. The information on how they define regulations on is available at www.heritage.org/Index/Property-Rights.

33. The information on how they define regulations on investments and financial markets are available at www.heritage.org/Index/Investment-Freedom and www.heritage.org/Index/Financial-Freedom.

34. How many days does it take to go through the red tape to start a business? How many procedures have to be done to start a business or obtain a license? How costly are those regulations to meet? See an explanation of their measure of "Business Freedom" at www.heritage.org/Index/Business-Freedom.

35. The property rights ranking for the United States fell from forty-fifth to fifty-fourth in rank. James Gwartney, Joshua Hall, and Robert Lawson, *Economic Freedom of the World: 2011 Annual Report* (Washington, DC: Cato Institute, 2011), www.cato.org/pubs/efw/.

36. Reddy, "Big Interview."

37. Paul Bedard, "6 Pages of Obamacare Equals 429 Pages of Regulations," *US News,* April 7, 2011, www.usnews.com/news/washington-whispers/articles/2011/04/07/6-pages-of-obamacare-equals-429-pages-of-regulations.

38. Ed Henry, "Obama Cuts Red Tape, But Businesses Want More," Fox News, August 23, 2011, http://politics.blogs.foxnews.com/2011/08/23/obama-cuts-red-tape-businesses-want-more.

39. Henry J. Pulizzi, "Obama Signs Credit-Card Overhaul Legislation into Law," *Wall Street Journal,* May 22, 2009, http://online.wsj.com/article/

SB124302235634548041.html and Clayton Closson, "President Obama Signs New Mortgage Law to Prevent Further Foreclosures," Associated Press, May 22, 2009, www.quickenloans.com/blog/ap-president-obama-signs-new-mortgage-law-to-prevent-further-foreclosures-5607.

40. "Cheerios Are a Drug? FDA's Surprising Letter to General Mills," Agence France Presse, May 13, 2009, www.alternet.org/health/139990; "General Mills' CEO Discusses Q1 2012 Results—Earnings Call Transcript," *Seeking Alpha*, September 21, 2011, http://seekingalpha.com/article/295088-general-mills-ceo-discusses-q1-2012-results-earnings-call-transcript.

41. Based on a telephone conversation with Susan Cruzan, in the FDA's press office, on June 18, 2009. See also a piece that I wrote for the *Washington Times*. Editorial, "Uh-oh, Cheerios," *Washington Times*, June 21, 2009.

42. Any time a family farm is set up as a business partnership or a corporation, children would be banned from doing chores. Even if the farms are not incorporated, children would not be allowed to work on other people's farms, even the farms of their grandparents. Rick Barrett, "Farms Could Face New Rules for Kid Workers," *Milwaukee Journal Sentinel*, November 22, 2011, www.jsonline.com/business/farms-could-face-new-rules-for-kid-workers-i3337e7-134368758.html.

43. Unsigned editorial, "Inside the EPA," *Wall Street Journal*, September 26, 2011, http://online.wsj.com/article/SB10001424053111904194604576582814196136594.html?mod=opinion_newsreel.

44. Mary Williams Walsh, "A.I.G. Reaches Deal to Repay Treasury and Fed for Bailout," *New York Times*, September 30, 2010, www.nytimes.com/2010/10/01/business/01aig.html?_r=1&hp; Mike Allen, "White House Hopes for Business Help," Politico, September 29, 2010, www.politico.com/news/stories/0910/42805.html.

45. "Hedge Fund Leader Blasts Obama for 'Bullying' and 'Abuse of Power,'" Yahoo Finance, May 6, 2009, http://finance.yahoo.com/tech-ticker/article/241837/Hedge-Fund-Leader-Blasts-Obama-for-%22Bullying%22-and-%22Abuse-of-Power%22?tickers=%5Edji,%5Egspc,GM,ARM,DAN,GT,XLF?sec=topStoriesccode=.

46. The entire quote from Lauria is this: ". . . was directly threatened by the White House and in essence compelled to withdraw its opposition to the deal under the threat that the full force of the White House press corps would destroy its reputation if it continued to fight. That's how hard it is to stand on this side of the fence." "Frank talks with Tom Lauria, who represents a group of lenders that object to the Chrysler sale," WJR Radio, May 1, 2009, www.wjr.com/Article.asp?id=1301727&spid=6525.

47. Theresa Cook, "White House Denies Charge by Attorney that Administration Threatened to Destroy Investment Firm's Reputation,"

ABC News *Political Punch*, May 2, 2009, http://abcnews.go.com/blogs/politics/2009/05/bankruptcy-atto/.

48. John Stoll, Jeff McCracken, and Kate Linebaugh, "U.S. Squeezes Auto Creditors," *Wall Street Journal*, April 10, 2009, http://online.wsj.com/article/SB123932036083306929.html.

49. Jerry Shenk, "Detroit High Life," *The American Thinker*, February 8, 2011, www.americanthinker.com/blog/2011/02/detroit_high_life.html.

50. John D. Stoll, Jeff McCracken, and Neil King Jr., "GM-Union Deal Raises U.S. Stake," *Wall Street Journal*, May 27, 2009, http://online.wsj.com/article/SB124335377570854805.html#mod=testMod.

51. James Kelleher and David Bailey, "U.S. Automakers See Tests from Old, New Threats," Reuters, January 11, 2011, www.reuters.com/article/2011/01/11/retire-us-autoshow-idUSTRE7090AN20110111?pageNumber=2. The union was originally supposed to get 55 percent of Chrysler. John D. Stoll and Sharon Terlep, "GM Offers U.S. a Majority Stake," *Wall Street Journal*, April 28, 2009, http://online.wsj.com/article/SB124083476254259049.html.

52. Holman Jenkins, "GM Bankruptcy? Tell Me Another," *Wall Street Journal*, April 1, 2009, http://online.wsj.com/article/SB123853988781575499.html.

53. Unsigned editorial, "Kicking the Tires on the General Motors Deal," *Washington Post*, June 3, 2009, www.washingtonpost.com/wp-dyn/content/article/2009/06/02/AR2009060203217.html.

54. Austan Goolsbee interview, "Obama Unveils Tough Terms for GM, Chrysler Recovery Efforts," *PBS NewsHour*, March 30, 2009, www.pbs.org/newshour/bb/business/jan-june09/ledeautos_03-30.html.

55. Goolsbee also pretty much repeated what he had said in his just-mentioned PBS *NewsHour* interview: "What we've seen over past months is the bondholders in some cases holding out, thinking that the government will step in and bail out the car companies and we'll get paid off. . . . I think what the president outlined in his remarks pretty clearly was that that's not going to happen and everybody has got to put some skin in the game."; Reuters, "GM Talks Likely to June 1, Not Past: Obama Adviser," Reuters, May 22, 2009, www.reuters.com/article/2009/05/22/us-gm-bankruptcy-goolsbee-idUSTRE54L0T120090522.

56. Theresa Cook, "White House Denies Charge by Attorney that Administration Threatened to Destroy Investment Firm's Reputation," ABC News *Political Punch*, May 2, 2009, http://abcnews.go.com/blogs/politics/2009/05/bankruptcy-atto/.

57. Holman Jenkins, "GM Is Becoming a Royal Debacle," *Wall Street Journal*, April 22, 2009, http://online.wsj.com/article/SB124035637935940943.html.

58. Andrew Napolitano, "Federal Govt Is Violating U.S. Constitution," Fox News, April 2, 2009, http://comments.realclearpolitics.com/read.php? 42323,327649,327676,quote=1; Peter Whoriskey and Kendra Marr, "U.S. Plans Key Role in Naming GM Board," *Washington Post*, April 1, 2009, www.washingtonpost.com/wp-dyn/content/article/2009/03/31/ AR2009033101521.html; and Alan Abelson, "Shareholders Be Damned!," *Barron's,* April 27, 2009, http://online.barrons.com/article/SB1240613559 86854673. html#articleTabs_panel_article%3D1.

59. Theresa Cook, "White House Denies Charge by Attorney that Administration Threatened to Destroy Investment Firm's Reputation," ABC News *Political Punch*, May 2, 2009, http://abcnews.go.com/blogs/politics/ 2009/05/bankruptcy-atto/.

60. Dealbook, "Chrysler's Holdout Lenders Feel the Heat," *New York Times*, May 1, 2009, http://dealbook.nytimes.com/2009/05/01/are-chrysler-hedge-funds-being-unfairly-blamed/; Steven Pearlstein, "Claiming Unfairness, Hedge Funds Miss the Point," *Washington Post*, May 1, 2009, www .washingtonpost.com/wp-dyn/content/article/2009/04/30/ AR2009043003898.html?wprss=rss_business.

61. Paul Roderick Gregory, "Obama Didn't Save Union Jobs, He Saved Union Pay," Forbes.com, June 21, 2011, www.forbes.com/2011/06/21/bailout-autoworkers-unions.html.

62. In 2008, adding up all the employees who worked for General Motors, Ford, and Chrysler as well as their parts-supplier employees and car-dealer employees totaled approximately 1.6 million. As a comparison, take the four major airlines that filed for Chapter 11 bankruptcy after 9/11 (US Air and United in 2002; Northwest and Delta in 2005). Each airline was restructured by a bankruptcy court. In each case, creditors took losses and some employees lost jobs and agreed to concessions in wages and work conditions. But each airline emerged from bankruptcy and continued to operate as a going concern—planes continued to fly, and pilots, mechanics, and flight attendants continued to have jobs, though there were fewer of them and their pay was less. President Barack Obama, "Weekly Address: President Obama Hails Successes of the Restructuring of the Auto Industry, Calls on GOP Leaders to Stop Blocking Aid for Small Businesses," The White House, Office of the Press Secretary, July 31, 2010, www.whitehouse. gov/the-press-office/weekly-address-president-obama-hails-successes-restructuring-auto-industry-calls-go. For information on the number of jobs in the automobile industry, see Harold Myerson, "The Case for Keeping Big Three Out of Bankruptcy," *The American Prospect,* November 24, 2008.

63. "Chrysler Creditors Claim Death Threats Win Hearing Delay," Detroit News, May 4, 2009, www.rushlimbaugh.com/daily/2009/05/05/obama_ thugocracy_on_display_in_unconstitutional_chrysler_takeover.

64. Rattner writes: "Their original estimate for a Chrysler liquidation had been a net job loss in a wide range. . . . Now Goolsbee said that the job loss from Plan A would be around 25,000 and the loss from Plan B would be about 60,000, a difference of around 35,000 jobs—and a far cry from the 300,000 that had practically knocked Larry off his chair when the subject of a Chrysler liquidation first came up." Steven Rattner, *Overhaul: An Insider's Account of the Obama Administration's Emergency Rescue of the Auto Industry* (Boston: Houghton Mifflin Harcourt, 2010), 164.

65. Craig Karmin and Peter Lattman, "White House Says It Stands Behind Rattner," *Wall Street Journal*, April 18, 2009, http://online.wsj.com/article/ SB124001459464430971.html.

66. Ashby Jones, "Quadrangle Settles Pay-for-Play Charges; Partners Rip Rattner," *Wall Street Journal*, April 16, 2010, http://blogs.wsj.com/law/ 2010/04/16/quadrangle-settles-pay-for-play-charges-partners-rip-rattner/.

67. Dan Primack, "Ex-Car Czar Steve Rattner Settles Pay-to-Play Scandal," Fortune.com, December 30, 2010, http://finance.fortune.cnn.com/2010/ 12/30/ex-car-czar-steve-rattner-settles-pay-to-play-scandal/.

68. The economics here is pretty straightforward. In exchange for the protections normally provided to bondholders, they earn less money. Shareholders take the risks and on average they earn more. Sometimes, if the company goes bankrupt, shareholders lose everything. For bondholders, they don't face the downside risk of shareholders, but they also don't rake in the earnings when things go well. Taking away this protection from bondholders may let the Obama administration give money to those they like, but it raises the costs for companies to borrow in the future.

69. It hasn't just been the Obama administration that has pushed for these write-offs. In 2010, with the Democrats completely controlling Congress, there was a similar push there. "House Financial Services Committee Chairman Barney Frank is going after the four largest providers of U.S. mortgages to write down second mortgages to prevent 'a deepening crisis' in the U.S. housing market"; "Pressure Builds for U.S. Mortgage Loan Write-Downs," Reuters, March 8, 2010, www.reuters.com/article/2010/03/08/usa-housing-secondlien-idUSN0818028120100308. A more recent discussion on the Obama administration policy is available here: "Delinquent Homeowners to Get Mortgage Aid from Government," Reuters, June 4, 2011, www.cnbc .com/id/43281199.

"They seem to just try to coerce the industry into the loan-modification program," said David Watts, a strategist at analysis firm CreditSights Inc. "They're saying, 'We want you to do this program, and we're going to make sure you do it by helping you, possibly with money and possibly with a big fat stick.'"; "CitiGroup Expands Loan Modification Program after FDIC

Pressure," Federal Loan Modification, February 4, 2009, http://fedmod.tv/citigroup-expands-loan-modification-program-after-fdic-pressure/.

70. Louise Story, "U.S. Inquiry Eyes S&P Ratings of Mortgages," *New York Times*, August 17, 2011, www.cnbc.com/id/44184348.

71. Jane Mayer, "Covert Operations: The Billionaire Brothers Who Are Waging a War against Obama," *New Yorker*, August 30, 2010, www.newyorker.com/reporting/2010/08/30/100830fa_fact_mayer.

72. Ben Smith, "White House Denies Eyeing Koch Tax Returns," Politico, September 21, 2010, www.politico.com/blogs/bensmith/0910/White_House_denies_eyeing_Koch_tax_returns.html.

73. Glenn Thrush, "Treasury Analyzes Goolsbee Remark," Politico, October 6, 2010, www.politico.com/politico44/perm/1010/tax_claims_reviewed_42857716-18fe-483d-9869-7cead282dd31.html.

74. Letter from Russell George, Inspector General, IRS, to Senator Charles E. Grassley, dated September 28, 2010, www.weeklystandard.com/sites/all/files/docs/Sen.%20Grassley%20-%20Acknowledgement%20Letter.pdf.

75. "Walking Dead: Congress Edition," *Mother Jones*, December 7, 2010.

76. Frank Beckman, "White House Wrong to Lean on Ford," *Detroit News,* September 30, 2011, http://detnews.com/article/20110930/OPINION03/109300331/1008/opinion01/White-House-wrong-to-lean-on-Ford and Daniel Howes, "Ford Pulls Its Ad on Bailouts," *Detroit News*, September 27, 2011, www.detnews.com/article/20110927/OPINION03/109270322/Howes--Ford-pulls-its-ad-on-bailouts. The *Washington Post*'s Greg Sargent reported that Ford and the Obama administration denied that there had been any pressure from the White House on Ford to pull the ad. Yet, sometimes, a few well-placed pointed questions are enough to get people to get a message. Greg Sargent, "Another White House Scandal . . . That Is Being Denied by the Parties on Both Sides," *Washington Post*, September 27, 2011, www.washingtonpost.com/blogs/plum-line/post/another-white-house-scandal--that-is-being-denied-by-the-parties-on-both-sides/2011/03/03/gIQAM5tY2K_blog.html.

77. Editorial, "Kneecapping Financial Bosses," *Washington Times*, December 23, 2009, www.washingtontimes.com/news/2009/dec/23/kneecapping-financial-bosses/.

78. President Barack Obama, "Obama Tells Bankers: Make Loans, Modify Mortgages," The White House, Office of the Press Secretary, December 14, 2009, http://blogs.suntimes.com/sweet/2009/12/obama_kicks_bankers_make_loans.html.

79. Unsigned editorial, "Government thuggishness," *Washington Times,* August 24, 2009, www.washingtontimes.com/news/2009/aug/24/government-thuggishness/.

80. Mike Allen, "House Demands Compensation Data," Politico, August 19, 2009, www.politico.com/politico44/perm/0809/compensationn_watch_d4882f2f-46d6-413f-9679-f518a7e923b3.html.

81. President Obama said: "Right now, at the time when everybody's getting hammered, [insurance companies are] making record profits and premiums are going up." Congressional Quarterly, "Transcript of Obama Prime-Time News Conference," Washington Post, July 22, 2009 http://voices.washingtonpost.com/44/2009/07/22/transcript_of_obama_prime-time.html.

82. "Insurance Co. Profits: Good, But Not Breaking Records," FactCheck.org, August 5, 2009.

83. Democrat House Speaker Nancy Pelosi claimed: "[Insurance companies] are the villains. They have been part of the problem in a major way. They are doing everything in their power to stop a public option from happening."; "Pelosi Lashes Out Against Insurance Companies," Reuters, July 30, 2009, http://in.reuters.com/article/2009/07/30/usa-healthcare-insurance-idINWNA021320090730.

84. David Kirkpatrick and Duff Wilson, "One Grand Deal Too Many Costs Lobbyist His Job," New York Times, February 12, 2010, www.nytimes.com/2010/02/13/health/policy/13pharm.html.

85. Editorial, "Kathleen Spitzer: The Administration Targets a Drug CEO in a Troubling Precedent," Wall Street Journal, May 2, 2011, http://online.wsj.com/article/SB10001424052748703655404576293232066996982.html.

86. Sam Baker, "HHS grants 106 new healthcare waivers," The Hill, August 19, 2011, http://thehill.com/blogs/healthwatch/health-reform-implementation/177581-hhs-grants-106-new-healthcare-waivers.

87. Information on the percentage of the private sector population belonging to unions is available at: www.bls.gov/cps/. The share of waivers granted to unions is available at: Bureau of Labor Statistics, "Union Members Survey," United States Department of Labor, January 21, 2011, www.bls.gov/news/release/union2.nr0.htm; Tom Fitton, "Why Did Unionized Companies Get So Many Obamacare Waivers?" Biggovernment.com, September 12, 2011, http://biggovernment.com/tfitton/2011/09/12/why-did-unionized-companies-get-so-many-obamacare-waivers/.

88. David Willman, "Cost, Need Questioned in $433-Million Smallpox Drug Deal," Los Angeles Times, November 13, 2011, www.latimes.com/news/nationworld/nation/la-na-smallpox-20111113,0,6456082,full.story; "Questions Arise Over $433M Smallpox Drug Contract to Company Tied to Donor," Fox News, November 12, 2011, http://topstories.foxnews.mobi/quickPage.html?page=17224&external=1214818.proteus.fma&pageNum=-1.

89. Obamacare involved two separate bills: the main legislation that was 2,407 pages (www.cbsnews.com/htdocs/pdf/Senate_health_care_bill.pdf?tag= contentMain;contentBody) and a separate reconciliation bill of 153 pages, www.cbsnews.com/htdocs/pdf/House_reconciliation_package_031810 .pdf?tag=contentMain;contentBody.

90. Paige Winfield Cunningham, "More than Half Health Care Deadlines Missed by Obama Administration," *Washington Times*, November 3, 2011, www.washingtontimes.com/blog/inside-politics/2011/nov/3/more-half-health-care-deadlines-missed-obama-admin/.

91. Jim Angle, "Employers Consider Dropping Insurance Plans Once Health Law Provisions Take Effect," Fox News, November 1, 2011, www.foxnews .com/politics/2011/11/01/employers-consider-dropping-insurance-plans-once-health-law-provisions-take/. Ricardo Alonso-Zaldivar, "Health Overhaul to Force Changes in Employer Plans," Associated Press, June 11, 2011, www .breitbart.com/article.php?id=D9G993800&show_article=1. One example of Obama's frequent promise of people being able to keep their health care coverage is available at: President Barack Obama, "Remarks by the President in Town Hall on Health Care, Central High School, Grand Junction, Colorado," The White House, Office of the Press Secretary, August 15, 2009, www .whitehouse.gov/the_press_office/Remarks-By-The-President-In-Town-Hall-On-Health-Care-Grand-Junction-Colorado/.

92. Ron Suskind, *Confidence Men: Wall Street, Washington, and the Education of a President* (New York: Harper, 2011).

93. Michael D. Shear, "Polling Helps Obama Frame Message in Health-Care Debate," *Washington Post*, July 31, 2009, www.washingtonpost.com/ wp-dyn/content/article/2009/07/30/AR2009073001547.html.

94. Suskind, *Confidence Men*; Peter Dreier, "Lessons from the Health-Care Wars," *The American Prospect*, March 27, 2010, http://prospect.org/article/ lessons-health-care-wars-0.

95. Suskind, *Confidence Men*, 158.

96. This quote is from Suskind, *Confidence Men*, 194. The discussion on who was alienated by the deal is from Dreier.

97. President Barack Obama, "Weekly Address: President Obama Debunks 'Phony Claims' about Health Reform; Emphasizes Consumer Protections," The White House, Office of the Press Secretary, Saturday, August 22, 2009, www.whitehouse.gov/the-press-office/weekly-address-president-obama-debunks-phony-claims-about-health-reform-emphasizes-.

98. Ricardo Alonso-Zaldivar, "Competition Lacking among Private Health Insurers," Associated Press, August 22, 2009, www.breitbart.com/article .php?id=D9A7VCQG0.

99. American Medical Association, "Competition in Health Insurance," American Medical Association, 2007, www.ama-assn.org/ama1/pub/upload/mm/368/compstudy_52006.pdf.

100. Agency for Healthcare Research and Quality, Center for Financing, Access and Cost Trends, 2008 Medical Expenditure Panel Survey-Insurance Component, www.meps.ahrq.gov/mepsweb/data_stats/summ_tables/insr/state/series_2/2008/tiib2b1.pdf.

101. The entire insurance market: Market concentration measures when "self-insured" companies are included, shown in table below.

State	Market share of full insurance market for state's largest firm	Share of individuals enrolled in private insurance who have self-insured plans	Market share of largest full insurance firm in the total insurance market	Market share of second-largest full insurance firm in the total insurance market	Market share of full insurance market for largest two firms
Alabama	83%	57.1%	35.6%	2.1%	37.8%
Rhode Island	79%	38.5%	48.6%	9.8%	58.4%
Hawaii	78%	37.9%	48.4%	12.4%	60.9%
Maine	78%	52.1%	37.4%	4.8%	42.2%
Vermont	77%	54.4%	35.1%	5.9%	41.0%
Montana	75%	49.5%	37.9%	5.1%	42.9%
Arkansas	75%	61.4%	29.0%	2.3%	31.3%
Iowa	71%	67.9%	22.8%	2.9%	25.7%
Wyoming	70%	71.0%	20.3%	4.4%	24.7%
Missouri	68%	61.2%	26.4%	4.3%	30.7%
South Carolina	66%	62.7%	24.6%	3.4%	28.0%
Michigan	65%	51.8%	31.3%	3.9%	35.2%
Louisiana	61%	58.4%	25.4%	5.4%	30.8%
Georgia	61%	65.3%	21.2%	2.8%	23.9%
Alaska	60%	60.7%	23.6%	13.8%	37.3%
Indiana	60%	66.0%	20.4%	5.1%	25.5%
Kentucky	59%	55.9%	26.0%	4.4%	30.4%
Connecticut	55%	49.1%	28.0%	5.6%	33.6%
North Carolina	53%	59.2%	21.6%	8.2%	29.8%
Maryland	52%	54.7%	23.6%	8.6%	32.2%

102. Based on email correspondence with Reed Cherlin at the White House on September 14 and 15, 2009.

103. "But having a public plan out there that also shows that maybe if you take some of the profit motive out, maybe if you are reducing some of the administrative costs, that you can get an even better deal, that's going to incentivize the private sector to do even better. And that's a good thing," President Obama told the nation during his July 22nd press conference. President Barack Obama, "News Conference by the President," The White House, Office of the Press Secretary, Saturday, July 22, 2009, www.whitehouse.gov/the_press_office/News-Conference-by-the-President-July-22-2009.

Chapter 6

We Have Seen What Happened under Obama. So Now What Do We Do?

T he simple answer is for the government to spend less, tax less, borrow less, and regulate less. But that advice is a little like answering the question, "And how do you get from Pakistan to China" with the simple, direct, and accurate answer, "Cross the Himalayas!" There is a little more to it than that.

Americans who want to restore American economic might to where we are creating millions of new jobs each year, growing our economy faster than Europe, indeed faster than China each and every year, and increasing the standard of living for every American year after year have a clear but difficult path before us.

Our own history and common sense show us what can be done. We have done it before. We know from painful recent experience what not to do. We also know that there are forces and special spending interests that profit from the present troubles.

The challenge is to do three things at the same time year after year: grow the economy, reduce the size and scope of the government, and do so in a way that you can confidently explain your goals, plans, and successes to the American people clearly enough to win elections every two years. Reform government, create economic growth, and win the election. Repeat again and again until we have restored American unchallenged economic preeminence. It is no good to have the perfect plan if you cannot explain it to the nation. Successful businessmen remember that the customer is always right. The customer has the dollar and if you wish to earn it you have to satisfy his or her concerns. It is not enough for you to believe in your product. You have to convince the customer that he wants, he needs, your product. And your product has to be good. It has to perform as advertised. Retail stores have a no-questions-asked return policy for their merchandise. In politics, the return policy is that if the customer is not happy with how you have governed, they return *you* to the private sector. In governing a free society, national leaders must earn the opportunity to govern every two years at election time. The voter is always right in the sense that she has her vote and you had better be able to explain why you deserve her vote.

Every two years, we must speak clearly to the American people and ask permission to continue on the path to limited government, which we believe goes hand in hand with jobs, higher wages, and overall economic growth.

Both citizens and elected officials determined to execute a U-turn on the road to serfdom and keep America on the right path for generations to come need bifocal vision. They need the ability to see the distant future, the perfect policy goal, and to articulate that goal so that a majority of Americans also see it, understand it, and want to move in that direction. But while describing the "shining city on the hill" is inspirational and necessary, the hard work of moving a deliberately unwieldy national government over time to achieve that goal is more perspiration. That is where we need to look down at the political world right before us so that while we move to the distant goal we don't put our feet down wrong and falter. Bifocal vision forces us to keep one eye on the ultimate goal and the other focused on the day-to-day politics of change.

If we set a goal of reducing the top income tax rate any American is forced to pay to Washington to 10 percent, there will be years and perhaps decades while we first must make the case for avoiding Obama's goal of increasing the top rate to 50 percent and then arguing for dropping the rate to 25 percent and then 20 percent and then lower.

This is not an easy task. Elections are often about unfurling banners of bold colors and demands for radical change, while governing is (when we are in charge) too often about "three yards and a cloud of dust."

Leading a successful movement to liberty demands that leaders manage expectations at the same time they inspire and encourage all Americans to insist on reaching for the stars. If this were easy, someone would have done it already.

How do we restore constitutionally limited government and make America the most powerful economic engine in the world again—creating jobs, opportunity, wealth, and higher income faster than all the other nations of the world?

If this were a novel, we would flip forward to the last chapters of *Atlas Shrugged,* where the politicians who had screwed up the economy with taxes and regulations and spending hand the decisions over to John Galt, who, by fiat, removed the layers of excess government to free up the economy. If we were in Plato's *Republic,* the philosopher-king could undo the bad laws and regulations of previous kings and, voilà: freedom.

But America is a constitutional republic, with elected representatives chosen in democratic elections. How to get from here to greater freedom is a two-part question. First, what is our destination, and second, how do we win enough elections decisively enough, over a long enough period, to turn around and bring under control the overgrown government that now makes us poorer by reducing liberty when it was created to allow us to achieve prosperity by establishing and protecting liberty?

Understand the Two Competing Political Coalitions in America

In the United States today, there are two competing coalitions. They gather around and in support of the two major political parties, the Republicans and Democrats.

Decades ago, one might have written about the struggle for liberty without focusing on the two parties. There were advocates of limited government in both the Republican and Democrat parties and certainly committed statists in each as well. Following the Civil War, the two parties were largely regional parties. Those born north of the Mason-Dixon line were Republicans. Their party affiliation was driven by regionalism, a sense that the Grand Old Party was the party of national unity. Had not the Civil War proved that? Democrats were from the Southern states that had fought for secession. They had lost but were not about to join the party that destroyed Dixie and humiliated them during Reconstruction.

There were waves of immigration into the United States, and immigrants settling in the Northern states often joined the Democratic Party if they felt excluded and unwanted by the Republicans.

During the lifetime of Ronald Reagan, the two parties sorted themselves out in a more rational way. No longer would little old ladies in Mississippi who agreed with Ronald Reagan on everything vote for George McGovern because Sherman had been mean to Atlanta "recently." Nor would older folks in Maine who agreed with Ted Kennedy on all matters political continue to vote for Ronald Reagan because the Union officer at Little Round Top was from Maine.

Those who wanted limited government—from whatever region or faith tradition—moved to the Reagan Republican Party. Those who viewed growth in government power as a good thing became Democrats.

We know that some conservative individuals—such as Ronald Reagan—left the Democratic Party and became advocates of liberty and joined the Republican Party, and some liberal Republicans, such as New York Mayor John Lindsay, moved to the Democratic Party. The migration of conservatives to the Republican Party and liberals to the Democratic Party have made the parties more internally consistent and organized around principle and policy.

As a result, the hopes and aspirations of Americans who wish to move forward to limited government and unlimited personal opportunity have one political vehicle: the modern Reagan Republican Party. The opposition is organized today through and around the modern liberal Democratic Party.

The modern Reagan Republican Party is in fact a coalition of groups and individuals that have one thing in common. On their primary political issue—the issue that bring them to politics and motivates their vote—they want one thing from the government: They wish to be left alone.

If the component parts of the Republican Party were seated around the table you would see first, those taxpayers who are most concerned with keeping taxes low and lower. They do not want the government to tax others. They simply wish taxes minimized so as to interfere less with their economic lives and choices. Also at the table are small businessmen, the self-employed, entrepreneurs, independent contractors, professionals who wish to run their businesses and professional lives freed of excessive government regulation as well as taxes. Farmers, businessmen, and homeowners who wish their property rights respected and protected. Next at the table are those who vote in support of the Second Amendment. Gun owners, 12.5 million hunters, 7 million concealed-carry permit owners who ask for nothing other than that they be allowed to maintain and exercise their right to keep and bear arms for self-protection, the protection of their homes and families, and to hunt and target shoot without government interference. Also active are the two million homeschoolers, those parents who wish full parental choice in education. And those Americans of faith whose most important goal in life is to practice their faith and transmit it to their children. Evangelical Protestants, conservative Catholics, Orthodox Jews, Muslims, and Mormons who ask only for religious liberty and for the state to keep the First Amendment in mind and in law. Importantly, one also finds those Americans who work for the government whose job it is to maintain and protect the liberty of all Americans: the armed forces and the police and the judicial system.

Critics of the freedom movement often claim advocates of liberty are "antigovernment." Nonsense. The Constitution sets up a limited government to protect our rights. The U.S. army works to keep foreigners from taking our freedom and the police and judiciary work to keep annoying people from breaking into our homes and cars and stealing our stuff. Americans are not antigovernment. They oppose government growing to the point that it endangers and tramples on liberty. We know this is the history of most governments in most centuries of world history. Americans are not antigovernment just as cancer doctors are not anti-cell. Cancer doctors are opposed to cells that are out of control and threaten to kill the person they were designed to serve.

Step one for individuals, political leaders, and movements desiring to fight for liberty is to understand the nature of the Leave Us Alone coalition and to focus on maintaining its cohesion and strength. Winning will require teaching more Americans that they should see their goals and future as part of the Leave Us Alone coalition. One should constantly be on the lookout for those groups and individuals whose challenges in life are caused by too much government. They are tomorrow's activists and leaders in the Leave Us Alone coalition.

In American politics, the movement demanding greater liberty truly is indivisible. Theoretically, one could find a homeschooling parent who supported higher taxes. But if you are voting to protect your ability to homeschool (a practice largely illegal in most states just 20 years ago) the candidate you vote for will also have promised tax-payers that he will not raise taxes.

Not everyone voting for limited-government candidates is person-ally consistent in the demand for limited government. But when they cast their vote on their moving issue—low taxes or property rights or less regulation or the Second Amendment or parental rights or school choice or religious liberty—they are voting for a candidate who sup-ports low taxes *and* property rights *and* less regulation *and* the Second Amendment *and* parental rights *and* school choice *and* religious liberty.

When 41 states enacted concealed-carry gun laws that require state and local governments to give law-abiding citizens over *either 18 or 21* a permit to carry a concealed weapon, the number of Americans who carry concealed weapons increased. That is a large increase in the number of Americans who are increasingly sensitive to their Second Amendment rights. They care more and are more likely to vote. And when they vote, they vote for candidates committed to the Second Amendment, abolishing the death tax, and reforming abuses such as the EPA's overreach.

All efforts that expand one part of the Leave Us Alone coalition increase the voting strength of the entire coalition. More guns equals less crime is true. More gun owners also leads to lower taxes, school choice, and less regulation overall.

If you are looking to cut or abolish the capital gains tax, your allies are not simply those who focus on economic growth, they include the entire Leave Us Alone coalition.

The Takings Coalition

The converse is true. Those who have combined into the left are the various wings of the Takings Coalition—which view the proper role of the government as taking money, power, and freedom from some and giving it to the government to control—work as one movement.

The modern Democratic Party, made up of all the moving parts of the Takings Coalition, would array itself around a conference table as follows. Up front are the paying customers: the labor union bosses, the billionaire trial lawyers, the government workers' unions, and the two wings of the dependency movement (those locked into welfare dependency and those who earn more than $90,000 a year managing that dependency, making sure none of them get jobs and become Republicans). Also at the table are the *coercive utopians,* which get government grants to tell the rest of us how to live our lives. These are the special interests that pass laws mandating cars too small to hold your entire family, toilets that too often don't flush completely, and lightbulbs that produce so little light that you think you have glaucoma. And on the Sabbath, they require you to put the green glass and the white glass and the brown glass in different containers for the recycling priests. These foodies, greenies, safety phalangists, slow growth, NIMBY types have a list of things you must and must not do that is slightly longer and more tedious than Leviticus.

Here we see the differences in the two competing coalitions.

Those of us on the center-right have a common interest in limited government, as each person or group wishes to be left alone in his respective area of life.

But on the left, the various tendencies can get along only as long as we are stupid enough to keep tossing tax dollars into the center of their table. Then the Takings Coalition members can get along like in the movie scene when the gangsters all meet after the bank robbery and the gang leader hands out the cash: "One for you and one for you."

Should we say "no new taxes" and mean it and put our foot on the air hose and stop throwing tax dollars at the Takings Coalition, then the various parts of the left sitting around the Takings Coalition table will begin to look at each other more like the second to the last scene of those lifeboat movies in which they begin to wonder whom they are going to throw overboard and whom they are going to eat.

Refuse to increase taxes . . . reduce government spending . . . and the Left turns on itself. For the Takings Coalition, the American Left, the modern Democratic Party, is not made up of friends and allies. It is made up of competing parasites. If we do not let them gnaw on taxpayers, they will just as cheerfully turn on the spendthrift special interest sitting next to them. Our job is to stop tax hikes, limit spending, and then when we meet the Left in battle in elections every two years, there will be fewer of them and they will be shorter.

Step One: Never Raise Taxes

Maintain the Republican brand as the party that will never raise your taxes.

Refusing to raise taxes is the necessary, but not sufficient, first step to limited government. Step two is to stop the government from spending so much money. But we never get to step two if we fail to stop tax increases dead in their tracks.

If the government can raise a dollar in taxes it never begins the conversation of reforming government or reducing its size or scope. It will continue to do everything it has been doing and add on new barnacles paid for with new taxes.

The Taxpayer Protection Pledge was created in 1985 by Americans for Tax Reform, the group organized by President Reagan to be the taxpayer group advocating what became the Tax Reform Act of 1986, which dropped the top tax rates for individuals and companies from 50 percent to 28 percent.

The Taxpayer Protection Pledge is a simple written commitment by a candidate for office that he will oppose and vote against any and all efforts to increase taxes. No net tax hikes. Tax reform that is revenue neutral, say, eliminating deductions or credits and reducing marginal tax rates on a dollar-for-dollar basis, is fine. The goal of the pledge was and is to facilitate real tax reform and make sure promises of tax reform never become a Trojan Horse for tax increases.

In 2011, 238 sitting members of the House of Representatives (out of 435) and 41 senators (out of 100) have signed the Taxpayer Protection Pledge to their voters. There were only six Republicans in the House and seven Republicans in the Senate who had failed to sign the Pledge. In newspaper interviews, all but one of the 13 non-Pledge signers have said that while they had some objection to signing pledges, they oppose any and all net tax hikes. (The one exception was Northern Virginia congressman Frank Wolf, an appropriator who fought against the Republican caucus to keep earmarks, who actually endorsed the $2 trillion tax increase recommended by Obama's tax increase commission known as the Simpson-Bowles Commission.)

Almost all of the Republicans running in 2010 for the House and Senate signed the pledge. Only two Democrats—out of hundreds—running for the House or Senate signed the pledge. Thus one could walk into the voting booth dead drunk and vote for the Republican and against the Democrat and know with Ivory Soap certainty that one had just voted for a candidate who would not raise your taxes and against a candidate who cheerfully would.

The Republican Party has, since 1994—when Republicans captured the House and Senate with all but a handful having signed the pledge—branded itself as the party that would not raise your taxes. Between 1993, when Clinton raised taxes with only Democrat votes, and 2009, when Obama raised taxes 16 days into his administration was a 15-year period with no tax hike passed in Washington DC. That was the longest period in American history with no tax increase. Voters knew: Elect a Republican congress or a Republican president, or both, and your taxes will not be raised.

Coca-Cola knows the value of a strong and protected brand. You can go into the store and pick up a bottle of Coke and toss it into your shopping cart without reading the label or asking the proprietor for a taste. You know what is in a Coca-Cola bottle. They have a strong brand and quality control. But if you got home and were two-thirds of the way through your bottle of Coke and looked down and noticed a rat head in what was left of your Coke, you would not think to yourself, "Now I may not finish the rest of this bottle of Coke, tonight." You would wonder about buying Coke in the future and you would mention this incident on Facebook and memorialize it on YouTube and then Coca-Cola would have a worldwide problem.

Republican elected officials who vote for tax increases are rat heads in a Coke bottle. They damage the brand for everyone else. This is not a victimless crime. It confuses small children about the nature of the world.

Republican absolute unity in stopping tax hikes is both sound policy—the Democrats would simply take the money and hire Democratic precinct workers with the cash—and it is sound politics. A Republican Party that will not raise taxes is more likely to win elections than one that will make no such commitment to voters.

This sounds like an easy strategy. Just say no. But the liberal spending interests are understandably unceasing in their demands for more and higher taxes. Modern Democrats are like a teenage boy on a prom date. He keeps asking for the same thing in different ways. One must say No, No, No. All evening. It does absolutely no good to say No, No, Yes.

Step Two: Keep the Focus on Spending, Not the Deficit

The world would be safer if there was a popular economic version of the *Screwtape Letters,* the clever book by Christian writer C. S. Lewis that purports to be letters from Screwtape, a senior demon, to a junior "tempter" named Wormwood, teaching him how to wield the best arguments and tactics to undermine a Christian's religious faith.

In arguing against the secular equivalents of Screwtape, one notes that the arguments for bigger government and against expanding liberty are repeated throughout history again and again despite their transparent wrongheadedness. Every generation has to be inoculated against this recurring virus, not once as children, but every year when the same virus shows up in public places like restrooms, kindergarten classrooms, and cable television.

The first act of legerdemain or misdirection employed by advocates of larger government is to trick you in to focusing on the deficit rather than total government spending. This is partly the fault of conservatives, who, back in the 1950s, believed themselves destined to lose the political struggle to limit government and thought they were, in William F. Buckley's immortal and depressing words, "standing athwart history yelling 'Stop.'" Conservatives believed they could not win arguing against government spending, so they attacked "deficit spending" to win the support of Americans concerned with debt and borrowing. Deficit was an intensifier. Conservatives realized the problem was spending, but believed *deficit spending* was less popular with the public.

At the time, liberals mocked the focus on the deficit and proclaimed that "we owed the national debt to ourselves" and it was therefore not of concern.

The Left rediscovered the deficit when President Ronald Reagan fought to cut taxes in 1981. Then the Democrats decided they could make use of the public's aversion to deficit spending, but they conveniently dropped the word *spending* from "deficit spending" and railed against deficits, which is to say, they opposed reducing taxes. While the public might be convinced that deficit spending had something to do with government spending, they were distracted by the phrase *deficits* to believe that low taxes or tax cuts or the failure to raise taxes was the problem.

If we are to reduce the total spending by the government— federal, state, and local—we must be clear in our use of language. The government spends too much. The government should spend less. Deficit spending is simply that relatively small part of total spending that exceeds the government's ability and willingness to pick our pockets. Raising taxes does not solve the problem of excessive spending. It enables it. It feeds it.

If the problem facing America is the deficit, then there are two possible solutions. One, spend less. And two, increase taxes. Spending less is not very interesting to the organized spending interests and the politicians who love them. The second option—increasing taxes . . . now, that is a fascinating option. Any liberal reporter, commentator, or politician worth his salt can steer a conversation that began talking about the deficit to a single focus on tax increases in seconds.

Conservatives who want a productive national conversation about limited government must always focus on "government spending as a percentage of the national economy." The true cost of government is total spending. How painful that spending is depends on the size of the government compared with the size of the entire economy. A trillion-dollar government in a 2-trillion-dollar economy would be more burdensome than a trillion-dollar government atop a 10-trillion-dollar economy.

Federal government spending has averaged 21 percent of GDP over the years between 1970 and 1990. When Republicans captured the House and Senate in 1995, federal spending was 20.6 percent of GDP. In 2000, federal spending fell to 18.2 percent of GDP. During the Bush years, federal spending increased to 20.1 percent in 2006, when the Democrats captured the House and Senate, and 20.7 percent in 2008 when Obama was elected president. Government spending as a percentage of the economy was 25 percent in 2009, 24 percent in 2010 and 25 percent in 2011.

There are only two ways to reduce spending as a percentage of the economy. One, reduce government spending. Or two, grow the total economy. This is the discussion to have for the next 50 years. Reagan Republicans have hundreds of ideas of how to reduce, cut, or reform government spending in a downward direction. Modern Democrats have no interest in this. (Obama didn't even reduce the defense budget when he had complete Democratic control. He instead tripled the number of American soldiers in Afghanistan, bringing the cost of that effort to $100 billion a year.)

The second part of reducing government spending as a percentage of the economy is to grow the economy. Here, Democrats have one failed idea: Spend more money. Reagan Republicans have dozens of ideas that work.

Obama and Reid and Pelosi believed they knew how to fix the economy. When Obama was inaugurated, unemployment was 7.8 percent. They passed the Stimulus bill with only Democratic votes in the House. It was to spend $825 billion over two years. They had a theory, Keynesian economics, that when the government takes a dollar and spends it, it increases the total economy by two dollars.

When the government takes a dollar from someone who earned it through taxation—simply grabbing it—or through borrowing the dollar and then gives it to someone who is politically connected . . . the theory runs that there is now more money in the economy.

Imagine Obama, Harry Reid, and Nancy Pelosi standing at one side of a lake and each drawing one bucket of water from the lake. They then trot over to the far side of the lake, and in front of the MSNBC cameras, they pour the three buckets of water back into the lake, announcing that they are "stimulating" the lake to great depths. Now if you laugh at this, remember they plan to do this hundreds of billions of times, which would certainly make the lake deeper.

The theory is transparently silly. Unsurprisingly, it didn't work. The president promised that if we spent $920 billion, it would create four million jobs, and unemployment, then at 8.2 percent, would stay below 8 percent. Unemployment rose instead to 9 percent and 1.5 million fewer Americans had jobs at the end of the two-year spendathon.

Government spending to fix the economy was first tried by Herbert Hoover, who reacted to the collapse of the stock market on October 29, 1929, by increasing federal spending 57.3 percent. FDR further increased spending. Did the economy recover? The stock market did not regain the level of September 3, 1929, until November 23, 1954.

Republican plans to grow the economy are legion. Reduce marginal tax rates. Reform tort law. Spend less. Regulate less. Expand free trade.

Why would any Reagan Republican wish to shift from a debate on how to reduce the cost of government as a percentage of the total economy—for which Republicans have many solutions and Democrats have one failed idea—to a debate over the deficit, which would allow the Democrats to argue there are two possible solutions, spend less or tax more, and that they should have a seat at this table.

Step Three: Reform the Federal Tax Code to Tax Consumed Income One Time at One Rate

The ultimate goal is to reduce and reform the present income tax system so that all Americans pay one single, low tax rate on consumed income. Taxing income at one rate, one time, is a big improvement over the present mess. Today, when you earn a dollar, the federal government taxes it through the personal income tax. If you invest it with a bank, the government taxes the interest the bank pays you. If you then buy Apple stock with what you have left after taxes, the federal government taxes Apple's corporate profits. Then, if Apple pays you a dividend, that dividend is taxed. Should Apple stock appreciate in value, there is a capital gains tax to pay when you sell it, and if you are foolish enough to die at some point, the death tax can take up to half of what you have left.

Reducing marginal tax rates increases liberty by leaving you more of what you earned and it greatly strengthens the national economy. Under President Eisenhower, the top rate hit 92 percent. President John F. Kennedy cut marginal tax rates 22 percent across the board, and the top rate came down to 70 percent. Reagan cut marginal tax rates 25 percent across the board in the period 1981 to 1983, and the top rate fell to 50 percent, and was then lowered again as part of the Tax Reform Act of 1986 to 28 percent. So, if you were paying the top marginal tax rate on $100 earned in 1960, you kept 8 dollars. Kennedy's tax cuts would allow you to keep $30 dollars. Reagan's 1981 cut would net you $50 on every $100 you earned, and then after 1986, you could keep $72. For the same amount of extra work or investment, Reagan increased your take-home pay from $30 to $72. If you tax something, you get less of it.

Reducing marginal tax rates increases the incentive (or rather, decreases the disincentive) to work, save, and invest. It also increases the opportunity cost of leisure and consumption.

To maximize liberty and economic growth, our goal is to reduce the tax rate on income as much as possible.

The second goal is to tax that dollar one time, not again and again. That means abolishing the death tax, which is just another tax on income on which you have already paid taxes at least once. Ditto the capital gains tax, which is a second bite at the apple.

The government should not punish those who take their earnings and invest them. We will have more privacy if the government limits itself to watching you earn a dollar and takes some and then goes away. (Advocates of ending the income tax and shifting entirely to a national sales tax would point out that their tax allows the government to leave you alone until you buy something and they then watch, monitor, and tax that activity, and then go away again.)

Kill the Death Tax

Abolishing the death tax once and for all should be part of any tax reform package. It can also be enacted on its own merits. It need not wait for any grand deal. The death tax was first imposed to help finance the North's need for revenue to fight the Civil War. It was ruled unconstitutional, but reappeared after the Sixteenth Amendment was imposed, and has been with us ever since. Both houses of Congress voted to abolish the death tax in 2000, but President Clinton vetoed the bill. In 2001, Congress voted to phase out the death tax over time such that the death tax went to zero in 2010. But the tax was reimposed at 35 percent for 2011 and 2012.

Taxing the accumulated savings of an American when he dies is a tax on capital. While the tax raises only 1 percent of the federal government's tax take in a year, it confiscates and destroys $1.2 trillion in investment that is then no longer available to create jobs in the private sector. Ending this tax, which cuts small businesses and farms in half each generation, would create 856,000 jobs and increase GDP by $3 trillion over 10 years, according to a study by Steve Entin and Douglas Holtz-Eakin for the American Family Business Institute.

Taxing Only Consumed Income

One way to turn the present income tax into a tax on consumption (without risking the creation of a VAT [value added tax] or sales tax that might grow alongside the present income tax) would be to build on and expand on the concept behind 401(k)s and Individual Retirement Accounts (IRAs), that allow Americans to be taxed only once on money they save—pay a tax on money before you put it into a Roth IRA and then take it out tax-free in retirement or invest money pre-tax in a regular IRA and pay taxes when you take it out in retirement.

In both cases, savings build up over decades and the increase in the value of stocks or interest paid on bonds in your IRA is not double-taxed.

Today we also have Health Savings Accounts (HSAs) and Education Savings Accounts (ESAs). Legislation has been drafted to create two new accounts, one for retirement, the Retirement Savings Account (RSA), and one to help saving for home purchases, education, and so forth, called the Lifetime Savings Account (LSA). The RSA and LSA would replace many of the overlapping tax-free savings accounts. One could go further and simply establish a Universal Savings Account that would allow every American to save for education, health care costs, investments in their own businesses and retirement tax-free such that savings was taxed on the way in to such an account or on the way out . . . not twice.

A Universal Savings Account would turn the present income tax into the equivalent of a sales tax or consumption tax without creating a new tax system. It would simplify rather than complicate.

And not unimportantly, making it easier for Americans to save and invest creates more members of the Leave Us Alone coalition. A wonderful poll by Scott Rasmussen found that Americans who had at least $5,000 invested in the stock market were 18 percent more likely to be Republicans than those who had none. Every income group, race, gender, and age group became more Republican with shareownership. Want more Republicans? Sure, you can go door to door with copies of *Atlas Shrugged* or *Road to Serfdom*. Or you can change tax law to make it easier for Americans to become share-owners. In 1980, only 6 percent of Americans owned mutual funds. Today, 44 percent of Americans own mutual funds and 70 percent of households have an IRA or 401(k). This explains much of the growth of Republican strength over these recent decades.

Taxing Income at One Rate

Why should we move to tax income at one single rate, either through a flat income tax or a retail sales tax? Fairness? Well, taxation is all about using force to take money from people who earned it and giving it to the state, so fairness is not a big part of this transaction.

One of the great advantages of a flat tax is that is it more difficult to increase. In Massachusetts, the state constitution requires that the income tax have only one rate. They make a graduated or progressive income tax unconstitutional. This in the bluest of the blue states and home to the Kennedy clan. This means that when a politician wishes to begin some new social experiment and use the income tax to pay for it, he must face the entire electorate and explain "I have a really good idea . . . and you will all be paying for it." This gets the entire population listening and the bar is raised for what actually passes the laugh test as a "really good idea."

Five times the big spending interests in Massachusetts have put on the ballot through initiative or referendum an effort to amend the state constitution to allow a graduated or progressive income tax. Five times, in 1962, 1968, 1972, 1976, and 1994, this was defeated by the people of Massachusetts. The argument showed great wisdom on the part of Bay Staters. They understood that as long as there is one tax rate, the people of the state could not be turned against one another. A tax hike on the rich Kennedys was also a tax hike on the average citizen. Uncouple taxpayers and divide them into two or a dozen tax brackets and the politicians can first increase taxes on the rich and then come for the rest of us—with the Kennedys sitting out the efforts to tax the middle class after they were mugged first.

One rate unites taxpayers. The preference for most big government politicians is to promise their base new goodies at taxpayer expense, and then promise that they will only loot a small number of taxpayers—not you in the audience I am speaking to right now.

This is the Richard Speck theory of tax increases. If you cannot take on everyone in the room at once, bring them out of the room one at a time.

If you tax income at one rate, it is more difficult for the politicians to raise the tax, easier to lower (all gain), and keeps transparent who pays what (tougher to sell envy).

So what is the right tax rate? Here we seek the wisdom of Samuel Gompers, the most prominent labor leader of his time, who, when asked what workingmen wanted, replied, "More." What tax rate do we want—"a lower one."

Wisconsin Congressman Paul Ryan's 2012 budget plan calls for reducing the top rate on businesses and individuals to 25 percent from today's 35 percent and Obama's planned 45 or 50 percent. In October 2011, Texas Governor Rick Perry unveiled a flat rate of 20 percent for businesses and individuals. Former presidential candidate and businessman Herman Cain endorsed a 9 percent income tax, but added to it a 9 percent value added tax and a 9 percent sales tax.

How to get from here to there? From the top rate of 35 percent and a code riddled with exemptions and deductions to a single low rate with few, if any, deductions and credits?

One path is the one originally proposed by Steven Moore, who is now with the editorial page of the *Wall Street Journal* and whose plan was endorsed by Texas Governor and presidential candidate Rick Perry. Create a separate tax system parallel to the present mess. Create your perfect plan. Few deductions, one low rate. And then allow every American to choose. If you have organized your life around the IRS's preferences and do not wish to lose the deductions and credits you have structured your economic life around, then stay put. If you would rather have the lower rates, no death tax, no capital gains tax, and few deductions, then move into the new system.

This has one great advantage. It minimizes opposition to the reform. No one would have a justified fear of the new system. You don't have to move into it. Everyone correctly fears reforms when the politicians announce, "We have a great new idea; you will love it; you will be forced to do the following." If it is such a great idea, why do we have to be forced into it?

Step Four: Reforming the Corporate Income Tax

While we work to bring the federal personal income tax rate down, economic growth requires that we also reform the corporate income tax (CIT) at the same time. Roughly 3 million businesses pay the corporate income tax. Those are the Fortune 500 and most larger companies. About 20 million American businesses pay through the personal income tax system, as they are partnerships, entrepreneurs, or independent contractors or what are called Subchapter S corporations.

This is why we need to bring down both the personal and corporate rate together. Obama has called for bringing the federal corporate rate down from today's 35 percent toward 25 percent but he wants to hike the personal income tax rate to 50 percent. This would put smaller companies at a big disadvantage compared to the biggest companies. Oddly enough, the bigger companies are most friendly to government regulation (that conveniently kneecap small up-and-coming competitors).

The key components of reforming or reducing the corporate income tax are to reduce the combined average federal and state marginal tax rate from 39.2 percent in 2011 so that America is competitive with other nations. The average corporate income tax in the European nations is 25 percent. So to meet the minimum standard of being competitive with the European average (not the lower-tax countries) we need to reduce the federal corporate income tax to 20 percent so that when they are added to state income taxes, American products are taxed at a 25 percent corporate income tax rate—roughly equal to the European average.

Territoriality

When we hear liberals whine that "America is the only nation in the world that. . . ." we are usually being urged to do something stupid "like all the other kids in school." America is the only nation without its own national airline or a VAT or government-run health care or that has enshrined the right to gun ownership in its Constitution.

Every once in a while, though, America does something uniquely stupid. For example, our tort laws enrich billionaire trial lawyers while slowing down innovation, killing jobs, and bankrupting companies though junk science.

America's present worldwide tax policy is also unique. Other countries tax economic activity within their borders and do not tax economic activity outside their borders. A French company that runs a factory in France pays French corporate income taxes. If the French company builds a second factory in Ireland, those profits are taxed by Ireland, not France. An American company investing in a factory in Ireland must first pay Irish taxes, and should they bring their earnings back to America, must pay the difference between Ireland's *12.5 percent* corporate income tax and America's 39.2 percent. That is a roughly a 27 percentage point tax on companies foolish enough to bring money back to invest in the United States. This also means that an American firm investing and selling on a global scale is more profitable if owned by a German or French or Chinese company. American tax policy makes a worldwide business less valuable because it has to pay higher taxes if it is American.

The good news is that Republican leaders in the House Ways and Means committee are committed to moving United States tax policy to a territorial system—we tax stuff you do here, not there. And as a transition, they would allow a period of a year or two for companies to repatriate their overseas profits estimated in 2011 to be more than 1 trillion dollars. American firms would pay a federal 5.25 percent tax on earnings brought home rather than the present tax that can run as high as 35 percent. When this was done in 2005, American firms brought back more than $400 billion.

Expensing

When an American company buys a machine for $1 million, it is allowed to depreciate the value of that machine over its economic life. If the bureaucrats declare that machine's economic life to be 10 years, the firm can deduct from its profits (that is, not pay corporate income taxes on) $100,000 each year for 10 years.

The reform that even Democrats have supported going back to 1981 is to move to immediate expensing. Buy a machine for $1 million, and you deduct from your taxable earnings and profits that year the full $1 million. You don't pay tax on it because you don't have it because you spent it. This eliminates a thousand pages of the corporate income tax code. No one has to guess what the economic life of a piece of software or a computer is.

Full business expensing would increase GDP permanently by $30 billion to $60 billion per year, and increase domestic investment by $50 billion.

Step Five: No Value Added Tax

If the American left is to succeed in its drive to turn America into a European welfare state, they must impose a value added tax, or VAT, on top of all other taxes at the national level.

The average European VAT is 18.5 percent. The VAT is first introduced at a low level and with promises that other taxes will be reduced. But in Europe, each time the VAT was introduced, other taxes were increased more rapidly after the VAT appeared than before. A bigger government became more powerful, hungrier, and more capable of demanding yet higher taxes of all sorts.

Even as Americans demand lower taxes and less spending, there remains the very real danger that we could get saddled with a VAT. Politicians will approach the American business community and offer to reduce the burdensome corporate income tax, not through reforming the tax with lower rates, territoriality and expensing, but through replacing some of the corporate income tax with a VAT. That replacement would, of course, be temporary.

We have already seen this scenario begin to unfold with the 9-9-9 tax reform proposed by former Republican presidential candidate Herman Cain. Cain's plan promised to eventually replace the present personal, corporate, and Social Security taxes with the retail sales tax or Fair Tax. But his transition period includes creating a 9 percent income tax, a 9 percent sales tax, and a 9 percent Japanese-style VAT (a 9 percent tax on all wages paid and profits earned by a business).

So, for a transition period (who knows how long), there will be a VAT, a sales tax, and an income tax. Three needles in your arm drawing out blood to temporarily replace one needle. The Left would immediately begin the chant that the United States was the only nation without a corporate income tax. All three taxes could and would grow. Switzerland has the lowest VAT in Europe at 7.5 percent. Hungary has the highest VAT in Europe with a rate of 27 percent.

We do not have to travel to Europe to be warned of the dangers of creating new taxes in the hope that this will lead to lower taxes. In 1975, New Jersey had the nation's highest property taxes. To fix this, Democratic governor Brendan Byrne persuaded the legislature to impose an income tax in New Jersey for the first time. This would, he explained, reduce the property tax pain. Today, New Jersey has a sales tax, high property taxes, and an income tax. Connecticut was a slow learner, and in 1991, Governor Lowell Weicker sold his state on creating their first income tax in order to reduce property taxes. Now, Connecticut has both income and property (and sales) taxes, all growing rapidly.

If you have a large tapeworm inside you, the solution is not to swallow additional tapeworms in the hope that the new tapeworm will remain small. Taxes, like tapeworms, tend to grow at their own pace.

All taxes increase to the breaking point. To the point at which they break the political careers of politicians. Property taxes will rise to the point that they cost folks elections. Add an income tax and both the property tax and income tax will increase independently to the point at which elections are lost. Add a sales tax and you have three different taxes, each inching upward.

Lower-tax states tend to be missing either an income tax or a sales tax. Or in the case of New Hampshire, they have neither. (Everyone whines about the property taxes, but the smart ones remember New Jersey and Connecticut and avoid creating new taxes to add to the property tax.)

Fewer taxes means lower overall taxation.

Step Six: Add the Warren Buffett Line

Warren Buffett is a very rich liberal. He says he would like to pay more in taxes. But something is holding him back. Just what is not clear. Very much like the drunk in the bar who pretends that someone is holding him back from throwing a punch at another patron. "Let me at him."

Luckily, Louisiana Congressman Steve Scalise has introduced legislation titled "The Buffet Line" that will add to every tax return a simple line at the end where those who believe the government can spend their money better than they would add a few extra dollars beyond what they "owe" in taxes. Eight states already have what they call "tax me more" lines: Massachusetts, Arkansas, Kansas, Minnesota, Montana, New Hampshire, Oklahoma, and Virginia. It has the wonderful advantage that those politicians who want to raise taxes on everyone else will be able to show the world whether they have been taking their own advice or if they are hypocrites who think everyone else should pay more but they choose not to.

Step Seven: Never Repeat the Debacle of 1982 or 1990

The advocates of higher taxes have an endless number of ploys, all to the same end: badger, trick, and cajole Americans out of more of their earnings. One of their favorites—because it has worked twice, big time—is to offer a "grand bargain" that will reduce the deficit by having a secret committee come up with a combination of spending cuts and tax hikes.

President Ronald Reagan fell for this in 1982. The Democrats, led by the Speaker of the House, Massachusetts Congressman Tip O'Neill, promised Reagan that they would cut three dollars of spending for every dollar of tax increase he agreed to. This would reduce the deficit. Note the subtle shift away from controlling spending to focusing on the deficit. Taxes were raised by $215 billion over the following five years. According to the promised deal, federal spending should have declined by $645 billion from its baseline projection. Instead, adjusting for inflation, total spending rose by $177 billion beyond what it would have with without the deficit deal. The promise to cut $647 billion became a spending increase of $177 billion.

That worked so well for the Democrats that in 1990 they approached President George H. W. Bush and invited him out to a big summit held at Andrews Air Force Base where Bush (a cheaper date) was offered only two dollars of imaginary spending reductions for every one dollar of very real tax increases. Twenty-six different taxes were permanently created or hiked, and this increased taxation by $137 billion over five years. Spending should have been reduced by $274 billion. Instead, spending increased $23 billion over the projected baseline.

For Democrats, this had a double benefit. Taxes went up. Spending went up, and President Bush, who had overseen the expulsion of Iraq from Kuwait without getting stuck occupying the place for a decade and managed the collapse of the Soviet Union without a lot of blood on the floor, was defeated at the polls as punishment for raising taxes. Bush won only 38 percent of the vote in 1992.

When Democrats offer to reduce spending in return for higher taxes, run.

Republicans did learn from 1982 and 1990, and in 2011, they refused to allow tax increases be part of the deal to increase the debt ceiling. What happened? The deal included no tax hikes and $2.5 trillion in spending restraint. By taking taxes off the table, there was a real focus on spending. When taxes are on the table, spending restraint evaporates. Tax increases are what politicians do instead of reducing spending.

Step Eight: Reform Government to Reduce Spending

Adopt the Ryan Plan in Washington. See Figures 6.1 and 6.2. Wisconsin Congressman Paul Ryan wrote the Budget Resolution for 2012 that was passed by the House of Representatives on April 12, 2011, with all but four Republican House members voting aye. The Senate also voted on the Ryan Plan and it won the votes of 40

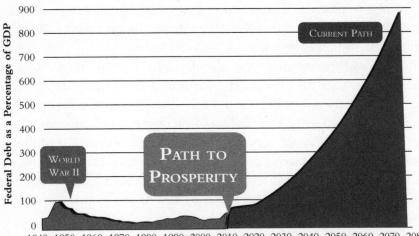

Figure 6.1 A Choice of Two Futures
SOURCE: OMB/CBO.

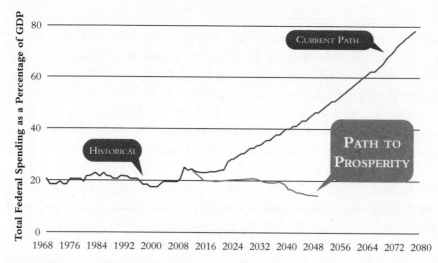

Figure 6.2   Total Federal Spending
SOURCE: CBO.

of the 47 Republican senators. These two votes demonstrate not simply Republican unity for a single budget but a path to prosperity. The Ryan Plan is also known as the Roadmap because it looks out decades and reforms government to bring spending down by six trillion dollars over one decade, reducing federal spending from 25 percent of GDP to 20 percent of GDP in 10 years and to 15 percent of GDP by *2050*.

The Ryan Plan is the outline for the federal government of an America that works. It is the antidote to Obama/Reid/Pelosi's forced march to the European welfare state. The reforms in the Ryan Roadmap will reform all entitlements to make them sustainable not for a year or two or pushing the collapse out past the budget window or the next election, but permanently.

Medicare is reformed to give citizens more control over their health care decisions, building on the model now available to Congressmen. Health care costs are lowered through reforming tort laws that drive up the cost of medicines and lead to unnecessary tests and hospital costs demanded by lawyers, not doctors.

Paul Ryan's fiscal year budget resolution, known as "The Path to Prosperity," also includes the following reforms:

Corporate welfare subsidies are ended. Earmarks permanently banned. Opens up America's energy resources to allow safe and environmentally sound use of America's coal, oil, and natural gas, creating millions of jobs and keeping energy prices low and determined by the market, not foreign governments. Reduces the federal workforce over three years by 10 percent through attrition. Freezes nonsecurity government bureaucracies to below 2008 levels and freezes that spending for five years. Reforming pay for federal workers, who now earn twice what taxpayers earn, on average. The plan freezes federal pay through 2015. Reforms the twin disasters that bankrupted us in 2007—Freddie Mac and Fannie Mae—so that taxpayers are not on the hook for their decisions, good or bad. Reducing farm subsidies by getting the government out of this key industry. Medicare and food stamps and housing subsidies are block-granted to the states. And capping discretionary spending for 2012, and establishing a binding cap on total federal spending as a percentage of the economy, enforced by sequester.

Reform Social Security for Younger Americans

Social Security, which had 16.5 American workers supporting each retiree in 1950, and in 2009 had three workers' payments supporting each retiree and in 2040 will see that ratio fall to where 2.1 Americans will pay taxes each year to support each retiree. The bad news for taxpayers and the Social Security system flows from good news. Life expectancy has increased from 68 years in 1950 to 78 years in 2009. This good news means that America must reform Social Security and all its pensions to become fully funded and sustainable. That means we need to shift from pay-as-you-go defined benefit systems that are sometimes accurately, if cruelly, labeled "Ponzi schemes," to fully funded defined contribution systems in which individuals contribute to a 401(k) equivalent whereby the money they save is controlled by them, not a bureaucracy of government or union or big business.

All plans to reform Social Security have two parts. First, all Americans at or near retirement will have no change in their benefits. Second, younger Americans will be given the option of moving to a defined contribution system through which their FICA taxes would be sent not to Washington to be spent that afternoon but invested in a personal savings account that will accumulate and grow. With conservative estimates of investment rates of return, the average 25-year-old who invested her FICA taxes in the stock market—even with all its ups and downs—would, upon retiring at 70 years old, would have accumulated lifetime savings of $3.5 million. If converted to an annuity, this would give her an annual pension of $140,000 per year. It's very safe to say this is three times more than what Social Security promises, but cannot afford to pay.

This personalization of Social Security is under way in other nations. The South American nation of Chile moved first and began this reform in 1980. Then, 90 percent of Chileans opted for the reformed system of individual control. Today, Chileans' accumulated pensions are about 60 percent of Chilean GDP ($120 billion). And citizens can retire and replace about 100 percent of their pre-retirement income, as opposed to the old system, which replaced about 50 percent of preretirement income.

Block-Grant All Means-Tested Welfare Programs

Ask an American to name one government reform that worked and he will likely name the Welfare Reform Act of 1996, which block-granted the Aid to Families with Dependent Children (AFDC) to the states and renamed the program "Temporary Assistance to Needy Families" (TANF). If a state had been receiving one billion dollars in federal tax money to pay for welfare, they were told that that money would now come in a block grant with fewer strings and would increase only with inflation. If the state could provide welfare less expensively than the feds had, they could keep the savings. Welfare rolls fell by 56 percent. Some states governed better than others. Indiana reduced its rolls by 39.4 percent. Wyoming by 74.2 percent. Hawaii alone increased its rolls by 7.4 percent.

The Ryan Plan endorsed by most Republicans in Congress would block-grant 77 different welfare programs, programs that target money to lower-income Americans: means-tested programs. This includes Medicaid, food stamps, and low-income housing. Telling states that they will receive for these programs what they received last year and the block grant will increase with inflation (but not faster) would save federal taxpayers more than $750 billion over 10 years and give 50 states the opportunity to run these programs free of federal regulations. Fifty different experiments competing to provide the best government at the lowest cost. Almost like the real world.

Keep the Ban on Earmarks

Congress banned earmarks, the process of having individual congressmen or senators stick pork-barrel spending projects into larger spending bills. Some argued that all the earmarks added together in, say, 2008, cost taxpayers only $20 billion within a federal budget of $3 trillion. Not big bucks. And that money was reprogrammed from other areas of the government, so in the short term, an earmark didn't cost taxpayers money that was not already going to be wasted elsewhere.

But this misses the actual damage done by earmarks. When Congressmen are expected by their local mayors, university presidents, and other would-be grant recipients to bring home the bacon, they are not focused on governing and certainly not focused on reforming government to cost less. And why should the federal government take a dollar from you and send it to a high school or community college in another state? Local or state taxpayers should pay for high school gymnasiums or university buildings. Worse, earmarks were the currency of corruption. They are what presidents, congressional leaders, and appropriators gave to congressmen and senators to buy their votes for things they would otherwise not stoop to support. Earmarks are the relatively small bribes paid to buy votes for bigger spending programs.

Earmarks are the broken windows of the overspending problem. If congressmen see everyone fighting to gain earmarks, no one believes that anyone is actually fighting for taxpayers in general. And they would be right.

Congressmen and their staffs freed from the time and effort needed to fight for spending earmarks are no longer raising federal taxes to shower money on local governments. When local governments think of this federal money as free, there is no limit to what they can demand and spend—because it is paid for by "others."

Transparency

In the age of the Internet, there is no reason that every single check written by federal, state, and local governments should not be available for every taxpayer to read in real time. Every contract entered into, be it your school district, town, city, county, state, or federal agency should be online in a searchable database. The bank balances of every government should be public information online. In the past, governments, such as California in 1978 or Virginia in 2004, have lied to citizens, demanding they raise taxes because the state had no money and revenues were depressed. It turns out that politicians have a bad habit of lying about how much cash is lying around in various bank accounts. There is no justifiable reason for this.

Attrition

Government has too many employees at all levels of government. But discussions of this create fears of massive layoffs. Better to take the long view and announce that your state, local government, and federal government will replace only one of every three retirees as a way to reduce government overhead without threatening the present workforce. The Postal Service had 900,000 employees in 2000. By 2009, that had declined to 700,000, and by 2011, it had fallen to 600,000. The Postal Service itself admits it needs only 400,000 employees. Another 200,000 can be reduced through attrition or voluntary buyouts.

Walk through your local state or federal government office. Which office could not function well with 10 or 20 percent fewer employees?

Reform the Number and Pay and Benefits of Government Workers

There are 2.2 million federal civilian workers, 1.5 million active-duty members of the armed forces, 5 million state employees in the 50 states, and 14.1 million local employees.

On average, Americans in the private sector earn $61,000 a year in pay, pension benefits, and health care benefits. State and local government workers earn $80,000 in pay, pension, and health care benefits. Federal workers are paid $120,000 in pay, pension, and benefits.

Hiring one federal worker at age 25 will cost taxpayers between $2.73 million and $8 million over his work life and retirement benefits, depending on how fast the employee is promoted (what GS level the employee achieves).

Competitively Bid All Government Jobs

Federal law requires that government look to see what jobs now being done by government workers could be done by the private sector. Even the Clinton administration found that to be upward of 850,000 jobs. Those jobs are required to be offered for competition to private firms. When this has happened, the average savings has been 30 percent, even if the government employees themselves won the bid—because they reorganized and provided the service at a lower cost. If all the available jobs were actually bid, it would save taxpayers $27 billion.

This could also be done in every state and local government.

Term-Limit Appropriators . . . Revive the Anti-Appropriations Committee

The old joke in Washington is that while there are two major parties in America, inside Washington, DC there are three parties: Republicans, Democrats, and Appropriators. Appropriators are those congressmen and senators who serve on the House and Senate Appropriations Committees, the committee that spends money. There are 50 Appropriators in the House and 30 in the Senate.

Unsurprisingly enough, those politicians who come to Washington determined to cut and slash and reform government on behalf of taxpayers who are handed the keys to the Treasury and become

Appropriators (Latin for *big spenders*) find they drift further and further from those who elected them.

Two reforms are key. First, Congress can and should term-limit membership on the Appropriations Committee to six years. They do this now on the Budget Committee. When a congressman is on the committee for just a maximum of six years, he does not become a spender for his entire career. Reformers do not ask to be on the Appropriations Committee because they are stacked with lifers opposed to reform. An Appropriations Committee that turned over regularly just might become the friend of taxpayers instead of their enemy.

Second, Congress could revive the Joint Committee on Reduction of Nonessential Federal Expenditures, which was created in 1941 at the urging of Virginia Senator Harry F. Byrd, who wanted to pay for some of World War Two by reducing spending in other programs. This was the anti-appropriations committee. Its job was to hold hearings, do studies, and propose legislation to reduce or end government spending programs. This committee ended the Civilian Conservation Corps in 1943, saving $289 million. It cut back the Work Projects Administration, savings $540 million in 1943, and ended it in 1944. The National Youth Administration, eliminated in 1944, saved $56 million.

Imagine the juicy targets, delightful hearings, and larger savings available to a rejuvenated anti-appropriations committee today, now that government spending is measured in billions and trillions instead of millions.

Sell Assets: Feds and States Should Sell Land, Mining Rights, and the Airwaves

When American citizens and businesses in the real world are in debt, they look to see what they can sell. Governments have accumulated ownership of trillions of dollars' worth of land, underground minerals, shale oil, natural gas, offshore oil and gas, and the valuable electromagnetic spectrum used by TV and radio stations, phone companies, and others.

Step Nine: Reduce the Regulatory Burden

We read the startling budget numbers: Federal spending has jumped from 21 percent in 2008 to 25 percent in 2011. We feel the cost of taxes: income taxes, sales taxes, property taxes. But the costly and silent killer of jobs and opportunity in America is government over-regulation.

Every year, Americans for Tax Reform calculates the true cost of government. Add up all federal, state, and local government spending and the cost of complying with regulations and you have the true cost of government. Refer to Figure 6.3.

In 2011, Americans worked 103 days to pay for federal spending, 44 days to pay for state and local government spending and 77 days for the cost of regulations imposed by federal, state, and local government. See Figure 6.4.

Reducing the cost and size of government will require a renewed focus on the cost of regulations. Why? Because taxpayers have had some success in stopping the federal and state governments from raising taxes. This had led to governments borrowing to continue spending. The Tea Party arose in opposition to overspending and earmarks and debt. Big-government politicians now find two doors closed, or at least well guarded: the tax hike door and the spending increase door. But they have discovered a third door, less well guarded, into the treasure room—the pockets and lives of the American people. That door is marked "Government Regulations." Certainly, the advocates of more government control through unelected bureaucracies telling us how to live our lives rarely raise the banner of regulations. They prefer words like *health,*

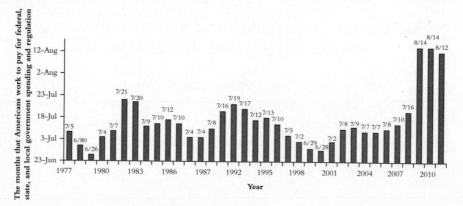

Figure 6.3 Cost of Government 1977 to 2011

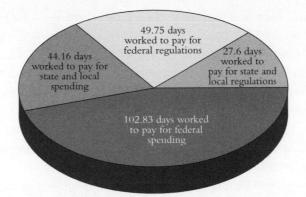

Figure 6.4   Cost of Government Day Components

safety, the environment, children, animal rights, and a variety of nice words that cover as a mask the unsmiling face of ever-larger government.

Today, federal and state regulations cost Americans more than $1.8 trillion each and every year. The Competitive Enterprise Institute's annual "Ten Thousand Commandments" study of government regulations points out that "at the end of 2009, the Code of Federal Regulations was 157,974 pages long. In 2010, 3,752 new rules hit the books—equivalent to a new regulation coming into effect every 2 hours and 20 minutes, 24 hours a day, 365 days a year."

Americans need to arm themselves against the onslaught of regulations as they once organized to limit taxes and spending.

One proposed law is the REINS act, the acronym flowing from its name, the "Regulations from the Executive in Need of Scrutiny" Act. This bill would do one simple thing: require that any regulation that costs the economy more than $100 million dollars be voted on by Congress.

Step Ten: Remember the States and Towns and Cities and Counties

There is understandably much focus on the taxation and spending and regulations flowing from our imperial city, Washington DC But if we are to wrestle big government to the ground and demand it serve us rather than vice versa, we need to keep an eye on how state governments and local governments are growing.

State and local government spent 8.83 percent of GDP in 1960, 10.44 percent in 1980, and 11.74 percent in 2010. Federal spending was fairly constant at about 21 percent of GDP until Obama drove it up to 25 percent in two years. The drift upward at the local level has been sustained and will be even more difficult to turn around.

Eighty percent of state and local spending goes to the costs of paying salaries, benefits, and pensions for government workers. In January 2011, there were 5 million employees of state governments and 14.1 million employees of local governments.

Total pay, benefit, and pension costs for a state and local worker average $80,000, almost $20,000 more than the average private sector worker is paid in total compensation, which is $61,000. That overpayment of $19,000 multiplied by 19.1 million state and local workers costs American taxpayers $361 billion each year.

A hiring freeze, or allowing government employment to be reduced by 10 percent through attrition—not firing anyone, but simply not replacing some of those who leave—would save taxpayers 10 percent of the cost of the 19.1 million workers who have an average total compensation package of $80,000 each, for a total of $152 billion saved each year.

Utah has led the way in reforming its pension system, as they have enacted a law drafted by State Senator Dan Liljenquist that requires that all state or local employees hired after July 1, 2011 would have a defined contribution pension where the state would contribute 10 percent of their salary (12 percent for fire and police) to their retirement account. Each worker would control his or her retirement account and would not have to wait for an artificial deadline to "vest." When they wanted to move to another state or another job their personal pension account would move with them. Taxpayers would know that they were not inheriting a hidden unfunded liability every time their town hired a new teacher.

Party Control of States

Figure 6.5 shows the 24 states in 2011 with a Republican governor and Republican control of both houses of the legislature and the

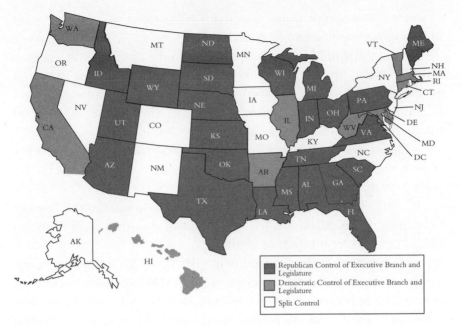

Figure 6.5 2011 Republican and Democrat Control of the States

eleven states with complete Democratic control, governor and legislature. Because states are writing their redistricting maps to govern elections for the next decade it is a wise bet that Red States will redistrict themselves to continue Republican control and Blue States will redistrict themselves to maintain Democratic control. Look for the Red States to reform their labor laws, tort laws, and tax laws to limit the size and scope of government and for the Blue States to move to a position somewhere between Greece and France as rapidly as they can.

Step Eleven: BBA Robust versus Weak

Once we take tax hikes permanently off the table, block-grant all welfare programs to the states, reform Social Security and government employee pensions so they are fully funded and controlled by workers rather than the government, and moved health care and education to consumer and parent-centered systems, we need constitutional protection against the government regrouping and fighting to return to its dominant and domineering position in America.

When the founding fathers wanted to be certain that religion would remain free of government control or help, they wrote it into the First Amendment. When they wanted to ensure the right of every American to keep and bear arms, they wrote the Second Amendment.

Where is the constitutional amendment to protect us from government spending and debt growing to where they threaten our liberty and national future?

In 2011, every single Republican senator co-sponsored the "Senate Consensus Amendment," S.J. Res. 10. Lead sponsors were Senators Mike Lee and Orrin Hatch of Utah.

This balanced budget amendment (BBA), endorsed by the entire Republican caucus, would require a balanced budget amendment each year and Congress could borrow money only with a three-fifths vote. It would require a two-thirds majority vote to increase taxes. Federal spending would be limited to 18 percent of GDP and no court could impose taxes on the American people.

This amendment protects against all the problems that previous weak or stripped-down balanced budget amendments have provoked. An amendment that required only a balanced budget would become an annual battering ram to demand higher taxes. Congress could overspend and then turn to voters and say, "Sorry, we are now constitutionally required to raise your taxes." Or worse, the Supreme Court could announce that they noticed overspending and they are forcing Congress to impose a tax increase to "balance the budget." If the justices get control of the tax code, there is no stopping them.

Even proposing a weak balanced budget amendment is counterproductive. It allows all the vulnerable Democrats to vote for the meaningless amendment—making them appear moderate or fiscally responsible—while knowing that the Democrats in the Senate would kill any actual amendment.

The path to a balanced budget or tax and spending limit amendment is for Republicans in the House and Senate to put forward for a vote the Senate consensus amendment and demand a vote, or at minimum, a procedural vote that everyone recognizes as the key vote for or against this amendment. Then proceed to the 2012 elections and defeat some of those Democrats who voted against a robust balanced budget amendment. Then repeat this process until there are 67 votes in the Senate and 290 votes in the House for the robust amendment.

What about compromising to win Democrats' votes by weakening the BBA. Perhaps enough Democrats might support—and we could live with—a three-fifths vote, rather than the larger two-thirds vote to raise taxes? The only conversation about weakening the Senate consensus amendment to win over Democrats should occur after the Democrats have a written amendment of their own that has at least 20 Democrats in the Senate and 49 in the House who have co-sponsored it. Otherwise, proponents of a robust BBA are negotiating with themselves and imaginary Democrats.

Step Twelve: Remember Archimedes and His Lever: Wear Bifocals

Archimedes wrote that if he were given a lever long enough and a fulcrum strong enough, he could move the earth. In politics, our lever is time. There is almost nothing that can be accomplished to reform government at the national, state, or local level this week or even this month. But there is nothing that cannot be accomplished in one generation. Building a coalition determined to end a government agency, reduce government spending, or put a long-lived tax to sleep can take many years and many election cycles.

It was argued that the civil rights movement did not change men's hearts, but when the hearts of old men gave out, the younger Americans who replaced them had grown up free of racial bigotry. Some changes require the electorate to change.

In the United States, when Congress or the state legislature or the governor or president will not work with the forces of freedom, the only civilized solution is to replace those politicians in the next election or the election after that. And elections come only every two years. And the good guys don't always get to win. Your candidate might be right on the key issues and yet forget to mention several DUIs. Sometimes the other team works harder or smarter.

Those looking to turn America around from its headlong rush toward becoming California or Greece must plan, work, and organize to win the next series of elections. Like the expanding early Roman Republic we must be persistent. It was not necessary for the Roman legions to win every battle, just that they win more battles than they lost and that they never quit. The law of large numbers gives you the advantage when your victory rate is above 50 percent and you never stop.

Looking ahead on the political battlefield of the next decade we see the following correlation of forces:

Republicans control the governorship and both houses of the legislature in 24 states marked in red on the map in Figure 6.5. They represent 51 percent of the population, and those states cast 266 electoral votes for president. Because Republicans will write the state legislative district lines in redistricting for the elections of 2012, 2014, 2016, 2018, and 2020, it is more likely than not that Republicans will redistrict to ensure they continue to control those state legislative bodies. One adds to that North Carolina, where Republican majorities in the House and Senate will redistrict themselves without any input (read *veto power*) from the governor.

Democrats control the governorship and legislature in 11 states: California, Illinois, Washington, Hawaii, Arkansas, West Virginia, Maryland, Delaware, Massachusetts, Connecticut, and Vermont. They will redistrict to maintain Democratic control of those states with the exception only of Arkansas, which will likely flip completely Republican in 2012. These states have 136 electoral votes and hold 25 percent of the national population.

At the national level, in 2011, Republicans controlled 242 members of the U.S. House of Representatives. A majority is 218. In November 2010, Republicans gained five seats in Pennsylvania, five seats in Ohio, two seats in Michigan, and two seats in Indiana. All states in which the Republicans will redistrict the national congressional seats to protect those gains. While life and politics are uncertain, the smart money would bet that the Republicans chose well when they had their Tea Party landslide in 2010—in time to rewrite the district lines for the next decade. The Democrats had their big tsunami wins in 2006 and 2008—too early to redistrict anything.

The House should remain with a comfortable Republican majority for a decade.

The struggle will be for the Senate and the presidency.

In 2012, there will be 23 Democratic Senate seats and 10 Republican seats up for election. Figure 6.6 shows that those Republicans elected in 2006 and up for re-election in 2012 tend to come from solid Republican states. After all, they survived the very bad election year of 2006. Only the hardiest trees remained standing in that storm.

Half of the Democrats running for Senate in 2012 are running in trending Republican states.

Two years later, it is more of the same. Only 13 Republicans in reasonably safe seats are up for election. Democrats have 20 Senate seats in play, including such Republican states as Alaska, Montana, North Carolina, South Dakota, Arkansas, New Hampshire, and Virginia.

In 2012 and 2014, there are 43 Democratic Senate seats up. If Republicans win a net of four they have a Senate majority. If they net 13, they have a filibuster-proof Senate vote of 60.

Hold the House. Win the Senate. Reach for real control of the Senate with 60 votes.

Then win the presidency in 2012, 2016, and/or 2020.

The sooner Republicans win control of the Congress and presidency, the sooner we can begin to turn the country around. The less painful the recovery. Reagan turned the nation around within three years of his election. It can be done.

But should Obama and the Democrats win back the House and keep the Senate, they will gain another four years of judicial appointments, bureaucratic edicts, and maintain the higher spending and taxes flowing from Obamacare. Then America will cease to be exceptional. We will have been pulled back into the European statist gravitational pull that was always there, stronger at times and weaker in our best days. They would reestablish a controlled society, ruled

DEMOCRATS

2012 (23 Democrats, 10 Republicans)

First Name	Last Name	Age on Election Day	State	State GOP Presidential Vote 2004	State GOP Presidential Vote 2008
Daniel	Akaka	86	HI	45.30%	27%
Jeff	Bingaman	67	NM	49.80%	41.78%
Sherrod	Brown	57	OH	50.80%	46.91%
Maria	Cantwell	52	WA	45.60%	40.48%
Benjamin	Cardin	67	MD	42.90%	36.47%
Thomas	Carper	63	DE	45.80%	36.92%
Robert P.	Casey, Jr.	50	PA	48.40%	44.17%
Kent	Conrad	62	ND	62.90%	53.07%
Dianne	Feinstein	77	CA	44.36%	36.95%
Kirsten	Gillibrand	43	NY	40.08%	36.03%
Carte	Goodwin	36	WV	56.10%	56%
Amy	Klobuchar	50	MN	47.60%	43.82%
Herb	Kohl	75	WI	49.30%	42.31%
Claire	McCaskill	57	MO	53.30%	49.43%
Robert	Menendez	56	NJ	46.20%	41.70%
Ben	Nelson	69	NE	66%	57%
Bill	Nelson	68	FL	52.10%	48.10%
Debbie	Stabenow	60	MI	47.80%	40.90%
Jon	Tester	54	MT	59.10%	49.43%
Jim	Webb	64	VA	53.70%	46.33%
Sheldon	Whitehouse	55	RI	38.70%	35.06%
Joseph	Lieberman	68	CT	44.00%	38.22%
Bernard	Sanders	69	VT	39.00%	30.45%

2014 (20 Democrats, 13 Republicans)

First Name	Last Name	Age on Election Day	State	State GOP Presidential Vote 2004	State GOP Presidential Vote 2008
Max	Baucus	68	MT	59.10%	49.43%
Mark	Begich	48	AK	61.10%	59.42%
Richard	Durbin	65	IL	44.50%	36.76%
Al	Franken	59	MN	47.60%	43.82%
Kay	Hagan	57	NC	56.90%	49.38%
Tom	Harkin	70	IA	49.90%	44.39%
Tim	Johnson	63	SD	59.90%	53.16%
Edward	Kaufman	71	DE	45.80%	36.92%
John	Kerry	66	MA	36.80%	35.99%
Mary	Landrieu	54	LA	56.70%	58.56%
Frank	Lautenberg	86	NJ	46.20%	41.70%
Carl	Levin	76	MI	47.80%	40.90%
Jeff	Merkley	54	OR	47.20%	40.40%
Mark	Pryor	47	AR	54.30%	58.72%
Jack	Reed	60	RI	38.70%	35.06%
John	Rockefeller	73	WV	56.10%	56%
Jeanne	Shaheen	63	NH	48.90%	44.52%
Mark	Udall	60	CO	51.70%	44.71%
Tom	Udall	62	NM	49.80%	41.78%
Mark	Warner	55	VA	53.70%	46.33%

REPUBLICANS

First Name	Last Name	Age on Election Day	State	State GOP Presidential Vote 2004	State GOP Presidential Vote 2008		First Name	Last Name	Age on Election Day	State	State GOP Presidential Vote 2004	State GOP Presidential Vote 2008
John	Barrasso	58	WY	68.90%	64.78%		Lamar	Alexander	70	TN	56.80%	56.85%
Scott	Brown	51	MA	36.80%	35.99%		Saxby	Chambliss	66	GA	58.00%	52.23%
Bob	Corker	58	TN	56.80%	56.85%		Thad	Cochran	72	MS	59.40%	56.18%
John	Ensign	52	NV	50.50%	42.65%		Susan	Collins	57	ME	45.00%	41.00%
Orrin	Hatch	76	UT	71.50%	62.25%		John	Cornyn	58	TX	61.10%	55.39%
Kay	Hutchison	67	TX	61.10%	55.39%		Michael	Enzi	66	WY	68.90%	64.78%
Jon	Kyl	68	AZ	54.97%	53.39%		Lindsey	Graham	55	SC	58.00%	53.87%
Richard	Lugar	78	IN	59.94%	48.91%		James	Inhofe	75	OK	65.60%	65.65%
Olympia	Snowe	63	ME	45.00%	41.00%		Mike	Johanns	60	NE	66%	57%
Roger	Wicker	69	MS	59.40%	56.18%		Mitch	McConnell	68	KY	59.60%	57.37%
							James	Risch	67	ID	68.40%	61.30%
							Pat	Roberts	74	KS	62.00%	56.50%
							Jeff	Sessions	63	AL	62.46%	60.32%

Figure 6.6 2012–2014 Senate

by a bureaucratic aristocracy that would tell us how we must live our lives.

Ten years. We will know who wins, what direction America turns, in the next decade. Our decade. Our struggle. The only thing between us and regaining a continental nation independent and free and growing in wealth and opportunity and liberty is a great deal of hard work.

Conclusion

Obama's Legacy

Yeah, I [voted for Obama in 2008]. My parents are dead for a long time, but my sister says, "You have to vote for Obama, for what it would have meant for Mom and Dad." I felt that, too. It's a huge thing. This [history of racism] has been the worst blot on this country. All of a sudden this charming, intelligent guy just blows it away. It was great. . . . I thought [Obama] was going to be more Clinton-like in his economics and politics. I was caught by surprise by how far left the guy is and how much he's hung on to it and, I would say, at considerable cost to his own standing.[1]

—*Nobel Prize–winning economist,*
Professor Robert Lucas,
University of Chicago

With campaign rhetoric frequently promising "Actually, I'm cutting more than I'm spending so that it will be a net spending cut" and slashing government deficits, President Obama portrayed himself as a nonthreatening economic moderate.[2] He even tried to paint himself to the right of his 2008 campaign opponent John McCain by attacking him for supporting some of the Bush deficits, which Obama claimed help cause the financial crisis. Instead, Obama delivered the largest spending increases and the largest deficits in American history. His proposals for new spending just kept coming. As late as February 2011, despite yet more promises to cut deficits, he was still proposing new government spending that would increase deficits by another $1.2 trillion over 10 years.[3] And later offers to cut spending were smoke and mirrors: Cuts would not have occurred until well after Obama had left office.

But whatever the broken promises, have Obama's policies left Americans better off than they were before he became president? The answer is clearly "no." Instead, we have endured the worst economic recovery since the Great Depression.

It has been quite a recovery with incomes for the median household falling and poverty rising. A year before the November 2012 election, unemployment remained stagnant at 9 percent—a full 1.2 percentage points above the figure when Obama became president. Despite more than five million more working-age people, there were two million fewer jobs. And the unemployed are finding themselves spending much more time looking for work; actually, the average time looking is twice as long as it was in the early 1980s, the previous all-time record.

Young adults have been hit particularly hard. Harvard economist Richard Freeman warns: "These people will be scarred, and they will be called the 'lost generation'—in that their careers would not be the same way if we had avoided this economic disaster."[4] Thirty-one percent of graduating college students still have not landed a job within six months after graduating, and the lag is even longer for those who leave college without graduating.[5] Outstanding unpaid student loans have exceeded $1 trillion for the first time in 2011.[6] These are record-setting rates of young people living with their parents and delaying marriage.[7]

The parallels to the Great Depression are unmistakable. It took over a decade before the United States recovered from the Great Depression, and even by 1940, the unemployment rate was still at 9.5 percent.[8] Economists have argued that all the New Deal regulations and rules unionizing the economy paralyzed companies and investments.[9] Franklin Roosevelt may have meant well, and the desire to do something is understandable, but the chaos created by government regulations and government spending made a bad situation even worse. Democrat politicians claim that President Obama is one of the most pro-business presidents, but it doesn't square well with the legions of Democratic businessmen who have pleaded with Obama to rethink his regulatory avalanche.

Rather than learning from the Great Depression and its failed Keynesian experiment, Obama's strategy has been to outspend the New Deal. The administration and its defenders keep repeating that things would have been even worse without all this new spending and deficits. But they remain silent on why our economy started faring so poorly relative to other countries as soon as the Obama Stimulus was enacted.

Whatever jobs might have been created or saved by the Obama Stimulus have been exorbitantly expensive. Take the Congressional Budget Office's (CBO) most optimistic estimates of the number of jobs created by the Stimulus, about 3.6 million, and compare it to the $700 billion of the $825 billion Stimulus that had been spent up through June 2011. The cost per job was about $200,000.[10] Their low-end estimate of 560,992 jobs implies a cost of about $1.25 million per job. Again, all these claims about job creation are quite debatable because many "might have existed without the stimulus package"—as the CBO acknowledged. In other words, the estimates ignore that the money has to come from someplace—and that loss means that these government jobs come at the expense of jobs someplace else.[11]

But some argue the cost is less. According to Associated Press reporter Calvin Woodward: "Any cost-per-job figure pays not just for the worker, but for material, supplies, and that worker's output—a portion of a road paved, patients treated in a health clinic, goods shipped from a factory floor, railroad tracks laid."[12] But this assumes that the government creates this money out of thin air, that the money wouldn't have been spent on anything else that was valuable. And that is simply false. The government has to borrow the money or raise taxes, taking it from elsewhere. Some argue that the government needs to spend, because the people they are taking the money from would have saved rather than spend it. But in reality, saved money ultimately gets spent, too. Leaving money in your bank account doesn't mean that it goes unspent. Instead, it simply means that it is lent out to someone else.[13]

Much of the $200,000-plus per job went to things besides paying workers. The job search site Monster.com presented an analysis of "relatively well-paying stimulus-boosted jobs you can get with no more than a four-year degree."[14] Among the lowest-paid ones were health information technicians with an associate's degree who would help create electronic medical records and those with a high school diploma installing weatherization insulation. Those two groups were expected to get jobs paying $29,000 and $31,000, respectively. Jobs at the high end were general and operations managers with four-year degrees who were expected to average $89,000. Many civil and industrial engineers as well as medical records systems analysts were expected to make in the low $70,000 range. In the middle range, there were lots of jobs paying around $40,000 to $50,000: rail track layers, electricians, physical therapy assistants, mechanical engineering technicians, and workers who extend broadband access to rural areas. Even including covering health insurance, retirement, and taxes, that is a long ways away from the at least $200,000 spent per job "saved or created."

The worsening economy has resulted in increasingly divisive rhetoric by Obama and his supporters. Take Paul Krugman's praise in late November 2011 that "'We are the 99 percent' is a great slogan."[15] Krugman wanted to take the idea even further to "99.9 percent," claiming that this "super-elite" weren't productive innovators, but largely CEOs who received unjustified "lavish paychecks" because executive pay is "set by boards of directors appointed by the very people whose pay they determine." If you only take the money from some shadowy undeserving elite, the huge Obama spending increases can continue. Krugman's argument resembles the slogans of European communist parties.

And it's not true. Even if one took every single dime that of the top 0.1 percent's "lavish" income, it wouldn't come close to paying for even one year of Obama's budget deficits—covering only half of it.[16]

Obama also rips into businessmen, asserting that they don't deserve what they are earning. At a Florida Democratic fundraiser in October 2011, Obama told a very receptive audience:

> But none of us make it on our own. Somebody—an outstanding entrepreneur like a Steve Jobs—somewhere along the line he had a teacher who helped inspire him. (Applause.) All those

great Internet businesses wouldn't have succeeded unless some-body had invested in the government research that helped to create the Internet. We don't succeed on our own. We succeed because this country has, in previous generations, made invest-ments that allow all of us to succeed. (Applause.)[17]

This is only partly true. Yes, we always stand on the shoulders of oth-ers who came before us. But just because the government subsidizes something doesn't mean that it wouldn't have been built on its own. Even when government subsidies are given out wisely, that doesn't mean that the projects wouldn't have been undertaken without the subsidy.

Most likely, the projects would have been undertaken somewhat later. Obama might not realize it, but in the 90 years before most states had established public schools, the vast majority of Americans did get an education.[18] Despite most people living on farms in rural areas, 93 percent of kids in states without public schools in 1860 were literate. Likewise with highways, which were privately built until after 1900.[19] Historically, railroads were overwhelmingly privately financed, and in those cases in which government subsidies were involved, the projects often faced financial problems.[20] The subway system in NYC was vir-tually all built and run by private companies until government price controls eventually bankrupted them and the government took over in 1940.[21]

Despite the massive government subsidies given out to favored billionaire Democrats by the Obama administration, many wealthy Democratic businessmen, from Steve Jobs to Mortimer Zuckerman to Ted Leonsis, warned Obama that his policies were going to drive American businesses overseas and discourage investment.[22] Incensed by Obama's then–chief of staff, Rahm Emanuel, who claimed that Obama is pro-business, Zuckerman ranted: "It is without question the most hostile administration to business and the role of business that we have had in decades, and he is saying that it isn't hostile to business. It is totally hostile to business."[23]

To top it off, the Obama administration is arrogant. They dis-play an ivory tower academic arrogance of supposedly knowing what is best for everyone. Consider Larry Summers's remarks after the March 2009 Health Care Summit: "We've gone from a moment when we've never had a less social science–oriented group [during the Bush administration], to a moment when we've never had a more social science–oriented group."[24]

Many have criticized the administration's casually made analysis before spending about a trillion dollars. Tom Sargent, who won the Nobel Prize for economics in 2011, was less than impressed: "[Obama's Council of Economic Advisers] calculations were surprisingly naive for 2009. . . . Back-of-envelope work can be a useful starting point or benchmark, but it does mischief when it is oversold."[25]

Things have not worked out well. Yet, President Obama has refused to rethink his positions and he keeps blaming others. The failure has been elsewhere. The United States isn't attracting new businesses because "we've been a little bit lazy."[26] Or the problem is because Americans have "lost our ambition, our imagination" or because we have "gotten a little soft."[27] Obama never considers that these problems may occur because the total corporate tax rate has remained at about 39 to 40 percent in the United States since 1988, while the rate has plummeted in other countries. Just between 1988 and 2011, the average total corporate tax rate for other developed countries fell from 44.3 percent to 25.1 percent.[28]

There are hundreds of trillions of dollars around the world available to invest, and there are obvious reasons they are not flowing into America. A tax structure that had once made the United States a relatively attractive place to invest now punishes investors. Why continue investing in the United States when investors get to keep 15 cents more of every dollar they make when they invest abroad?

Obama's supposed solutions will only make the problem worse. He doesn't want states and local governments competing against one another for foreign businesses and so wants to create a powerful federal government. The president may not believe that incentives matter, but reduced competition is going to kill job opportunities. Americans have not forgotten how to create wealth. Rather, big government has stopped wealth creation by punishing those who work hard and innovate.

Unfortunately, the phrase "he made things worse" has come to describe Obama's presidency. Time after time, from higher unemployment to lower house prices, Obama's policies have taken a bad situation and made it worse.

Notes

1. Holman W. Jenkins, Jr., "Chicago Economics on Trial," *Wall Street Journal,* September 24, 2011, http://online.wsj.com/article/SB1000142405311190 4194604576583382550849232.html?mod=opinion_newsreel.

2. "The Second McCain–Obama Presidential Debate," Commission on Presidential Debates, October 7, 2008, www.debates.org/index.php?page=october-7-2008-debate-transcrip.

3. Letter to the Honorable Daniel K. Inouye, "Preliminary Analysis of the President's Budget for 2012," Congressional Budget Office, March 2011, http://www.cbo.gov/doc.cfm?index=12103.

4. Associated Press, "Young Becoming 'Lost Generation' Amid Recession," CBS News, September 22, 2011, www.cbsnews.com/stories/2011/09/22/national/main20110000.shtml.

5. Melissa Korn and Lauren Weber, "How I Found My First Big Job," *Wall Street Journal,* November 10, 2011, http://online.wsj.com/article/SB10001424 052970203537304577028394060129950.html?mod=WSJ_hp_mostpop_read.

6. Tim Mak, "Unpaid Student Loans Top $1 Trillion," *Politico,* October 19, 2011, www.politico.com/news/stories/1011/66347.html.

7. Associated Press, "Young Becoming 'Lost Generation.'"

8. Michael R. Darby, "Three-and-a-Half Million US Employees Have Been Mislaid: Or, an Explanation of Unemployment, 1934–1941," *Journal of Political Economy* (February 1976): 1–16.

9. Harold L. Cole and Lee E. Ohanian, "New Deal Policies and the Persistence of the Great Depression: A General Equilibrium Analysis," *Journal of Political Economy* 112 (2004): 779–816.

10. Harvard professor Martin Feldstein provides a similar number to the $200,000, and Austan Goolsbee only weakly disagreed: "Well, I don't think I totally agree with that exact number."; Judy Woodruff, "How Do Tax Cuts, Hikes Fit into Obama's American Jobs Act?," *PBS NewsHour,* September 13, 2011, www.pbs.org/newshour/bb/business/july-dec11/taxes_09-13.html.

11. Congressional Budget Office, "Estimated Impact of the American Recovery and Reinvestment Act on Employment and Economic Output from April 2011 through June 2011," Congressional Budget Office, August 2011, 2, www.cbo.gov/ftpdocs/123xx/doc12385/08-24-ARRA.pdf.

12. Calvin Woodward, "FACT CHECK: GOP Math Suspect in Stimulus Debate," *Seattle Times,* November 2, 2009, http://seattletimes.nwsource .com/html/businesstechnology/2010183560_apusfactcheckstimulusmath .html.

13. Even if the government prints up the money it plans to spend, printing up money causes inflation and that inflation takes away a little of the purchasing power from everyone in the economy.

14. Dona De Zube, "High-Paying Stimulus Jobs," Monster.com, http://career-advice.monster.com/salary-benefits/salary-information/high-paying-stimulus-jobs/article.aspx; See also Laurence Shatkin, *Great Jobs in the President's Stimulus Plan* (New York: Jist Works, 2009).

15. Paul Krugman, "We Are the 99.9%," *New York Times,* November 24, 2011, http://www.nytimes.com/2011/11/25/opinion/we-are-the-99-9.html.

16. In 2010, there were 118,000 people in the top 0.1 percent of income earners. Taking all their income would raise $694 billion. Of course, once you threaten to take this money, people will either leave the country or stop working, so it is unlikely that the government would raise anything remotely close to the $694 billion. The numbers are from the Tax Policy Center, a project of the Urban Institute and the Brookings Institution, which provides a breakdown of the "Distribution of Cash Income and Federal Taxes by Filing Status and Family Type, Under Current Law, by Cash Income Percentile, 2010" (www.taxpolicycenter.org/numbers/displayatab.cfm?Docid=2975&DocTypeID=7).

17. "Remarks by President Obama at DNC Fundraiser at Sheraton Downtown Hotel, Orlando, Florida," Politisite.com, October 11, 2011, http://politisite.com/2011/10/11/remarks-by-president-obama-at-dnc-fundraiser-at-sheraton-downtown-hotel-orlando-florida/.

18. John R. Lott Jr., "Why Is Education Publicly Provided? A Critical Survey," *Cato Journal* 7, no. 2 (1987): 475–501.

19. Walter Block, Privatization of Roads and Highways: Human and Economic Factors (Auburn, Alabama: Mises Institute, 2009); see also Dan Klein, "The Voluntary Provision of Public Goods? The Turnpike Companies of Early America," *Economic Inquiry* 28 (1990): 788–812 and Dan Klein, John Majewski, and Christopher Baer, "Economic, Community and the Law: The Turnpike Movement in New York, 1797–1845," *Journal of Economic History* 26, no. 3 (1992): 469–512.

20. Thomas DiLorenzo, "The Role of Private Transportation in America's 19th-Century 'Internal Improvements' Debate," Sellinger School of Business and Management, Loyola College, Baltimore, Maryland.

21. *Reason* magazine, July 1976.

22. Steve Jobs was quoted earlier in this book. Ted Leonsis noted: "I voted for our president. I have maxed out on personal donations to his re-election campaign. I forgot his campaign wants to raise $1 billion. *That* is a lot of money—money—money—money! Money still talks. It blows my mind

when I am asked for money as a donation at the same time I am getting blasted as being a bad guy! Someone needs to talk our president down off of this rhetoric about good versus evil; about two classes and math." Ted Leonsis, "Class Warfare—Yuck!" *Ted's Take,* September 25, 2011, www .tedstake.com/2011/09/25/class-warfare-yuck/; Mortimer Zuckerman, "The Most Fiscally Irresponsible Government in U.S. History," *US News & World Report,* August 26, 2010, www.usnews.com/opinion/mzuckerman/ articles/2010/08/26/the-most-fiscally-irresponsible-government-in-us-history_print.html.

23. Mortimer Zuckerman, appearing on MSNBC's *Morning Joe,* July 9, 2010, http://youtu.be/SpDxlstrpU8.

24. Ron Suskind, *Confidence Men: Wall Street, Washington, and the Education of a President* (New York: Harper, 2011), 196–197.

25. Art Rolnick interview of Tom Sargent, "Modern Macroeconomics under Attack," *The Region,* Federal Reserve Bank of Minneapolis, September 2010, https://files.nyu.edu/ts43/public/personal/sargent_Mpls_interview.pdf.

26. Kimberly Schwandt, "President Obama: U.S. Gotten a Bit 'Lazy' on Attracting Businesses," Fox News, November 13, 2011, http://politics.blogs.foxnews .com/2011/11/13/president-obama-us-gotten-bit-lazy-attracting-businesses.

27. President Barack Obama, "We Have Lost Our Ambition, Our Imagination," Real Clear Politics Video, October 25, 2011, www.realclearpolitics.com/ video/2011/10/25/obama_we_have_lost_our_ambition_our_imagina-tion.html; President Barack Obama, "America Has Gone 'Soft,'" Real Clear Politics Video, September 29, 2011, www.realclearpolitics.com/ video/2011/09/29/president_obama_america_has_gone_soft.html.

28. See the OECD Tax Database, "Corporate and Capital Income Taxes" (www .oecd.org/document/60/0,3746,en_2649_34533_1942460_1_1_1_1,00 .html#C_CorporateCaptial).

Appendix

Looking at the Fifty States

T he following charts show how stimulus dollars per capita from the Recovery.gov website vary with the poverty, unemployment, bankruptcy, and foreclosure rates as well as per capita income for all 50 states. As can be seen further on, Alaska is such an extreme outlier that it drives the results. Yet, including this one extreme value leaves the results unchanged in six of the seven figures.

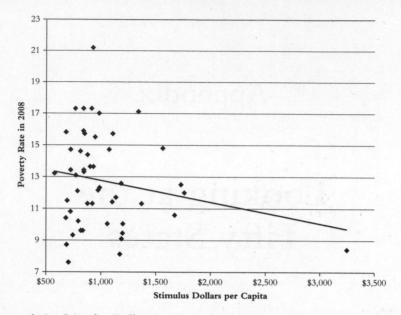

Figure A.1 Stimulus Dollars Per Capita by State and Poverty Rates in 2008 (including Alaska)

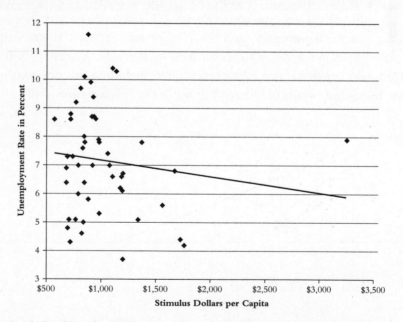

Figure A.2 Stimulus Dollars per Capita by State and Unemployment Rates (January 2009) (including Alaska)

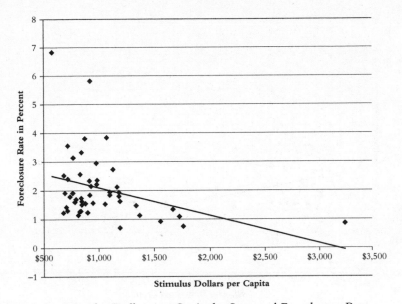

Figure A.3   Stimulus Dollars per Capita by State and Foreclosure Rate (December 2008) (including Alaska)

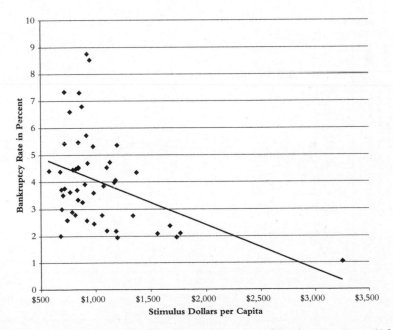

Figure A.4   Stimulus Dollars per Capita by State and Bankruptcy Rates (4th Quarter 2008) (including Alaska)

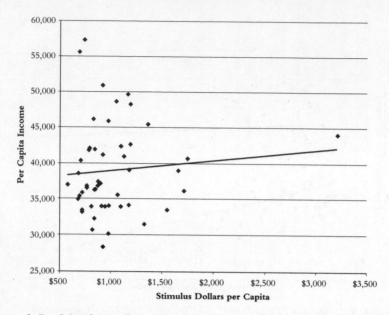

Figure A.5   Stimulus Dollars per Capita and Per Capita Income (4th Quarter 2008) (including Alaska)

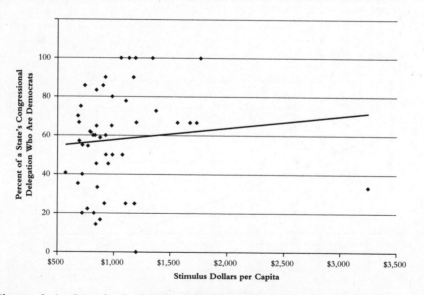

Figure A.6   Stimulus Dollars Per Capita by State and the Percentage of a State's Congressional and Senate Delegation that Are Democrats in 2009 (including Alaska)

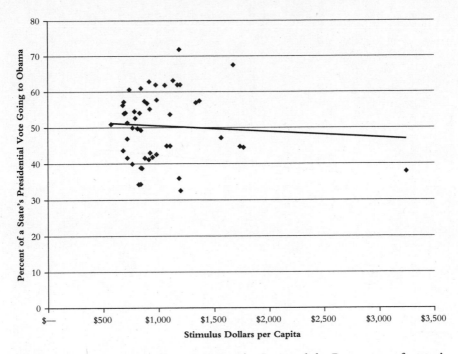

Figure A.7 Stimulus Dollars per Capita by State and the Percentage of a state's Presidential Vote Going to Obama (including Alaska)

About the Authors

Grover Norquist is president of Americans for Tax Reform (ATR), a taxpayer advocacy group he founded in 1985 at the request of President Ronald Reagan. ATR is a coalition of taxpayer groups, individuals, and businesses opposed to higher taxes at the federal, state, and local levels. It organizes the Taxpayer Protection Pledge, which asks all candidates for federal and state office to commit themselves in writing to oppose all tax increases. He chairs the "Wednesday Meeting," a weekly gathering of over 150 elected officials, political activists, and movement leaders. He serves on the board of the NRA, the American Conservative Union and the Nixon Center. He and his wife, Samah, and their daughters, Grace and Giselle, live in Washington, DC.

John R. Lott Jr. is an economist who has held research and/or teaching positions at the University of Chicago, Yale University, Stanford University, UCLA, Wharton, and Rice University, and was the chief economist at the United States Sentencing Commission during 1988 and 1989. He has published over 100 articles in academic journals. He is the author of six books, including *More Guns, Less Crime, Freedomnomics, The Bias Against Guns*, and *Are Predatory Commitments Credible?* Lott is a FoxNews.com contributor and weekly columnist. His opinion pieces have appeared in such places as the *Wall Street Journal*, the *New York Times*, the *Los Angeles Times*, the *New York Post*, *USA Today*, and the *Chicago Tribune*. He has appeared on such television programs as the ABC and NBC national evening news broadcasts, Fox News, *The NewsHour with Jim Lehrer*, and the *Today* show. He received his PhD in economics from UCLA in 1984.

Index